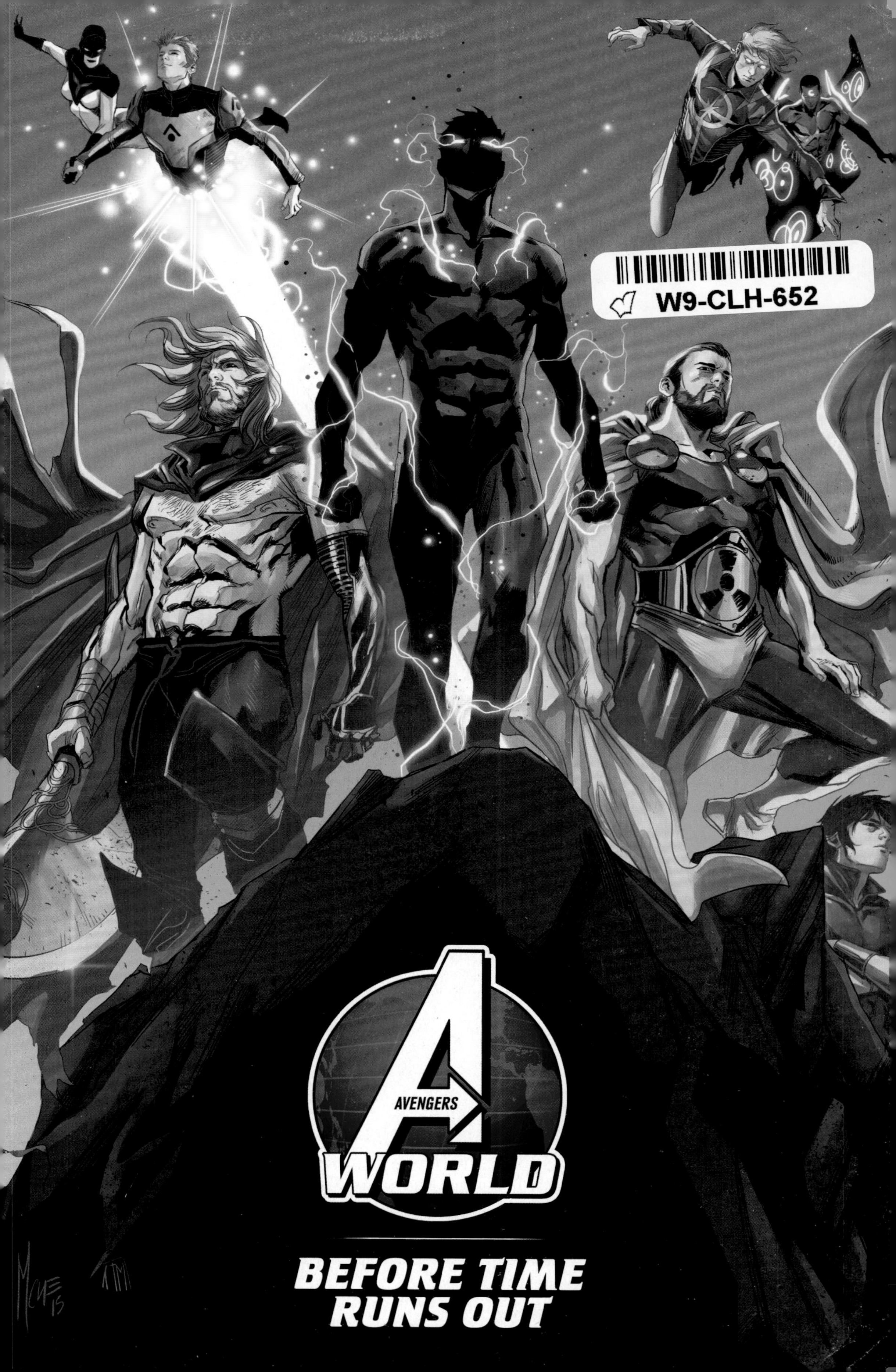
AVENGERS
WORLD
BEFORE TIME
RUNS OUT

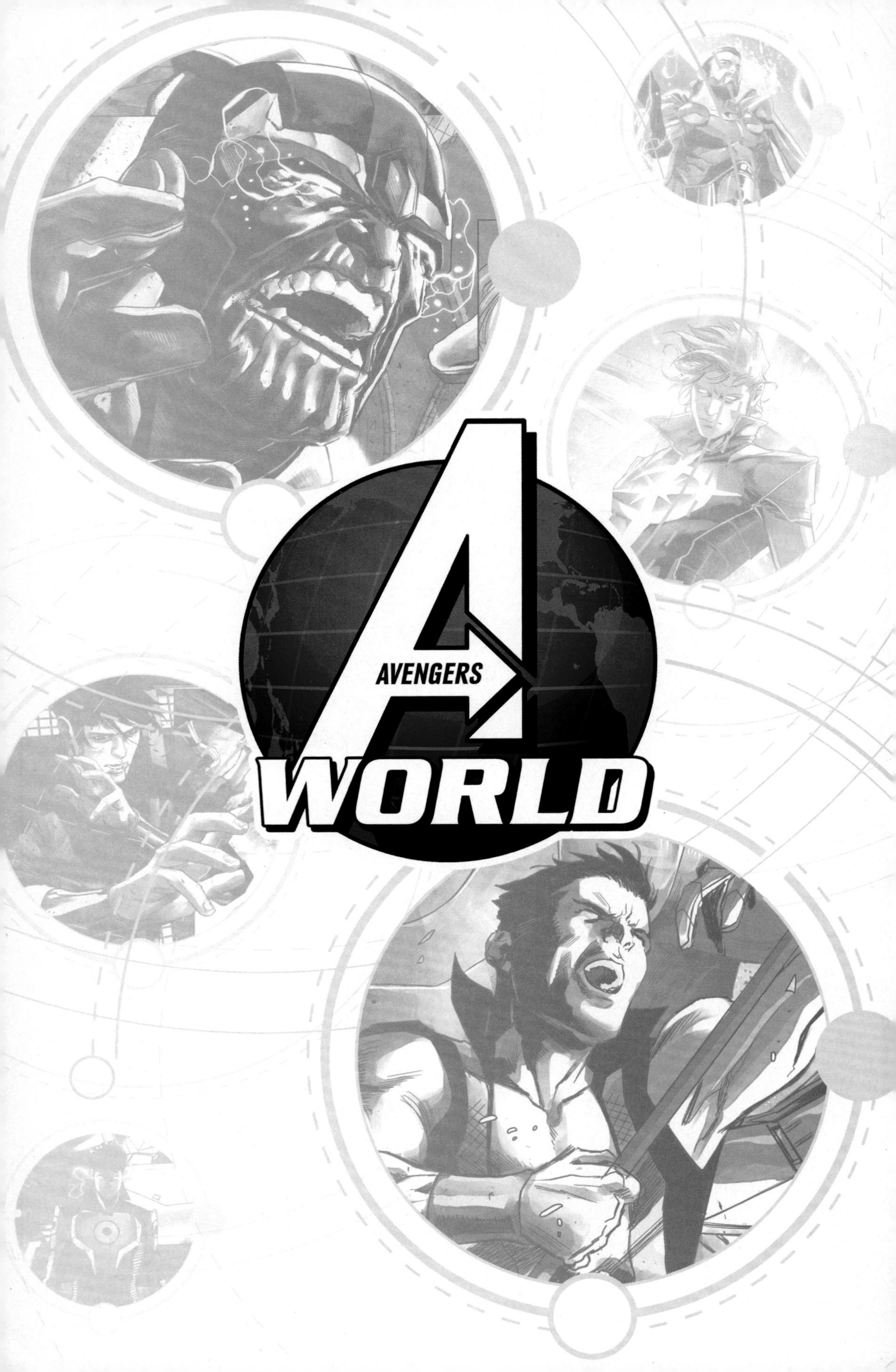
AVENGERS
WORLD

# BEFORE TIME RUNS OUT

## AVENGERS #34.2

WRITER: **SAM HUMPHRIES**
ARTIST: **BENGAL**
COLOR ARTIST: **DAVID CURIEL**
LETTERER: **VC's CORY PETIT**
COVER ART: **BENGAL**
ASSISTANT EDITOR: **JAKE THOMAS**
EDITORS: **TOM BREVOORT** WITH **WIL MOSS**

## AVENGERS WORLD #17-21

WRITER: **FRANK BARBIERE**
ARTIST: **MARCO CHECCHETTO**
COLOR ARTIST: **ANDRES MOSSA**
LETTERER: **VC's JOE CARAMAGNA**
COVER ART: **JEFF DEKAL** (#17-18 & #21), **W. SCOTT FORBES** (#19)
AND **SANFORD GREENE** & **RICO RENZI** (#20)
ASSISTANT EDITOR: **JON MOISAN**
EDITOR: **WIL MOSS**
EXECUTIVE EDITOR: **TOM BREVOORT**

**AVENGERS** CREATED BY **STAN LEE** & **JACK KIRBY**

Collection Editor: **Jennifer Grünwald** • Assistant Editor: **Sarah Brunstad** • Associate Managing Editor: **Alex Starbuck**
Editor, Special Projects: **Mark D. Beazley** • Senior Editor, Special Projects: **Jeff Youngquist**
SVP Print, Sales & Marketing: **David Gabriel** • Book Design: **Adam Del Re**

Editor in Chief: **Axel Alonso** • Chief Creative Officer: **Joe Quesada**
Publisher: **Dan Buckley** • Executive Producer: **Alan Fine**

**AVENGERS WORLD VOL. 4: BEFORE TIME RUNS OUT.** Contains material originally published in magazine form as AVENGERS #34.2 and AVENGERS WORLD #17-21. First printing 2015. ISBN# 978-0-7851-9252-7. Published by MARVEL WORLDWIDE, INC., a subsidiary of MARVEL ENTERTAINMENT, LLC. OFFICE OF PUBLICATION: 135 West 50th Street, New York, NY 10020.  **Printed in Canada.** ALAN FINE, President, Marvel Entertainment; DAN BUCKLEY, President, TV, Publishing and Brand Management; JOE QUESADA, Chief Creative Officer; TOM BREVOORT, SVP of Publishing; DAVID BOGART, SVP of Operations & Procurement, Publishing; C.B. CEBULSKI, VP of International Development & Brand Management; DAVID GABRIEL, SVP Print, Sales & Marketing; JIM O'KEEFE, VP of Operations & Logistics; DAN CARR, Executive Director of Publishing Technology; SUSAN CRESPI, Editorial Operations Manager; ALEX MORALES, Publishing Operations Manager; STAN LEE, Chairman Emeritus. For information regarding advertising in Marvel Comics or on Marvel.com, please contact Jonathan Rheingold, VP of Custom Solutions & Ad Sales, at jrheingold@marvel.com. For Marvel subscription inquiries, please call 800-217-9158. **Manufactured between 6/26/2015 and 8/3/2015 by SOLISCO PRINTERS, SCOTT, QC, CANADA.**

10 9 8 7 6 5 4 3 2 1

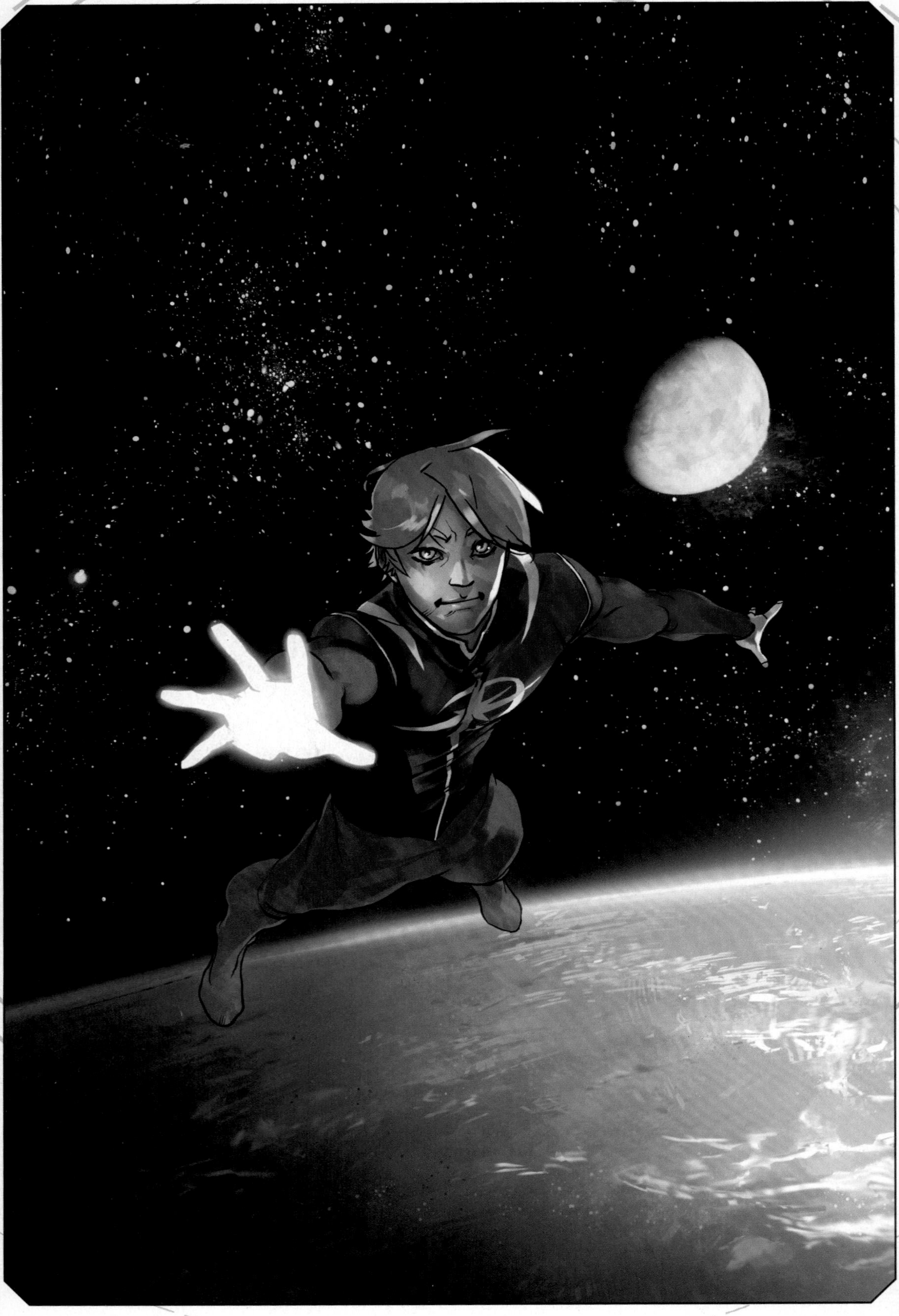

AVENGERS 34.2

# PREVIOUSLY IN AVENGERS

A WHITE EVENT CREATES/ALTERS HERALDS TO SHEPHERD A WORLD INTO ASCENDING TO A UNIVERSAL SCALE. A STARBRAND IS ONE SUCH HERALD.

BUT THE MACHINE WAS BROKEN. WHEN THE WHITE EVENT CHOSE NORMAL COLLEGE STUDENT KEVIN CONNOR IT DESTROYED HIS SCHOOL, KILLING EVERYONE BUT HIM.

STARBRAND'S VIOLENT CREATION AND UNDISCIPLINED POWER HAD CATASTROPHIC CONSEQUENCES.

FOR THE SAFETY OF THE ENTIRE PLANET, BOTH HE AND FELLOW HERALD NIGHTMASK WERE FORCIBLY SENT TO A GIANT DYSON SPHERE ENCIRCLING THE SUN.

IN THEIR ISOLATION, NIGHTMASK AIDED STARBRAND IN CONTROLLING AND UNDERSTANDING HIS POWERS. NOW THE TWO SONS OF BROKEN WHITE EVENTS CAN TAKE THEIR RIGHTFUL PLACE...

...AS HEROES HERALDING A BRAVE NEW WORLD.

# BIG CITY

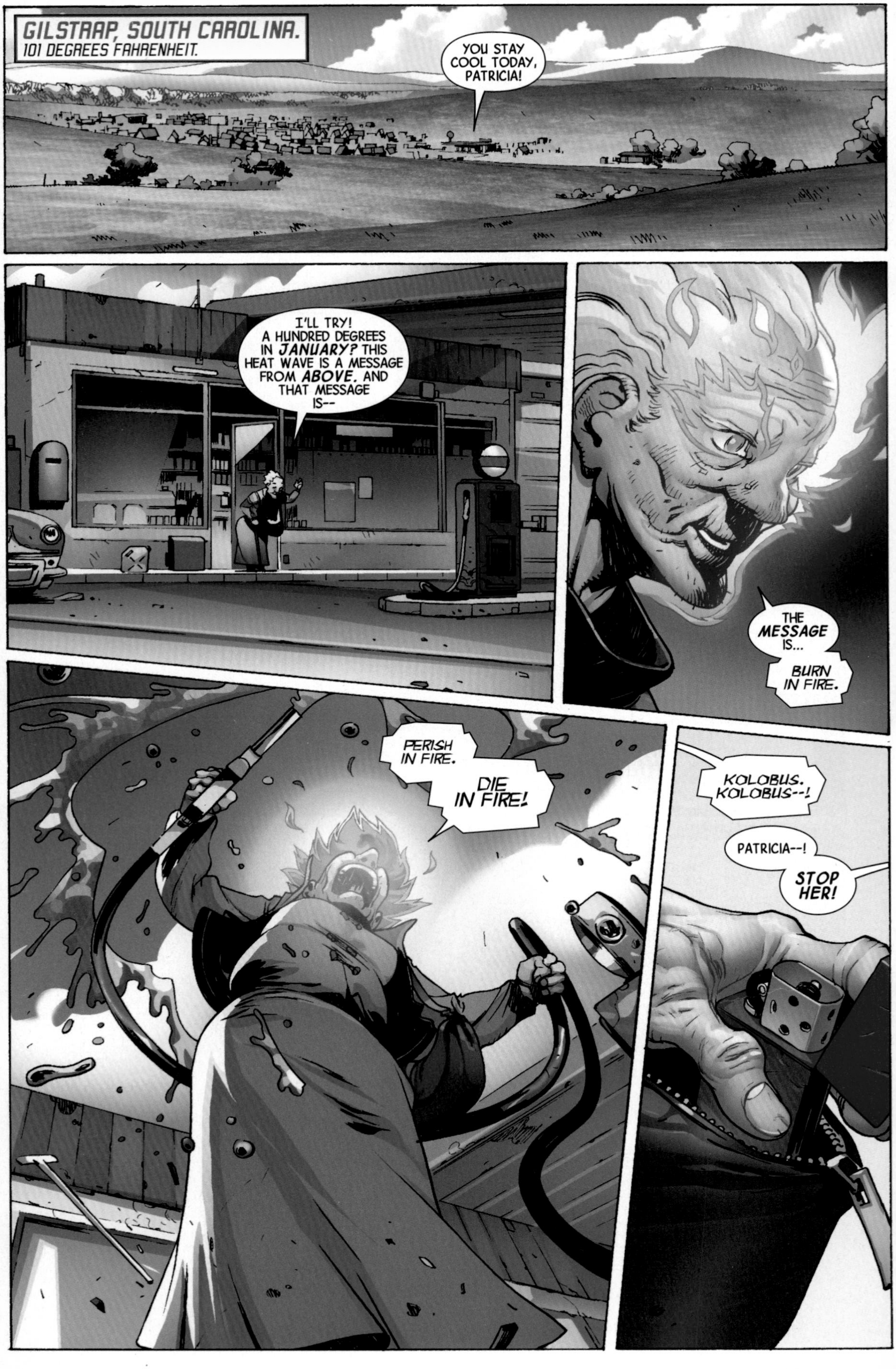
GILSTRAP, SOUTH CAROLINA.
101 DEGREES FAHRENHEIT.
YOU STAY COOL TODAY, PATRICIA!
I'LL TRY! A HUNDRED DEGREES IN JANUARY? THIS HEAT WAVE IS A MESSAGE FROM ABOVE. AND THAT MESSAGE IS--
THE MESSAGE IS...
BURN IN FIRE.
PERISH IN FIRE.
DIE IN FIRE!
KOLOBUS. KOLOBUS--!
PATRICIA--!
STOP HER!

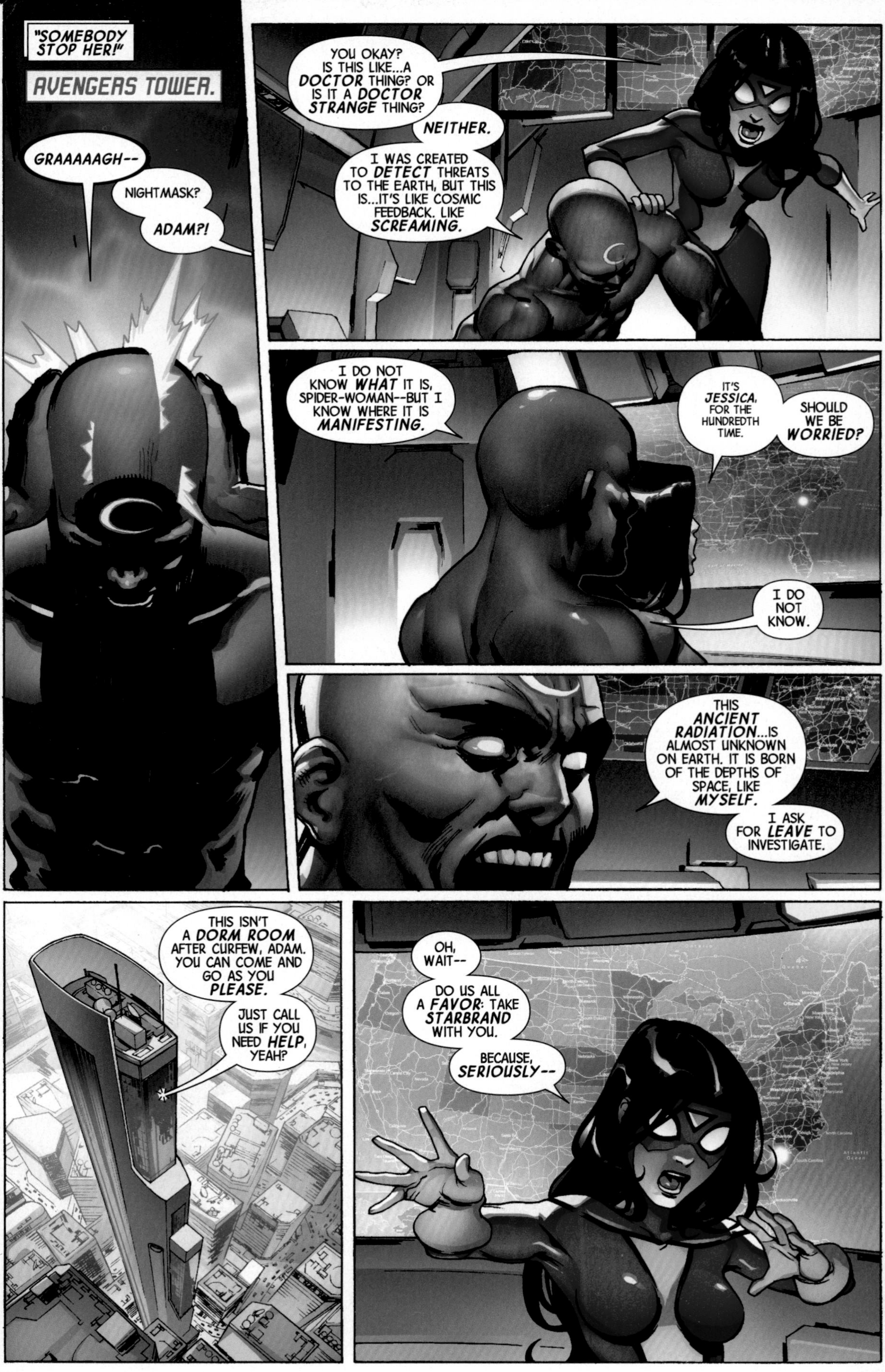
"SOMEBODY STOP HER!"
AVENGERS TOWER.
GRAAAAAGH--
NIGHTMASK?
ADAM?!
YOU OKAY? IS THIS LIKE...A DOCTOR THING? OR IS IT A DOCTOR STRANGE THING?
NEITHER.
I WAS CREATED TO DETECT THREATS TO THE EARTH, BUT THIS IS...IT'S LIKE COSMIC FEEDBACK. LIKE SCREAMING.
I DO NOT KNOW WHAT IT IS, SPIDER-WOMAN--BUT I KNOW WHERE IT IS MANIFESTING.
IT'S JESSICA, FOR THE HUNDREDTH TIME.
SHOULD WE BE WORRIED?
I DO NOT KNOW.
THIS ANCIENT RADIATION...IS ALMOST UNKNOWN ON EARTH. IT IS BORN OF THE DEPTHS OF SPACE, LIKE MYSELF.
I ASK FOR LEAVE TO INVESTIGATE.
THIS ISN'T A DORM ROOM AFTER CURFEW, ADAM. YOU CAN COME AND GO AS YOU PLEASE.
JUST CALL US IF YOU NEED HELP, YEAH?
OH, WAIT--
DO US ALL A FAVOR: TAKE STARBRAND WITH YOU.
BECAUSE, SERIOUSLY--

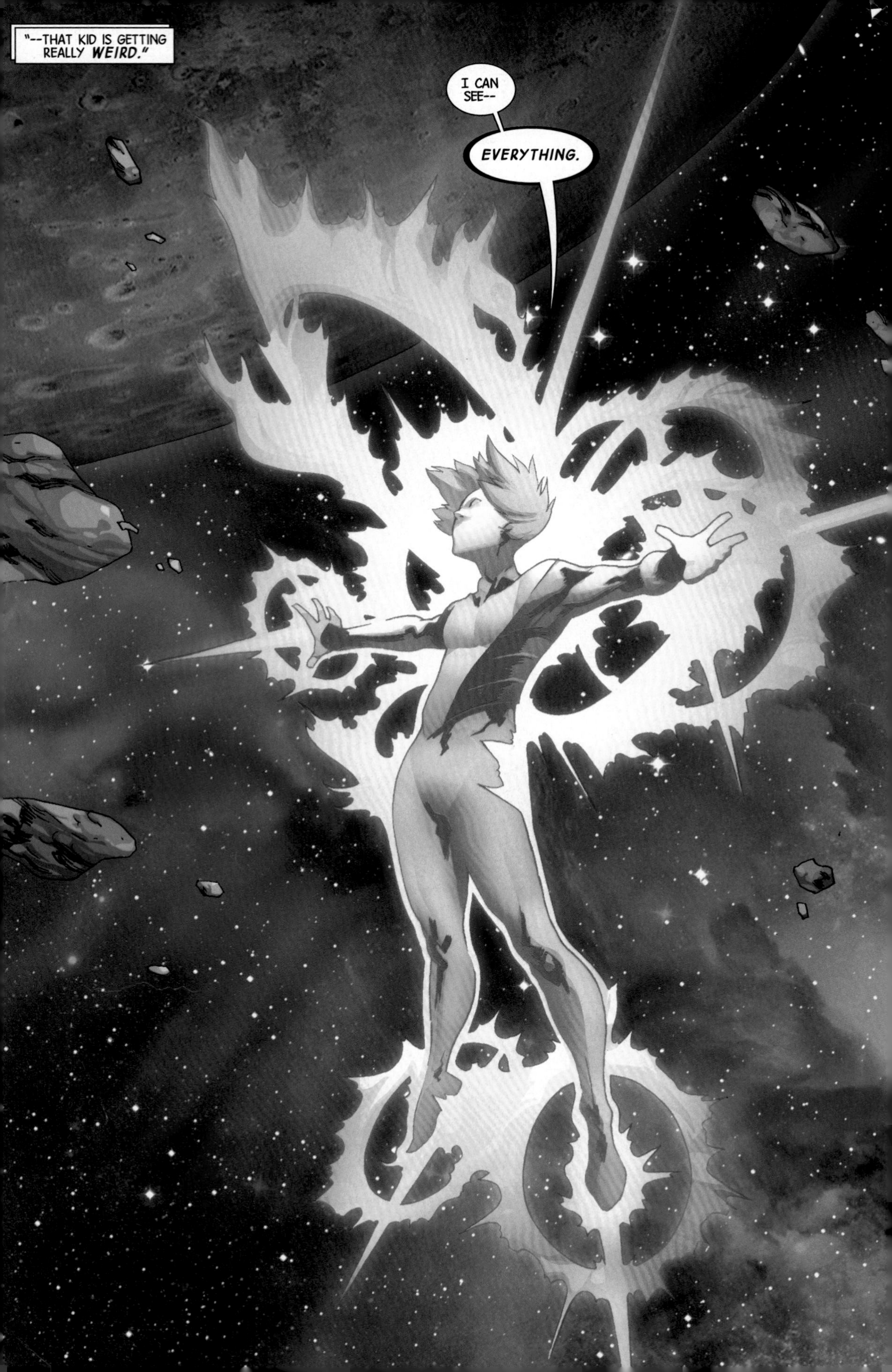
"--THAT KID IS GETTING REALLY WEIRD."
I CAN SEE--
EVERYTHING.

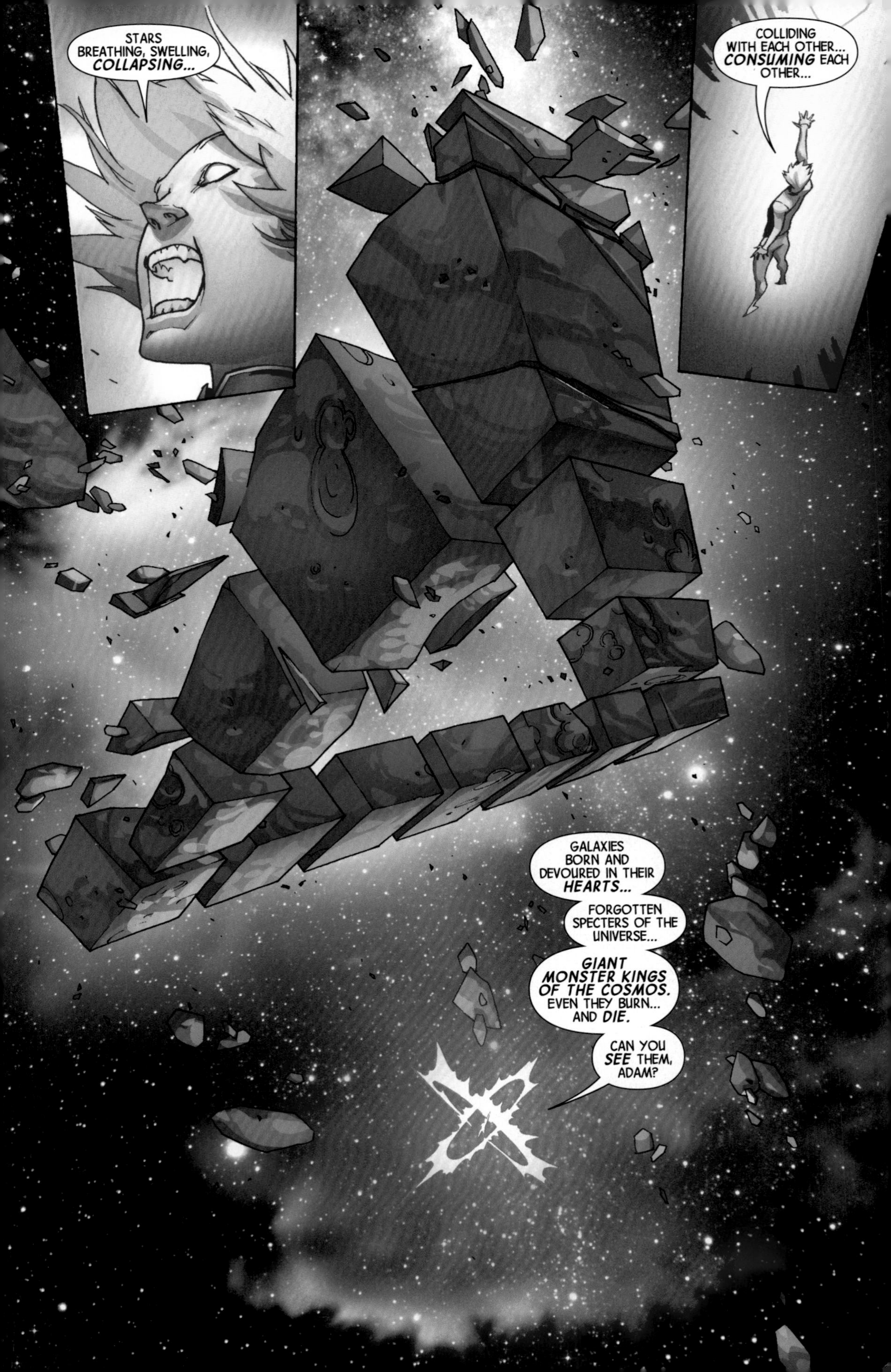

STARS BREATHING, SWELLING, COLLAPSING...
COLLIDING WITH EACH OTHER... CONSUMING EACH OTHER...
GALAXIES BORN AND DEVOURED IN THEIR HEARTS...
FORGOTTEN SPECTERS OF THE UNIVERSE...
GIANT MONSTER KINGS OF THE COSMOS. EVEN THEY BURN... AND DIE.
CAN YOU SEE THEM, ADAM?

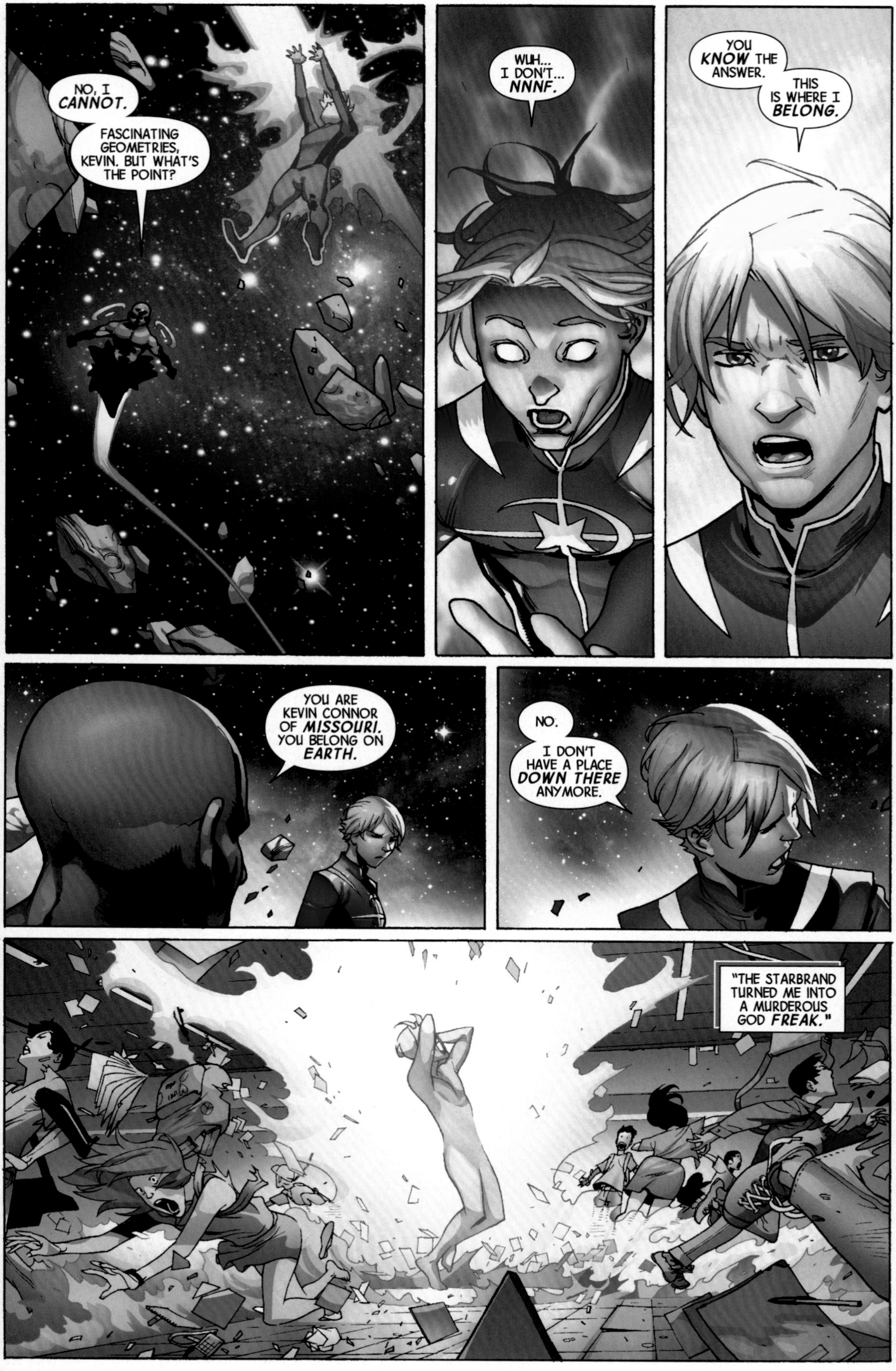
NO, I CANNOT.
FASCINATING GEOMETRIES, KEVIN. BUT WHAT'S THE POINT?
WUH... I DON'T... NNNF.
YOU KNOW THE ANSWER.
THIS IS WHERE I BELONG.
YOU ARE KEVIN CONNOR OF MISSOURI. YOU BELONG ON EARTH.
NO.
I DON'T HAVE A PLACE DOWN THERE ANYMORE.
"THE STARBRAND TURNED ME INTO A MURDEROUS GOD FREAK."

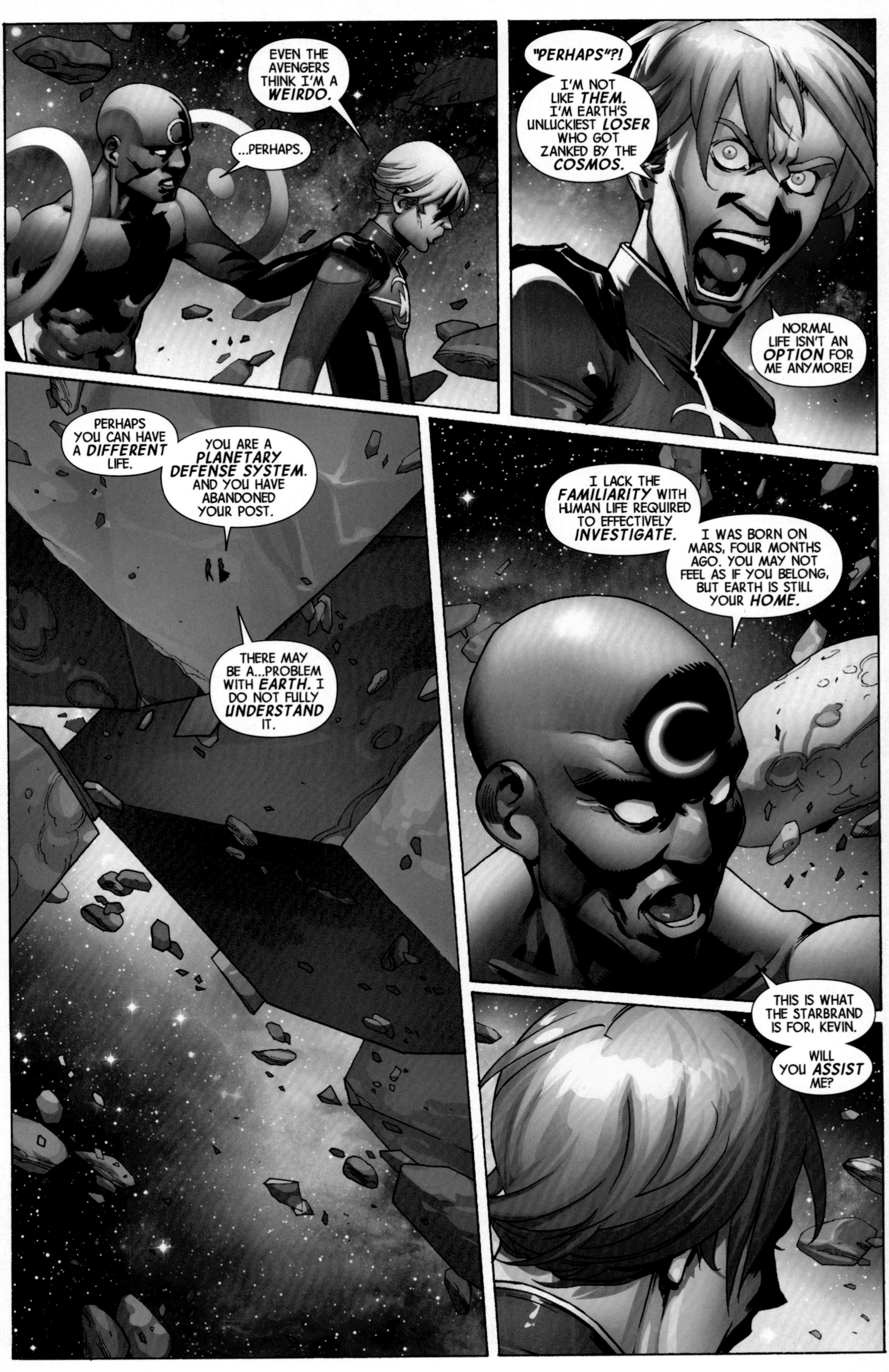
EVEN THE AVENGERS THINK I'M A WEIRDO.
...PERHAPS.
"PERHAPS"?!
I'M NOT LIKE THEM. I'M EARTH'S UNLUCKIEST LOSER WHO GOT ZANKED BY THE COSMOS.
NORMAL LIFE ISN'T AN OPTION FOR ME ANYMORE!
PERHAPS YOU CAN HAVE A DIFFERENT LIFE.
YOU ARE A PLANETARY DEFENSE SYSTEM. AND YOU HAVE ABANDONED YOUR POST.
THERE MAY BE A...PROBLEM WITH EARTH. I DO NOT FULLY UNDERSTAND IT.
I LACK THE FAMILIARITY WITH HUMAN LIFE REQUIRED TO EFFECTIVELY INVESTIGATE.
I WAS BORN ON MARS, FOUR MONTHS AGO. YOU MAY NOT FEEL AS IF YOU BELONG, BUT EARTH IS STILL YOUR HOME.
THIS IS WHAT THE STARBRAND IS FOR, KEVIN.
WILL YOU ASSIST ME?

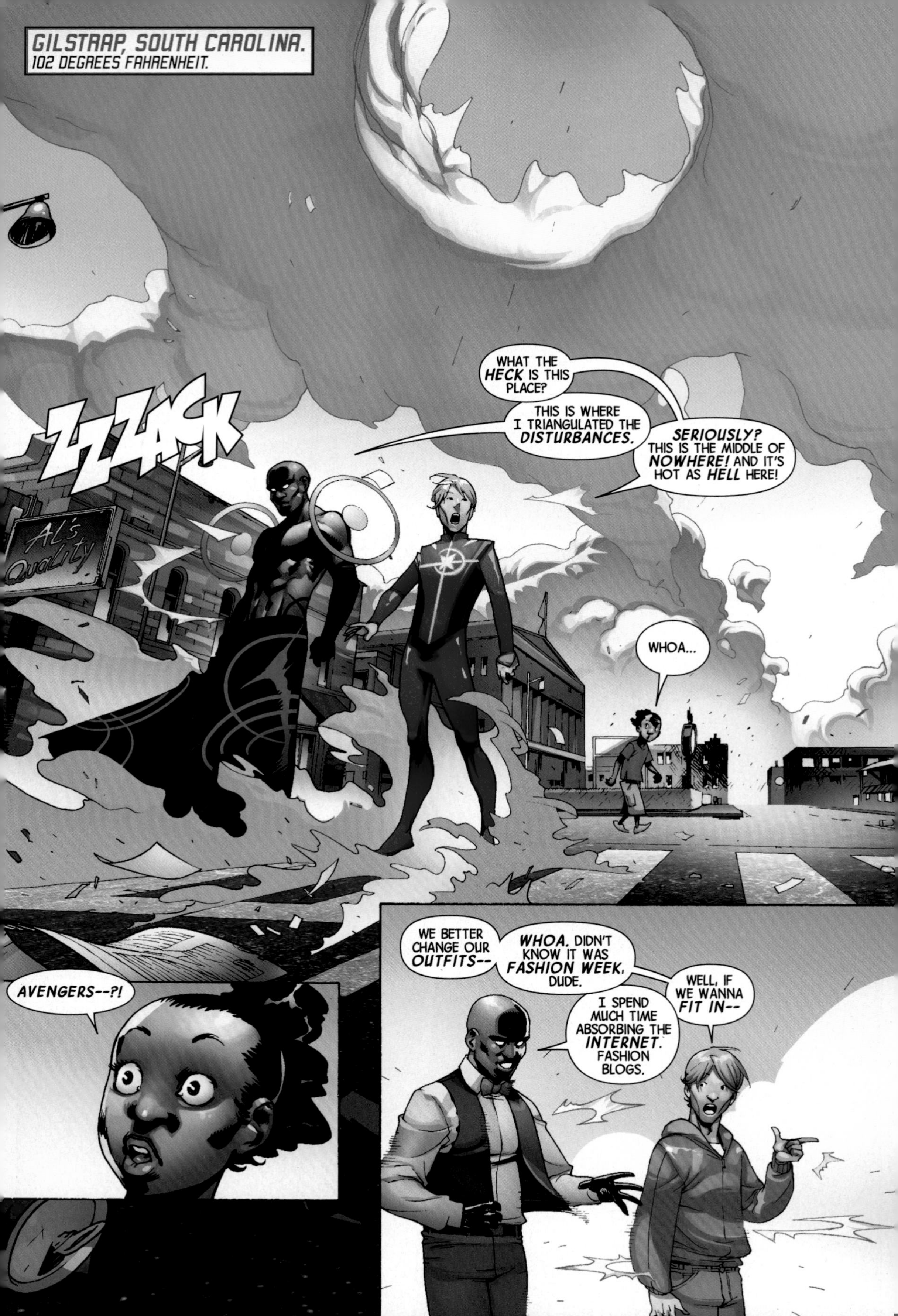
GILSTRAP, SOUTH CAROLINA.
102 DEGREES FAHRENHEIT.
ZZZACK
WHAT THE HECK IS THIS PLACE?
THIS IS WHERE I TRIANGULATED THE DISTURBANCES.
SERIOUSLY? THIS IS THE MIDDLE OF NOWHERE! AND IT'S HOT AS HELL HERE!
Al's Quality
WHOA...
AVENGERS--?!
WE BETTER CHANGE OUR OUTFITS--
WHOA. DIDN'T KNOW IT WAS FASHION WEEK, DUDE.
WELL, IF WE WANNA FIT IN--
I SPEND MUCH TIME ABSORBING THE INTERNET. FASHION BLOGS.

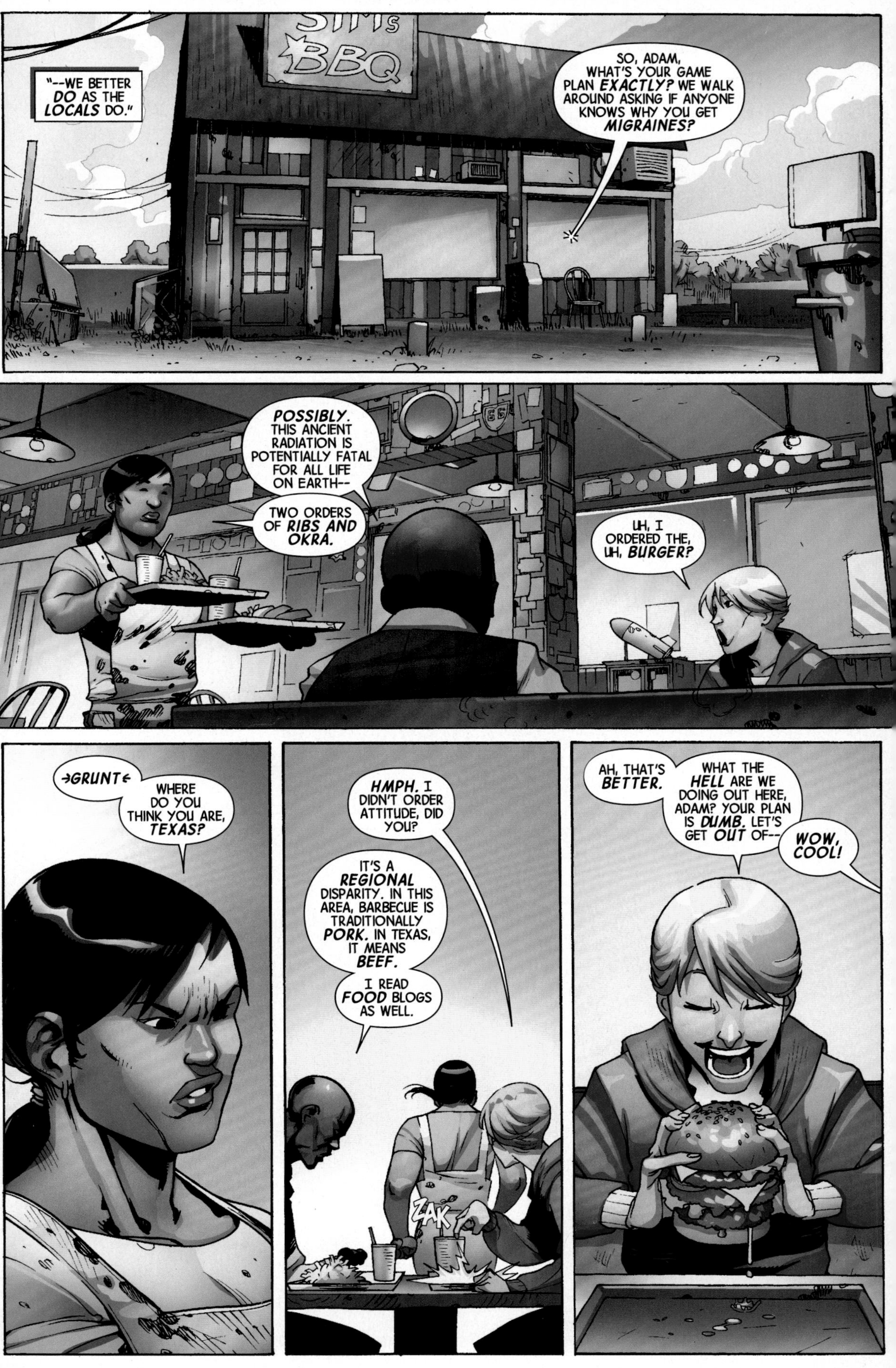
SIM'S BBQ
"--WE BETTER DO AS THE LOCALS DO."
SO, ADAM, WHAT'S YOUR GAME PLAN EXACTLY? WE WALK AROUND ASKING IF ANYONE KNOWS WHY YOU GET MIGRAINES?
POSSIBLY. THIS ANCIENT RADIATION IS POTENTIALLY FATAL FOR ALL LIFE ON EARTH--
TWO ORDERS OF RIBS AND OKRA.
UH, I ORDERED THE, UH, BURGER?
→GRUNT←
WHERE DO YOU THINK YOU ARE, TEXAS?
HMPH. I DIDN'T ORDER ATTITUDE, DID YOU?
IT'S A REGIONAL DISPARITY. IN THIS AREA, BARBECUE IS TRADITIONALLY PORK. IN TEXAS, IT MEANS BEEF.
I READ FOOD BLOGS AS WELL.
ZAK
AH, THAT'S BETTER.
WHAT THE HELL ARE WE DOING OUT HERE, ADAM? YOUR PLAN IS DUMB. LET'S GET OUT OF--
WOW, COOL!

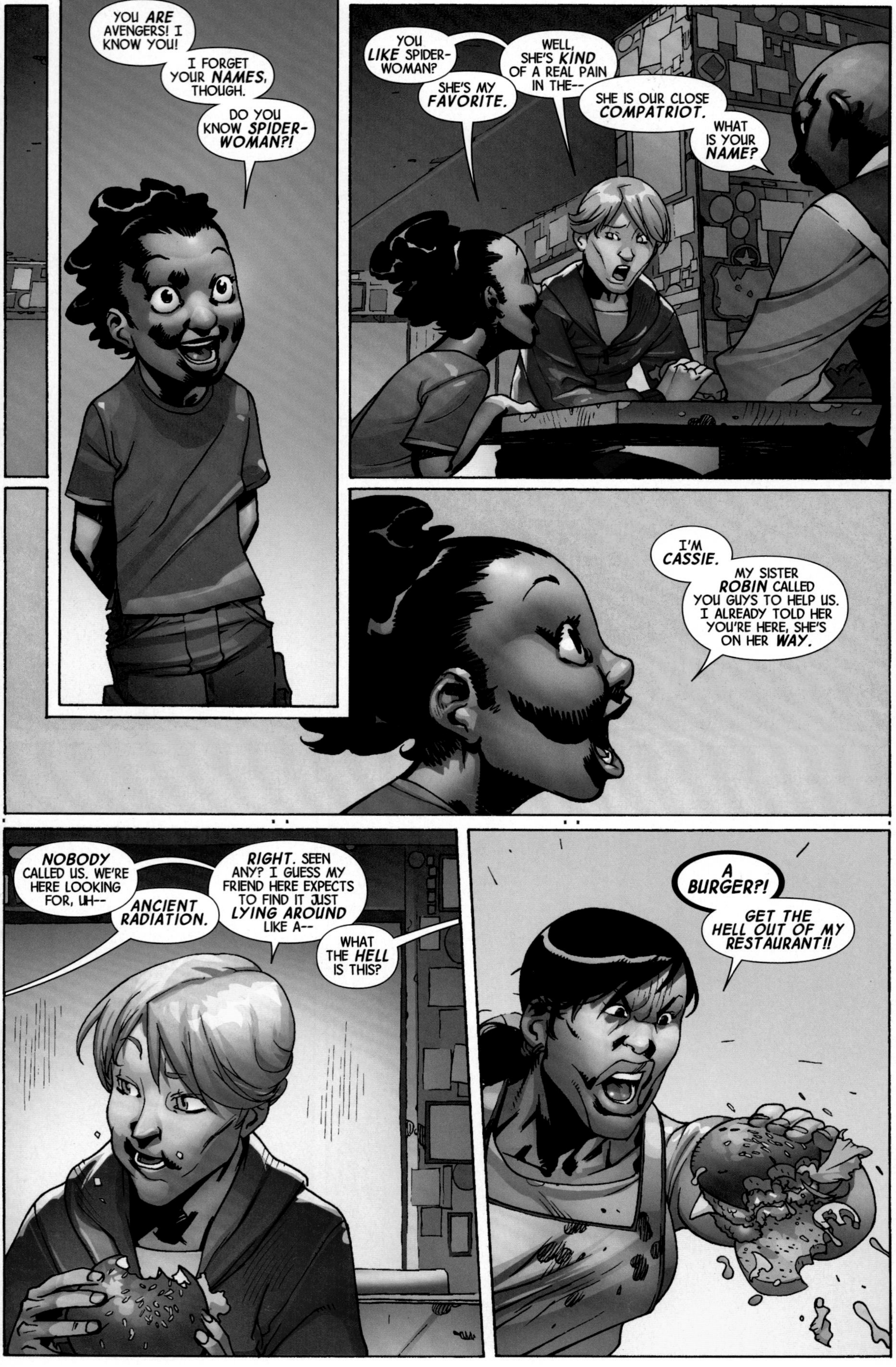
YOU ARE AVENGERS! I KNOW YOU!
I FORGET YOUR NAMES, THOUGH.
DO YOU KNOW SPIDER-WOMAN?!
YOU LIKE SPIDER-WOMAN?
SHE'S MY FAVORITE.
WELL, SHE'S KIND OF A REAL PAIN IN THE--
SHE IS OUR CLOSE COMPATRIOT.
WHAT IS YOUR NAME?
I'M CASSIE.
MY SISTER ROBIN CALLED YOU GUYS TO HELP US. I ALREADY TOLD HER YOU'RE HERE, SHE'S ON HER WAY.
NOBODY CALLED US. WE'RE HERE LOOKING FOR, UH--
ANCIENT RADIATION.
RIGHT. SEEN ANY? I GUESS MY FRIEND HERE EXPECTS TO FIND IT JUST LYING AROUND LIKE A--
WHAT THE HELL IS THIS?
A BURGER?!
GET THE HELL OUT OF MY RESTAURANT!!

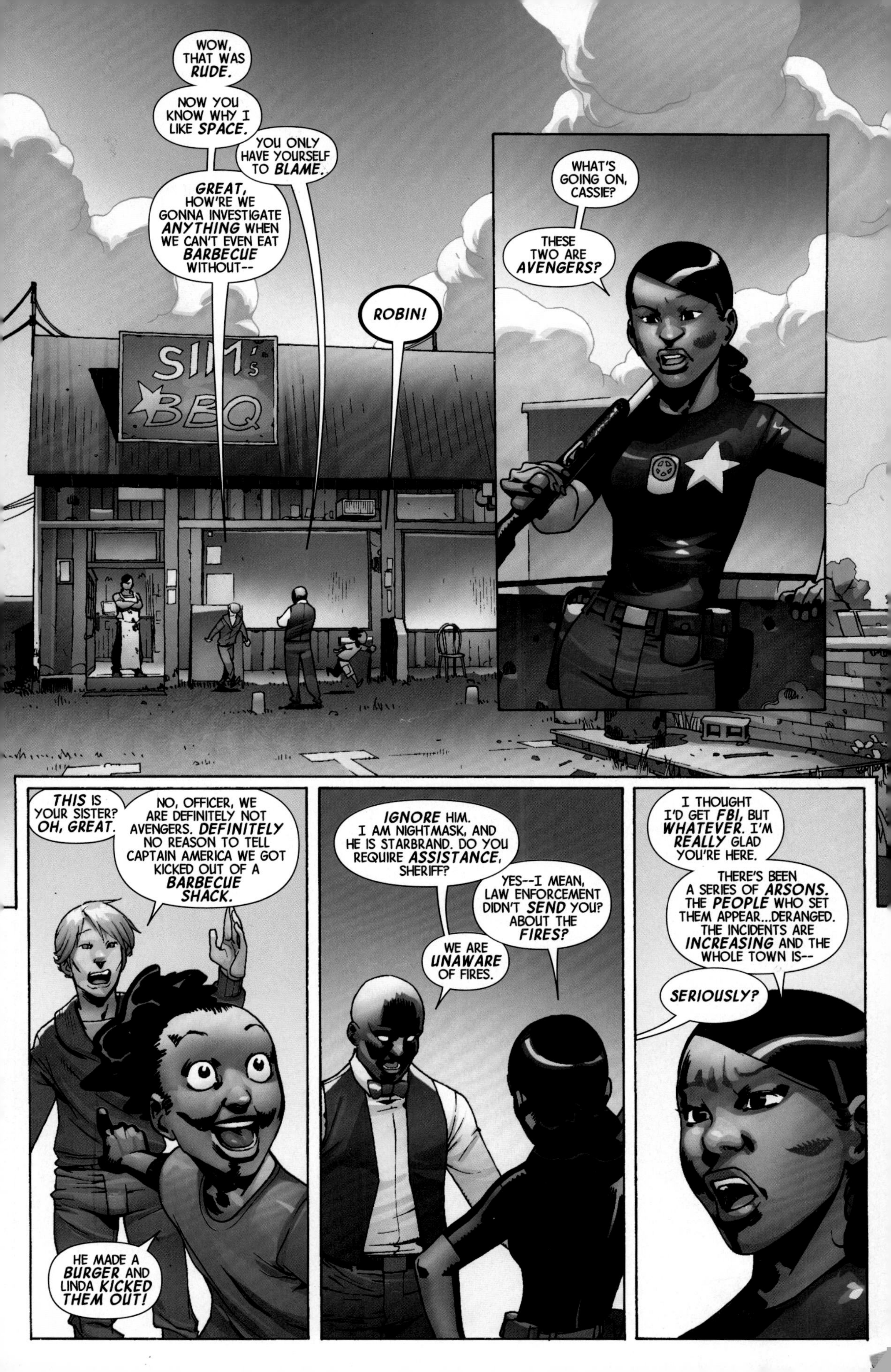
WOW, THAT WAS RUDE.
NOW YOU KNOW WHY I LIKE SPACE.
YOU ONLY HAVE YOURSELF TO BLAME.
GREAT, HOW'RE WE GONNA INVESTIGATE ANYTHING WHEN WE CAN'T EVEN EAT BARBECUE WITHOUT--
ROBIN!
SIM's BBQ
WHAT'S GOING ON, CASSIE?
THESE TWO ARE AVENGERS?
THIS IS YOUR SISTER? OH, GREAT.
NO, OFFICER, WE ARE DEFINITELY NOT AVENGERS. DEFINITELY NO REASON TO TELL CAPTAIN AMERICA WE GOT KICKED OUT OF A BARBECUE SHACK.
HE MADE A BURGER AND LINDA KICKED THEM OUT!
IGNORE HIM. I AM NIGHTMASK, AND HE IS STARBRAND. DO YOU REQUIRE ASSISTANCE, SHERIFF?
YES--I MEAN, LAW ENFORCEMENT DIDN'T SEND YOU? ABOUT THE FIRES?
WE ARE UNAWARE OF FIRES.
I THOUGHT I'D GET FBI, BUT WHATEVER. I'M REALLY GLAD YOU'RE HERE.
THERE'S BEEN A SERIES OF ARSONS. THE PEOPLE WHO SET THEM APPEAR...DERANGED. THE INCIDENTS ARE INCREASING AND THE WHOLE TOWN IS--
SERIOUSLY?

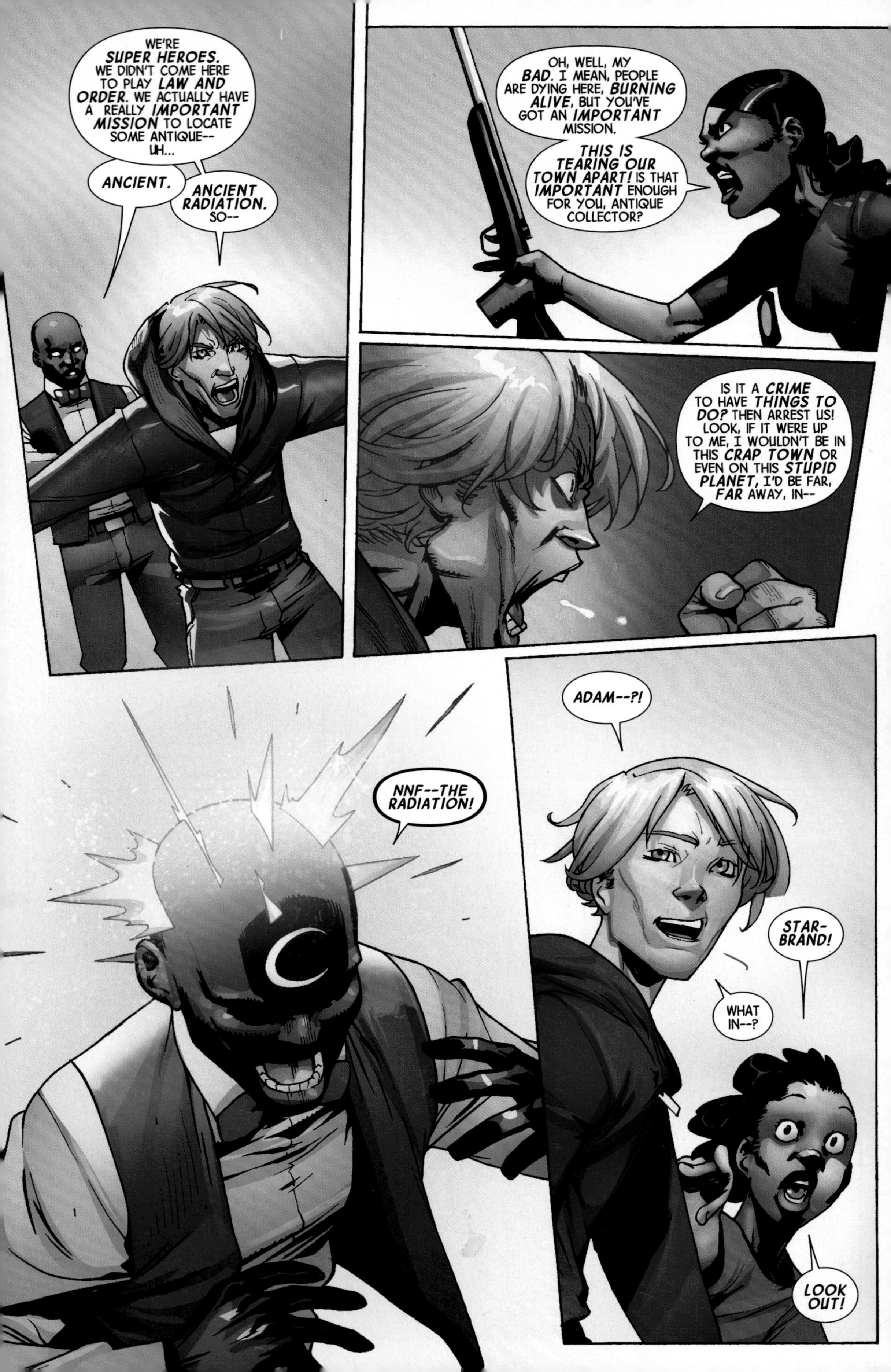
WE'RE SUPER HEROES. WE DIDN'T COME HERE TO PLAY LAW AND ORDER. WE ACTUALLY HAVE A REALLY IMPORTANT MISSION TO LOCATE SOME ANTIQUE-- UH...
ANCIENT.
ANCIENT RADIATION. SO--
OH, WELL, MY BAD. I MEAN, PEOPLE ARE DYING HERE, BURNING ALIVE, BUT YOU'VE GOT AN IMPORTANT MISSION.
THIS IS TEARING OUR TOWN APART! IS THAT IMPORTANT ENOUGH FOR YOU, ANTIQUE COLLECTOR?
IS IT A CRIME TO HAVE THINGS TO DO? THEN ARREST US! LOOK, IF IT WERE UP TO ME, I WOULDN'T BE IN THIS CRAP TOWN OR EVEN ON THIS STUPID PLANET, I'D BE FAR, FAR AWAY, IN--
NNF--THE RADIATION!
ADAM--?!
STAR-BRAND!
WHAT IN--?
LOOK OUT!

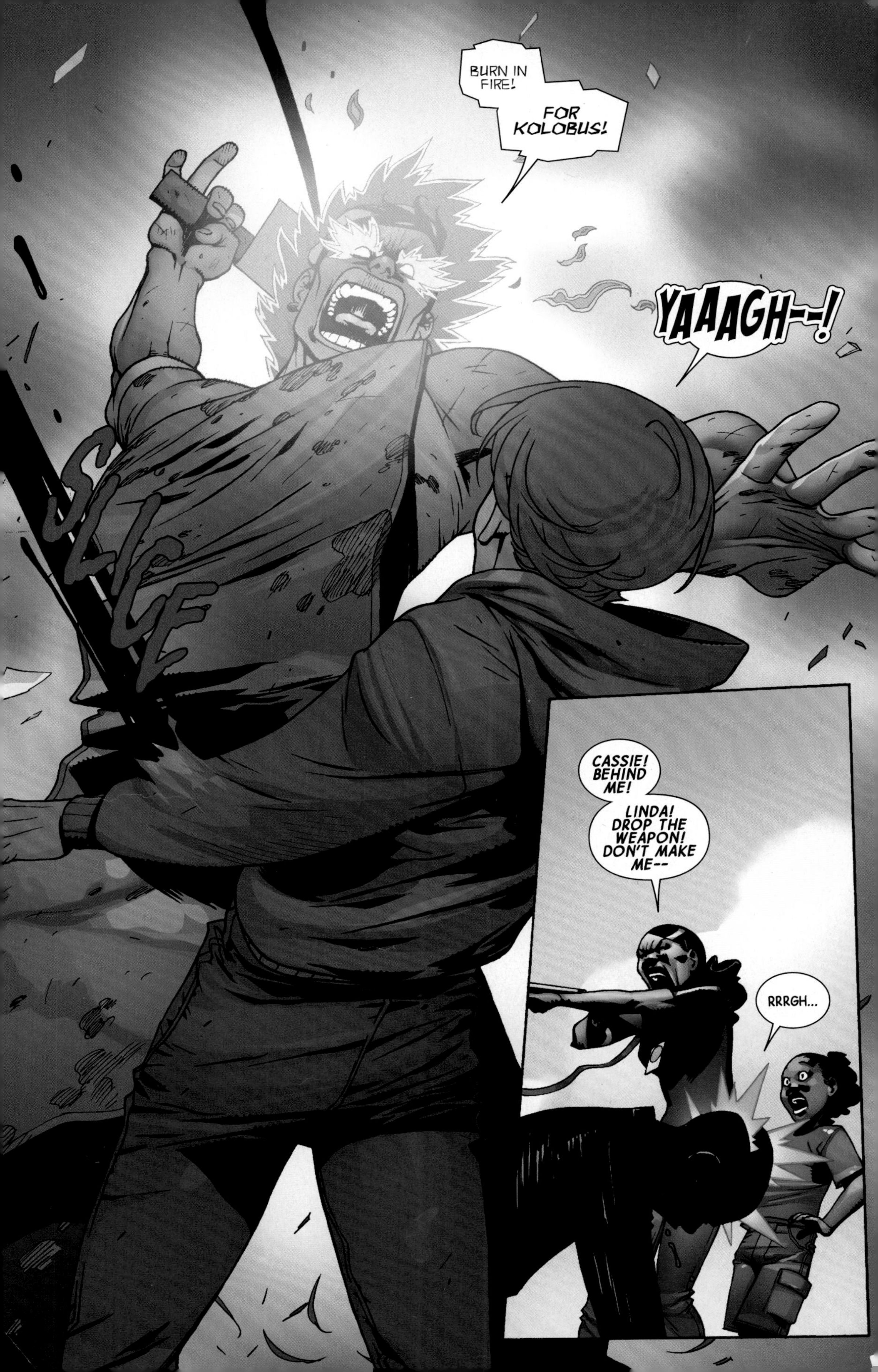
BURN IN FIRE!
FOR KOLOBUS!
YAAAGH--!
SLICE
CASSIE! BEHIND ME!
LINDA! DROP THE WEAPON! DON'T MAKE ME--
RRRGH...

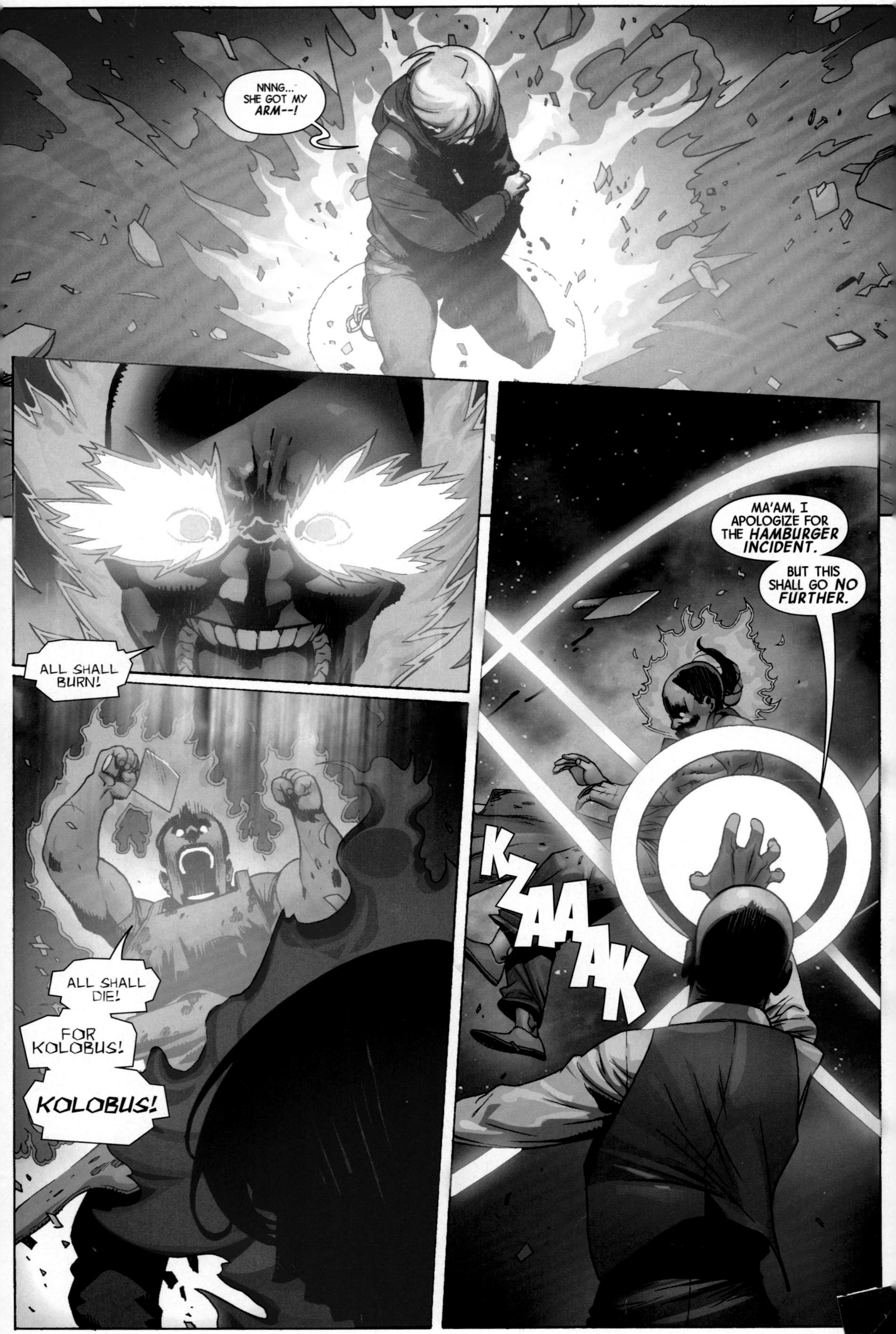
NNNG...
SHE GOT MY
ARM--!
ALL SHALL
BURN!
ALL SHALL
DIE!
FOR
KOLOBUS!
KOLOBUS!
MA'AM, I
APOLOGIZE FOR
THE HAMBURGER
INCIDENT.
BUT THIS
SHALL GO NO
FURTHER.
KZAAAAK

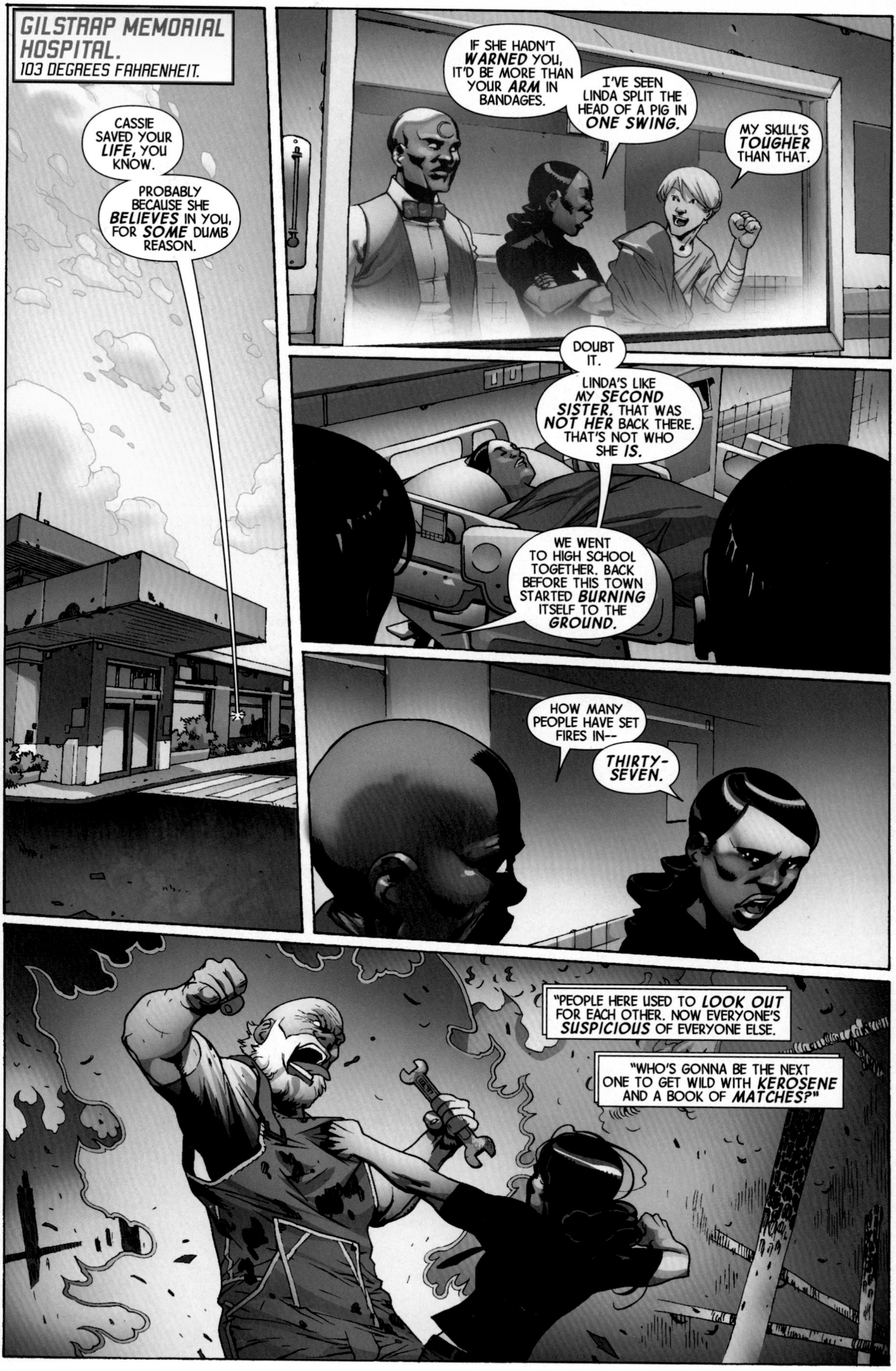
GILSTRAP MEMORIAL HOSPITAL.
103 DEGREES FAHRENHEIT.
CASSIE SAVED YOUR LIFE, YOU KNOW.
PROBABLY BECAUSE SHE BELIEVES IN YOU, FOR SOME DUMB REASON.
IF SHE HADN'T WARNED YOU, IT'D BE MORE THAN YOUR ARM IN BANDAGES.
I'VE SEEN LINDA SPLIT THE HEAD OF A PIG IN ONE SWING.
MY SKULL'S TOUGHER THAN THAT.
DOUBT IT.
LINDA'S LIKE MY SECOND SISTER. THAT WAS NOT HER BACK THERE. THAT'S NOT WHO SHE IS.
WE WENT TO HIGH SCHOOL TOGETHER. BACK BEFORE THIS TOWN STARTED BURNING ITSELF TO THE GROUND.
HOW MANY PEOPLE HAVE SET FIRES IN--
THIRTY-SEVEN.
"PEOPLE HERE USED TO LOOK OUT FOR EACH OTHER. NOW EVERYONE'S SUSPICIOUS OF EVERYONE ELSE.
"WHO'S GONNA BE THE NEXT ONE TO GET WILD WITH KEROSENE AND A BOOK OF MATCHES?"

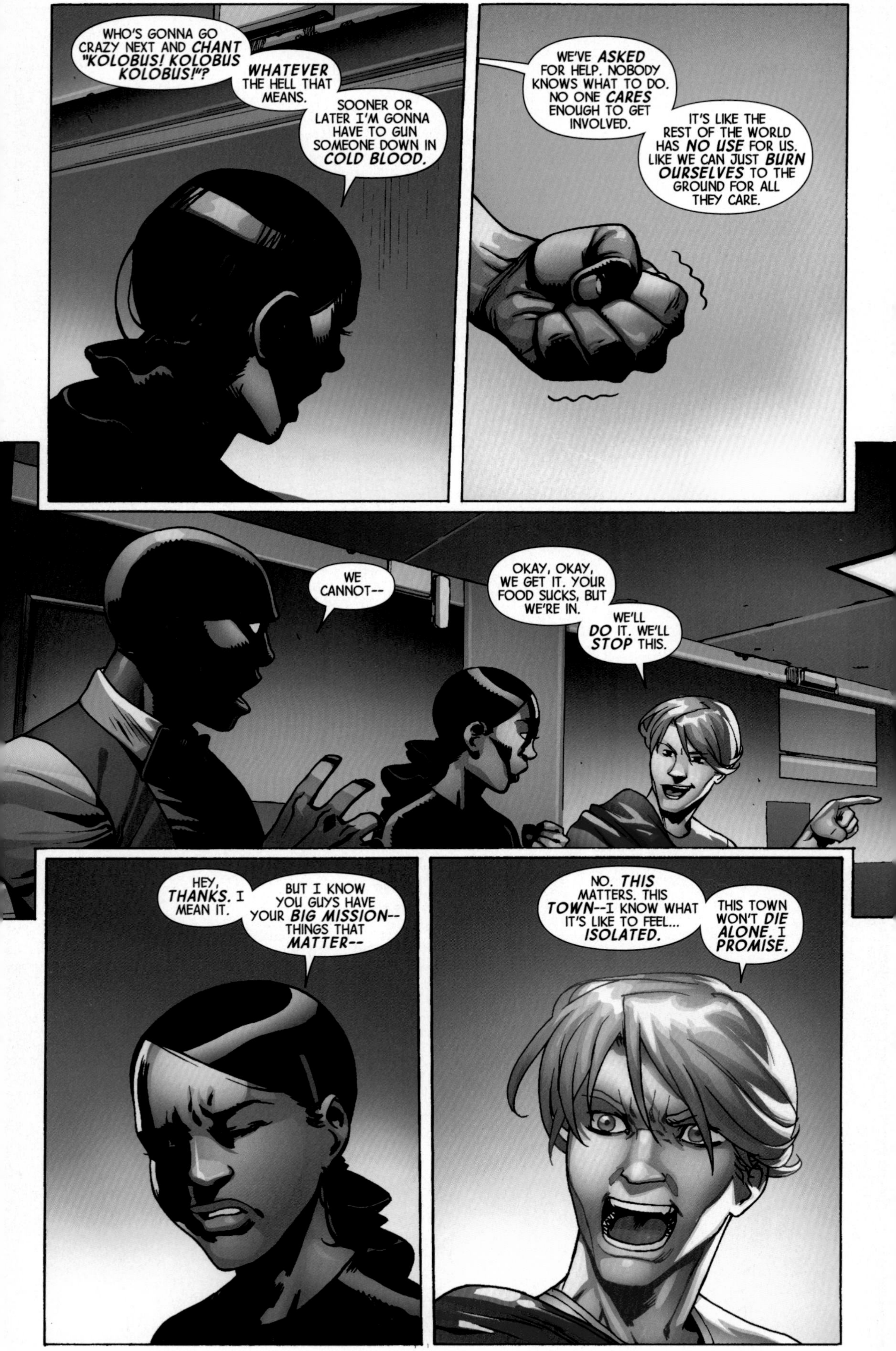
WHO'S GONNA GO CRAZY NEXT AND CHANT "KOLOBUS! KOLOBUS KOLOBUS!"?
WHATEVER THE HELL THAT MEANS.
SOONER OR LATER I'M GONNA HAVE TO GUN SOMEONE DOWN IN COLD BLOOD.
WE'VE ASKED FOR HELP. NOBODY KNOWS WHAT TO DO. NO ONE CARES ENOUGH TO GET INVOLVED.
IT'S LIKE THE REST OF THE WORLD HAS NO USE FOR US. LIKE WE CAN JUST BURN OURSELVES TO THE GROUND FOR ALL THEY CARE.
WE CANNOT--
OKAY, OKAY, WE GET IT. YOUR FOOD SUCKS, BUT WE'RE IN.
WE'LL DO IT. WE'LL STOP THIS.
HEY, THANKS. I MEAN IT.
BUT I KNOW YOU GUYS HAVE YOUR BIG MISSION-- THINGS THAT MATTER--
NO. THIS MATTERS. THIS TOWN--I KNOW WHAT IT'S LIKE TO FEEL... ISOLATED.
THIS TOWN WON'T DIE ALONE. I PROMISE.

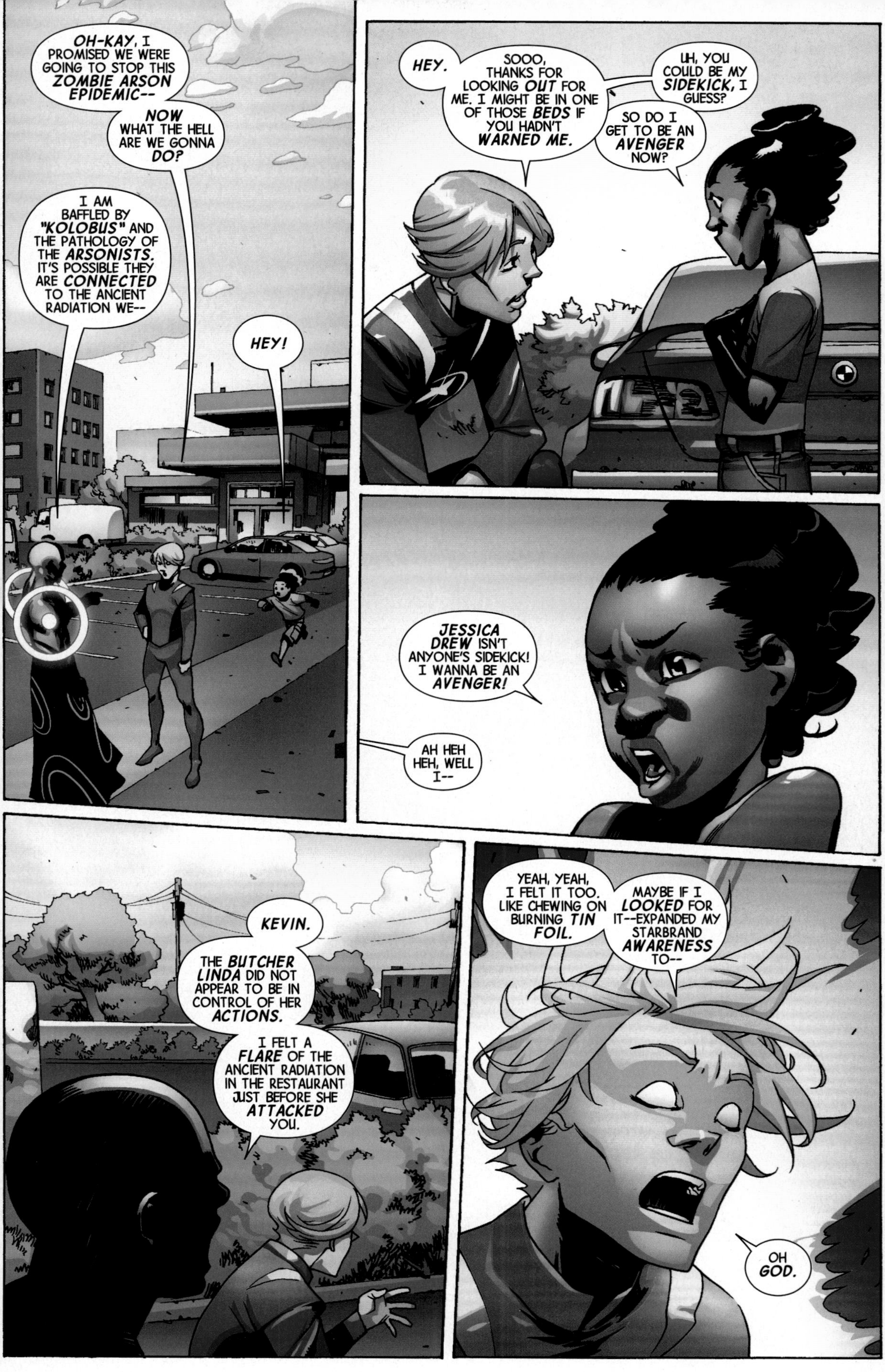
OH-KAY, I PROMISED WE WERE GOING TO STOP THIS ZOMBIE ARSON EPIDEMIC--
NOW WHAT THE HELL ARE WE GONNA DO?
I AM BAFFLED BY "KOLOBUS" AND THE PATHOLOGY OF THE ARSONISTS. IT'S POSSIBLE THEY ARE CONNECTED TO THE ANCIENT RADIATION WE--
HEY!
HEY.
SOOO, THANKS FOR LOOKING OUT FOR ME. I MIGHT BE IN ONE OF THOSE BEDS IF YOU HADN'T WARNED ME.
UH, YOU COULD BE MY SIDEKICK, I GUESS?
SO DO I GET TO BE AN AVENGER NOW?
JESSICA DREW ISN'T ANYONE'S SIDEKICK! I WANNA BE AN AVENGER!
AH HEH HEH, WELL I--
KEVIN.
THE BUTCHER LINDA DID NOT APPEAR TO BE IN CONTROL OF HER ACTIONS.
I FELT A FLARE OF THE ANCIENT RADIATION IN THE RESTAURANT JUST BEFORE SHE ATTACKED YOU.
YEAH, YEAH, I FELT IT TOO. LIKE CHEWING ON BURNING TIN FOIL.
MAYBE IF I LOOKED FOR IT--EXPANDED MY STARBRAND AWARENESS TO--
OH GOD.

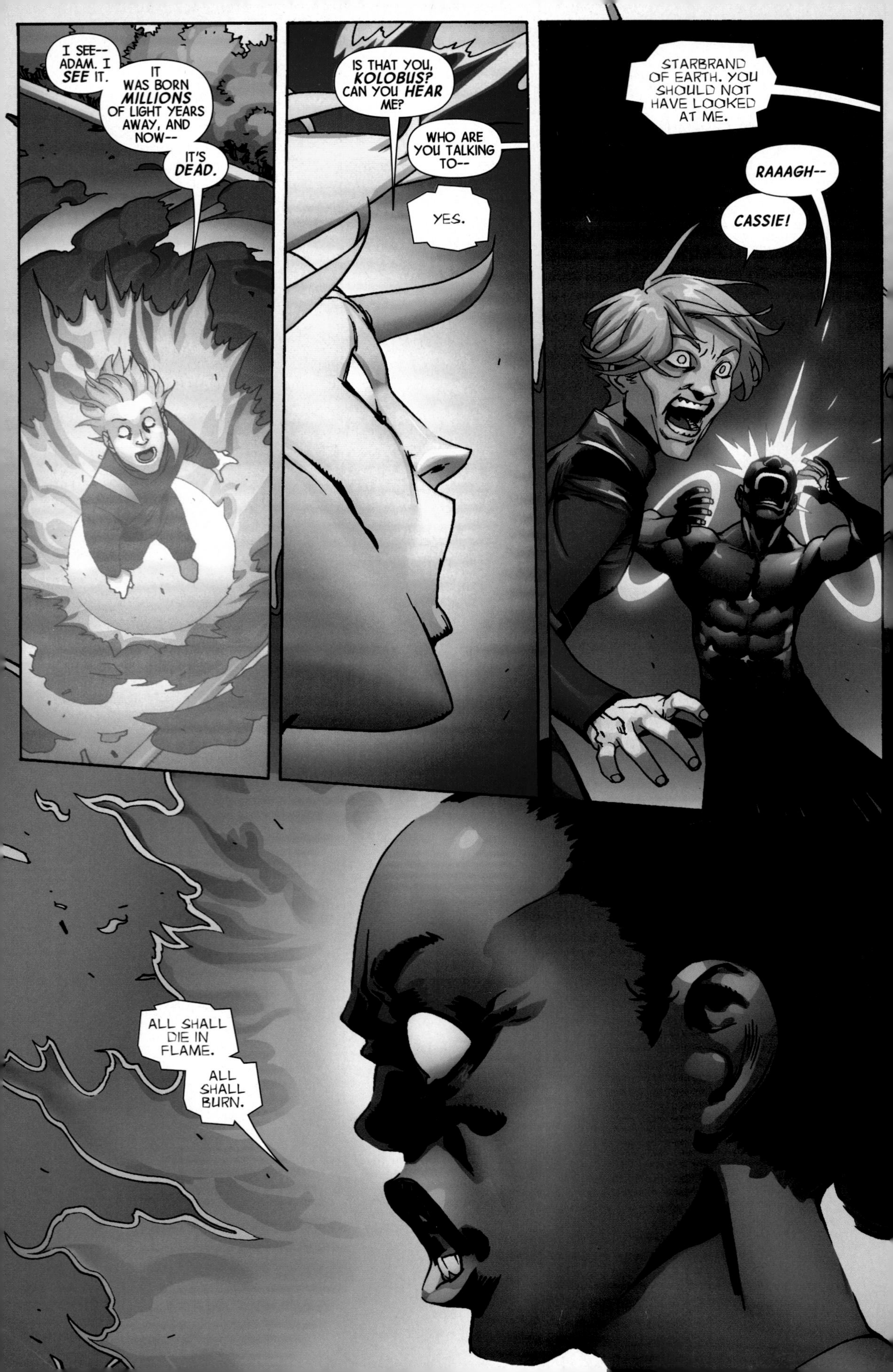
I SEE-- ADAM. I SEE IT.
IT WAS BORN MILLIONS OF LIGHT YEARS AWAY, AND NOW--
IT'S DEAD.
IS THAT YOU, KOLOBUS? CAN YOU HEAR ME?
WHO ARE YOU TALKING TO--
YES.
STARBRAND OF EARTH. YOU SHOULD NOT HAVE LOOKED AT ME.
RAAAGH--
CASSIE!
ALL SHALL DIE IN FLAME.
ALL SHALL BURN.

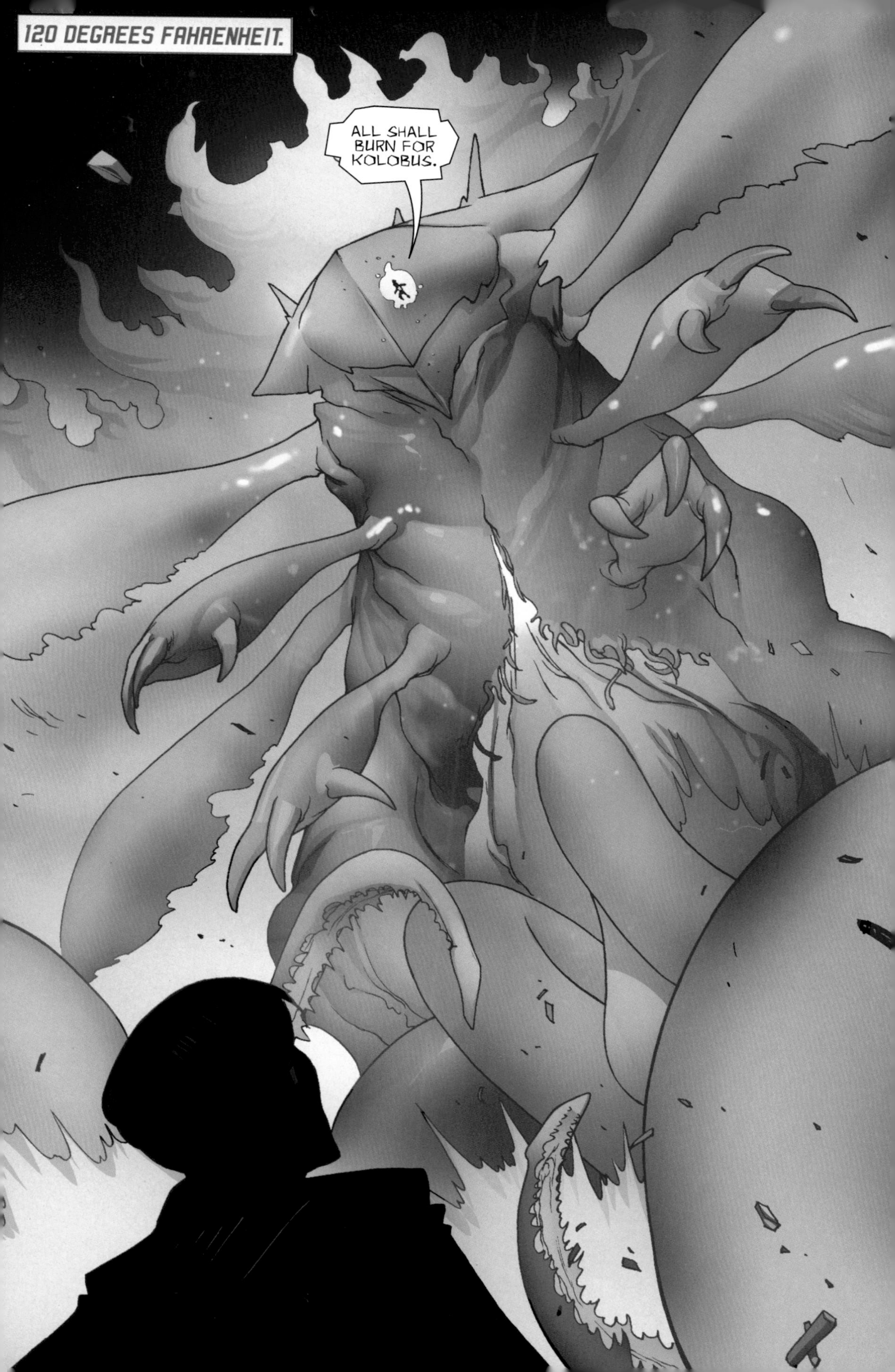
120 DEGREES FAHRENHEIT.
ALL SHALL BURN FOR KOLOBUS.

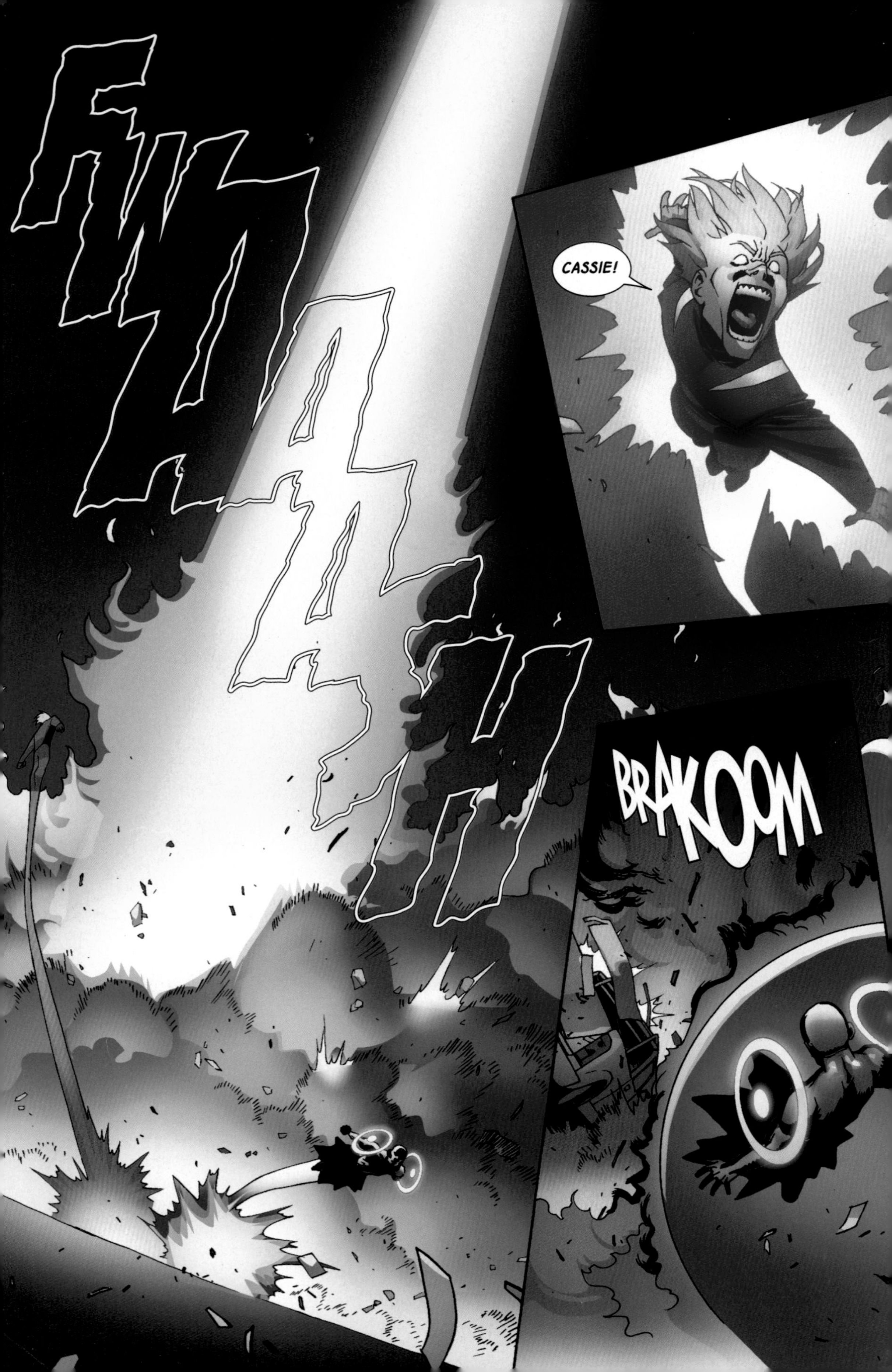
CASSIE!
BRAKOOM

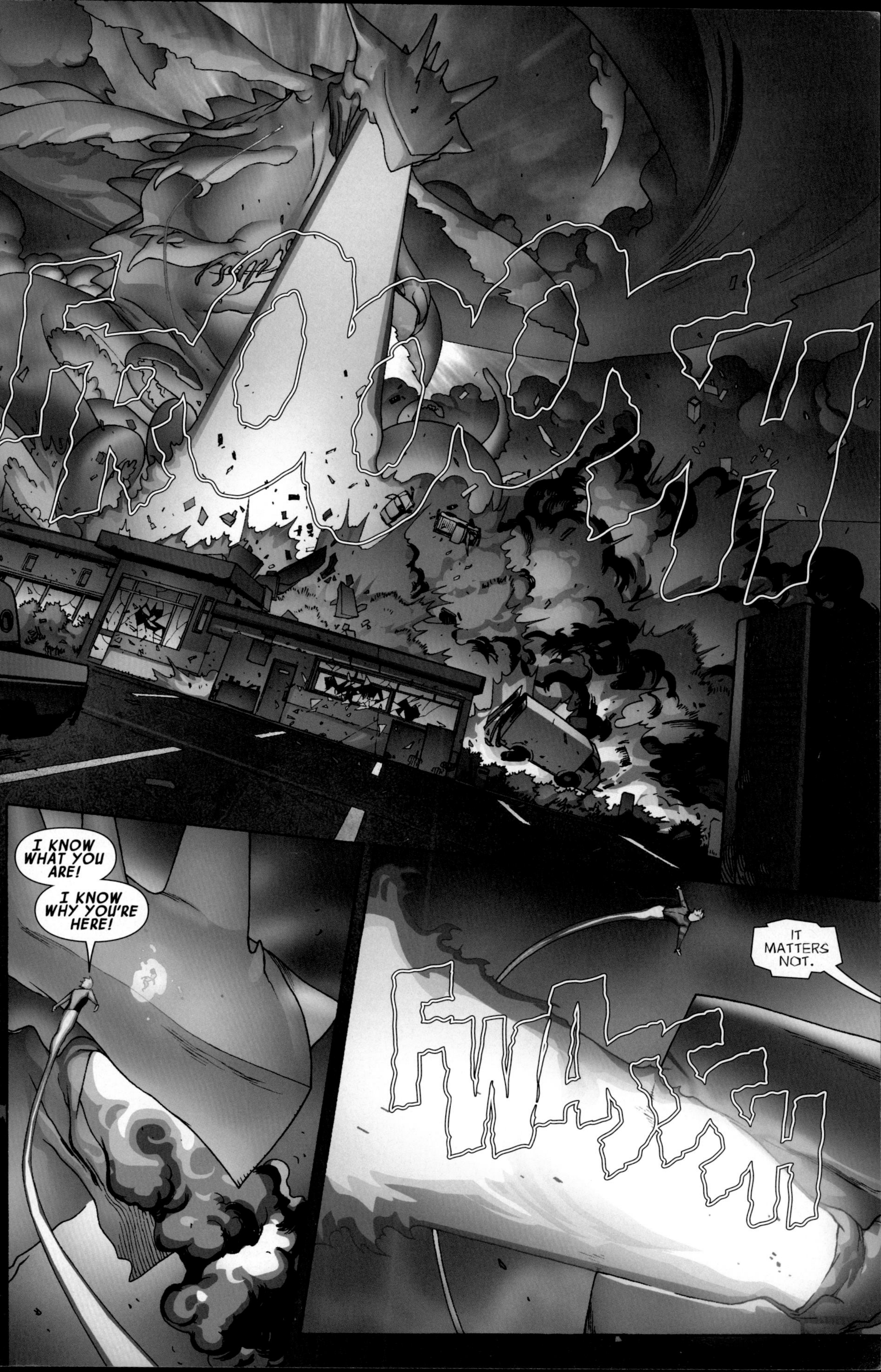
I KNOW WHAT YOU ARE!
I KNOW WHY YOU'RE HERE!
IT MATTERS NOT.

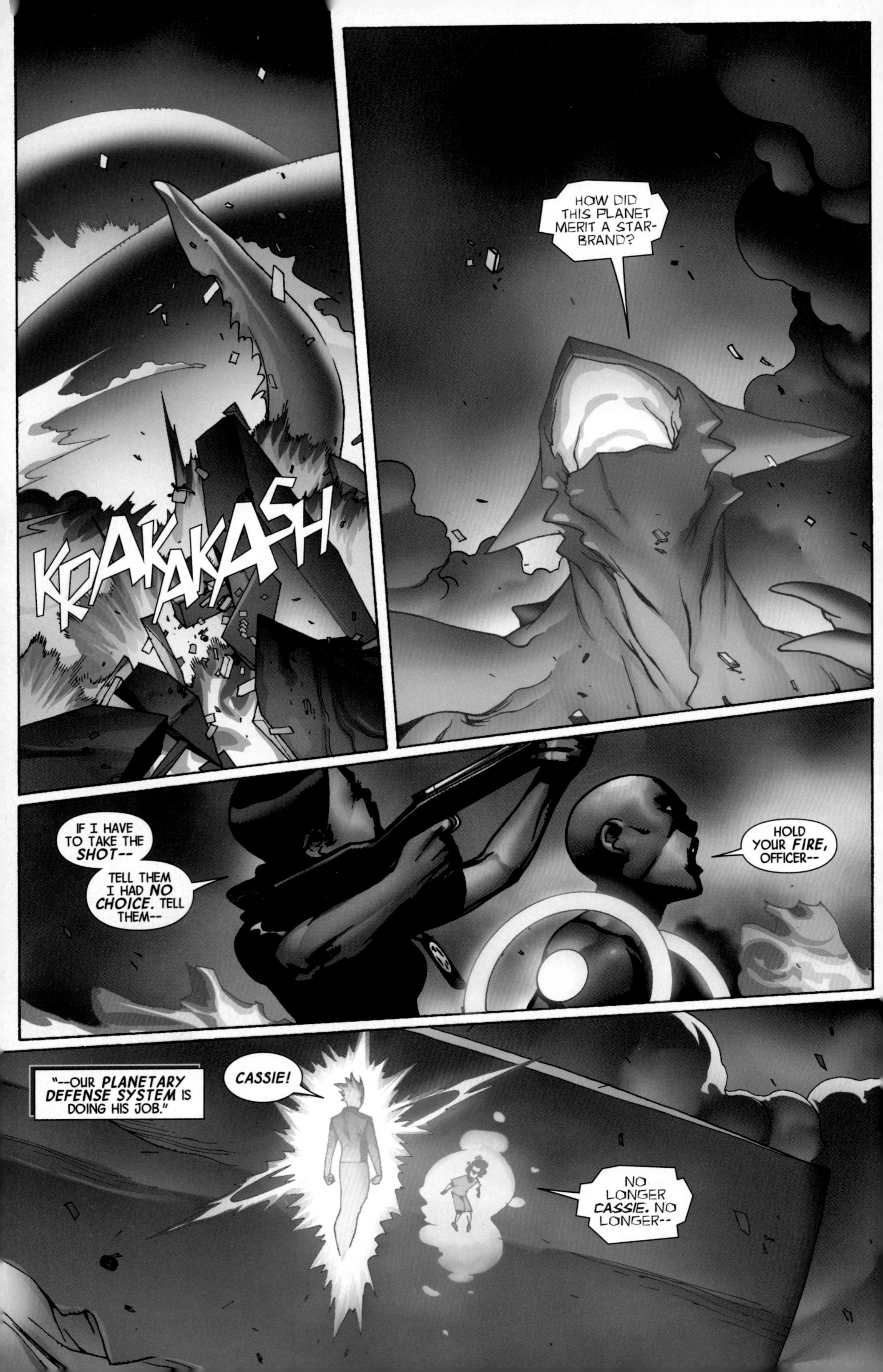
KRAKAKASH
HOW DID THIS PLANET MERIT A STAR-BRAND?
IF I HAVE TO TAKE THE SHOT--
TELL THEM I HAD NO CHOICE. TELL THEM--
HOLD YOUR FIRE, OFFICER--
"--OUR PLANETARY DEFENSE SYSTEM IS DOING HIS JOB."
CASSIE!
NO LONGER CASSIE. NO LONGER--

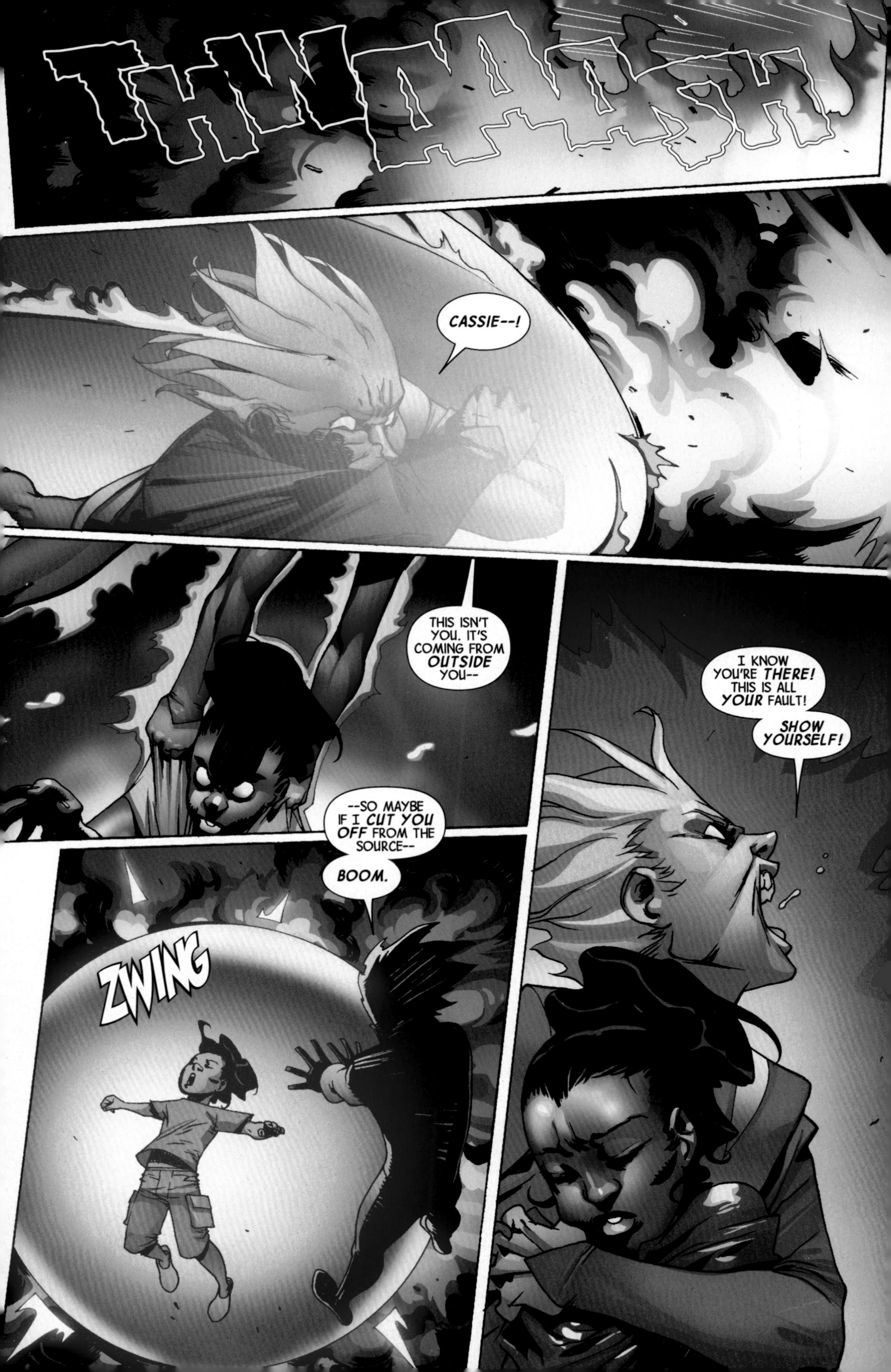
THWAASH
CASSIE--!
THIS ISN'T YOU. IT'S COMING FROM OUTSIDE YOU--
--SO MAYBE IF I CUT YOU OFF FROM THE SOURCE--
BOOM.
ZWING
I KNOW YOU'RE THERE! THIS IS ALL YOUR FAULT!
SHOW YOURSELF!

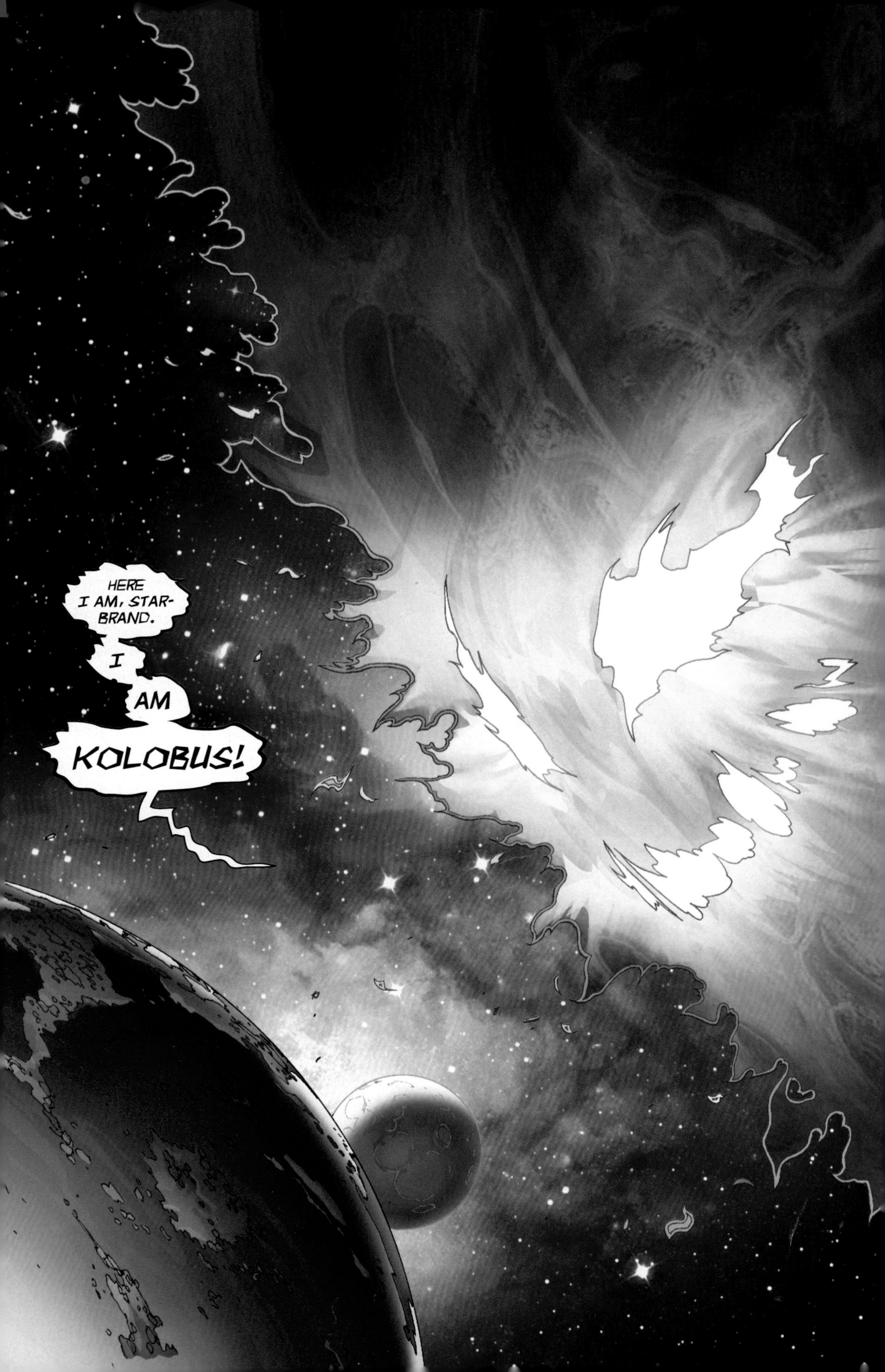
HERE I AM, STAR-BRAND.
I AM KOLOBUS!

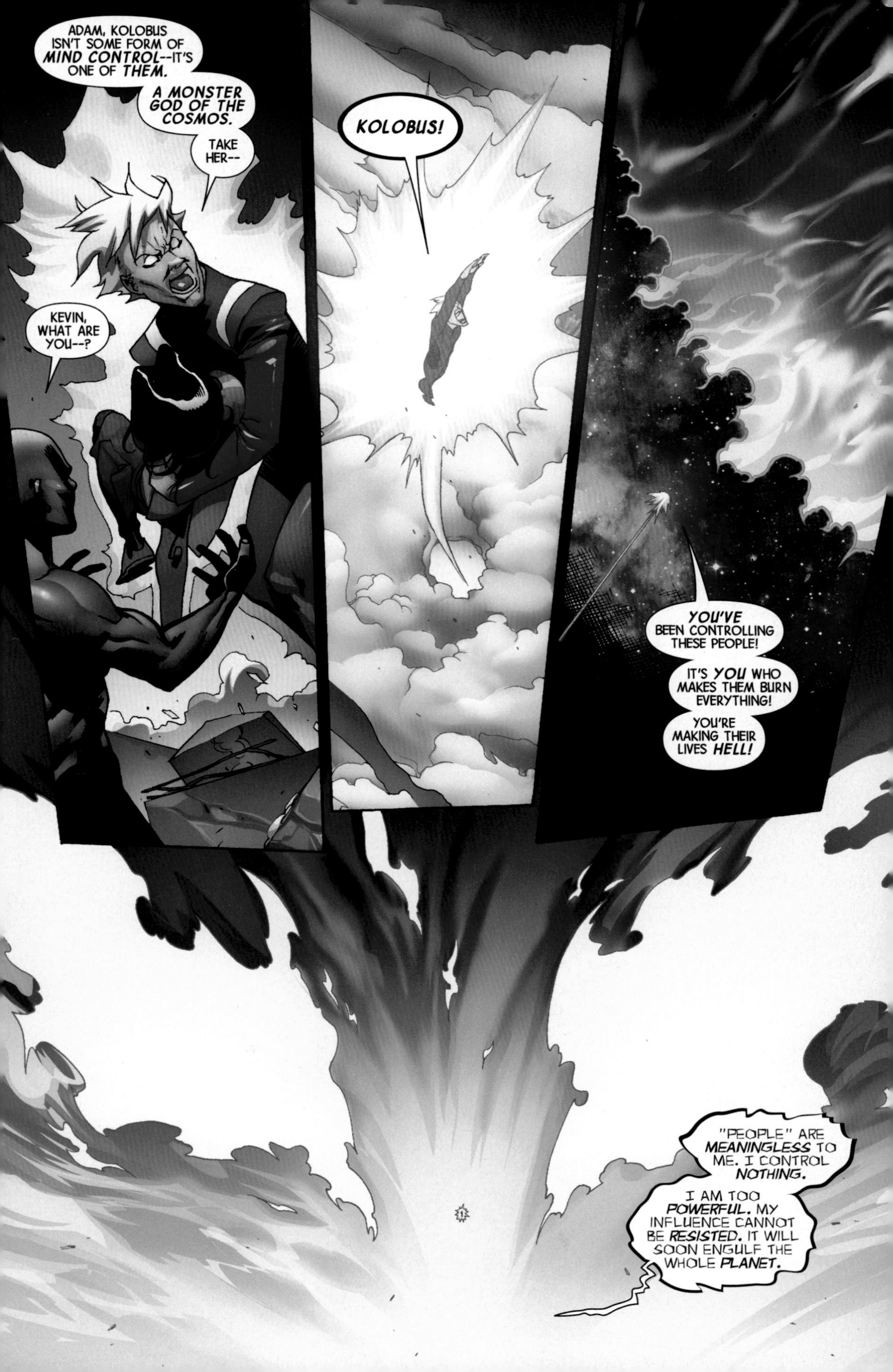
ADAM, KOLOBUS ISN'T SOME FORM OF MIND CONTROL--IT'S ONE OF THEM.
A MONSTER GOD OF THE COSMOS.
TAKE HER--
KEVIN, WHAT ARE YOU--?
KOLOBUS!
YOU'VE BEEN CONTROLLING THESE PEOPLE!
IT'S YOU WHO MAKES THEM BURN EVERYTHING!
YOU'RE MAKING THEIR LIVES HELL!
"PEOPLE" ARE MEANINGLESS TO ME. I CONTROL NOTHING.
I AM TOO POWERFUL. MY INFLUENCE CANNOT BE RESISTED. IT WILL SOON ENGULF THE WHOLE PLANET.

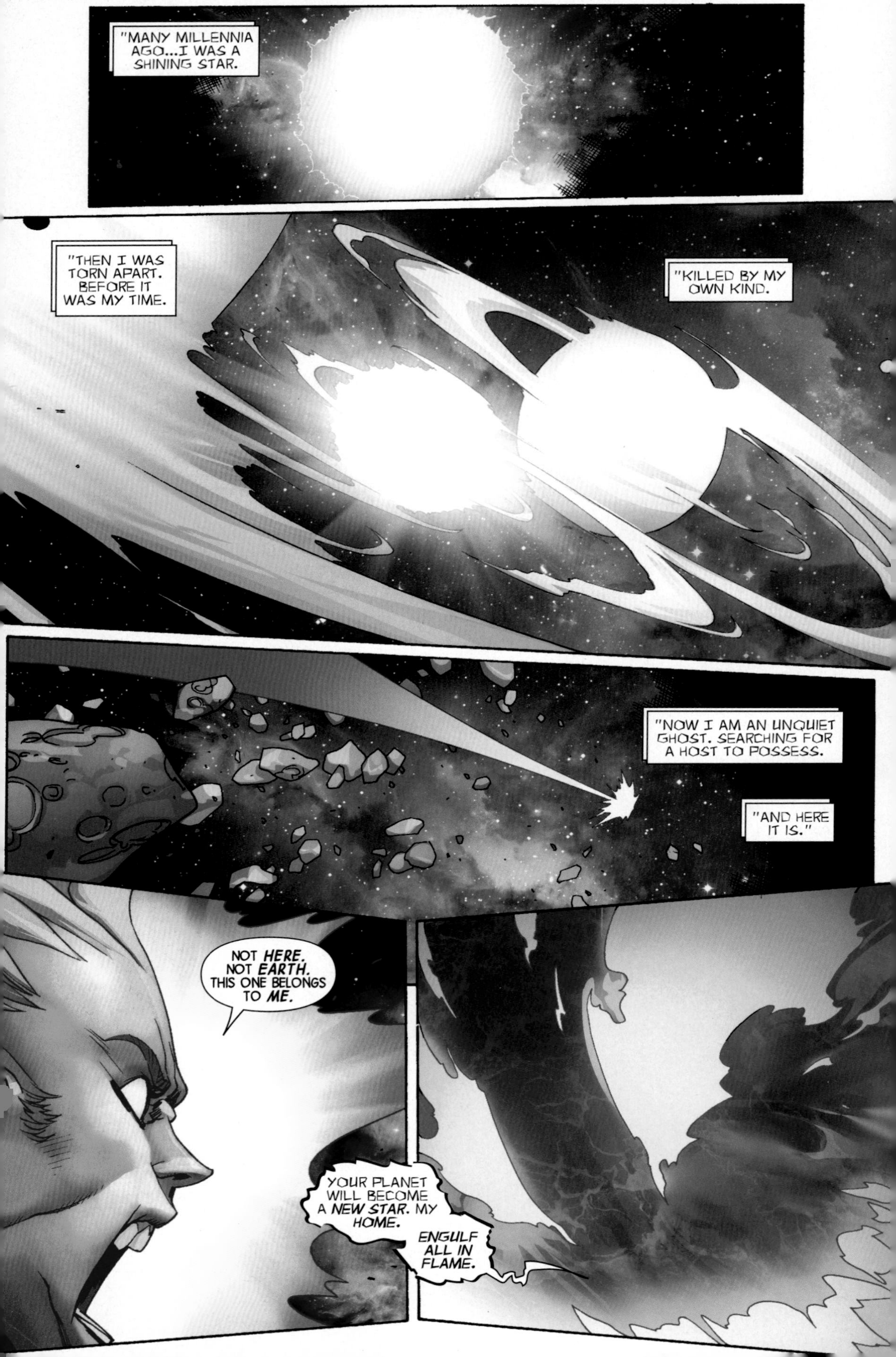

"MANY MILLENNIA AGO...I WAS A SHINING STAR.
"THEN I WAS TORN APART. BEFORE IT WAS MY TIME.
"KILLED BY MY OWN KIND.
"NOW I AM AN UNQUIET GHOST. SEARCHING FOR A HOST TO POSSESS.
"AND HERE IT IS."
NOT *HERE*. NOT *EARTH*. THIS ONE BELONGS TO *ME*.
YOUR PLANET WILL BECOME A *NEW STAR*. MY *HOME*.
*ENGULF ALL IN FLAME.*

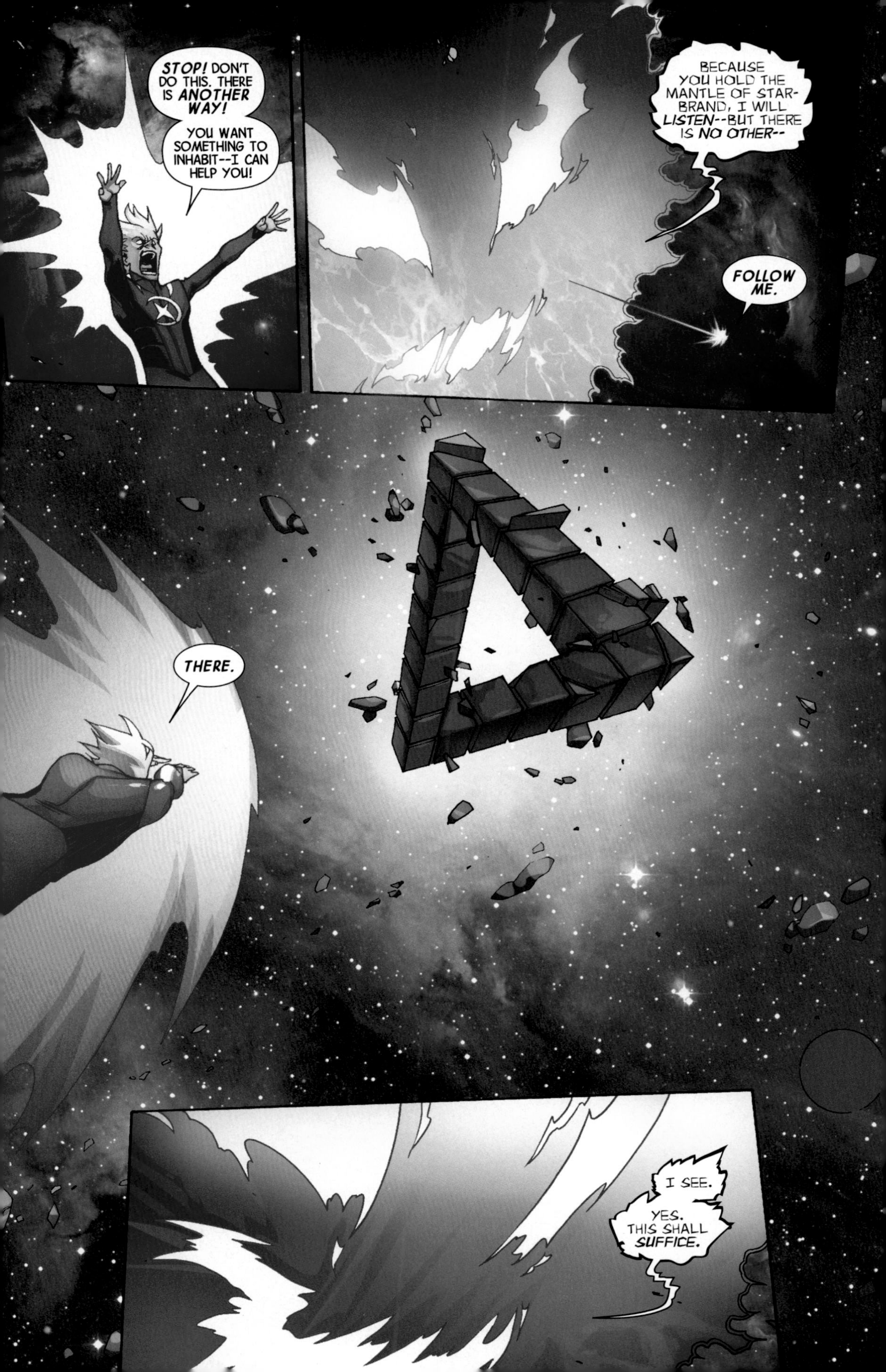
STOP! DON'T DO THIS. THERE IS ANOTHER WAY!
YOU WANT SOMETHING TO INHABIT--I CAN HELP YOU!
BECAUSE YOU HOLD THE MANTLE OF STAR-BRAND, I WILL LISTEN--BUT THERE IS NO OTHER--
FOLLOW ME.
THERE.
I SEE.
YES. THIS SHALL SUFFICE.

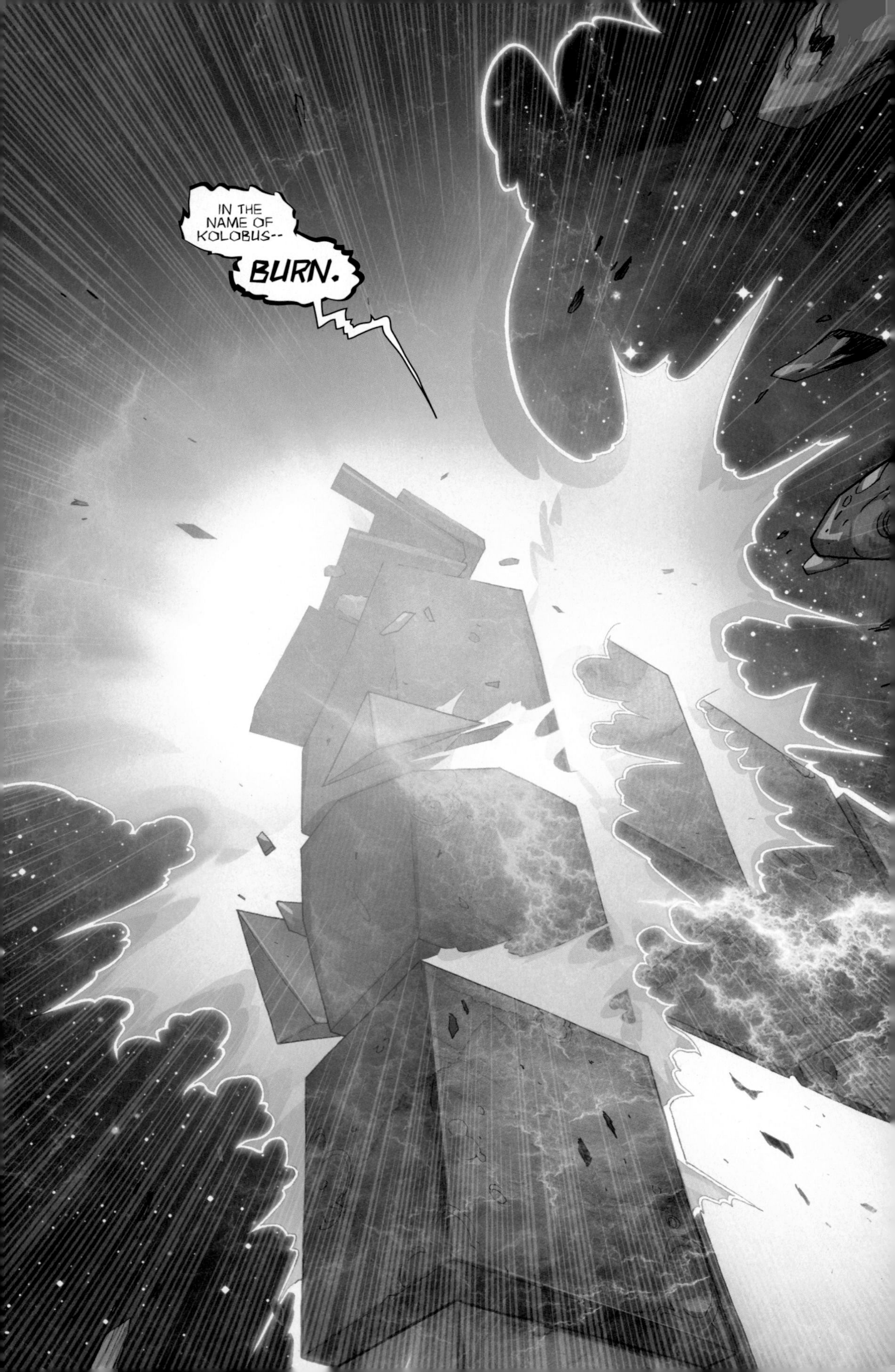
IN THE NAME OF KOLOBUS--
BURN.

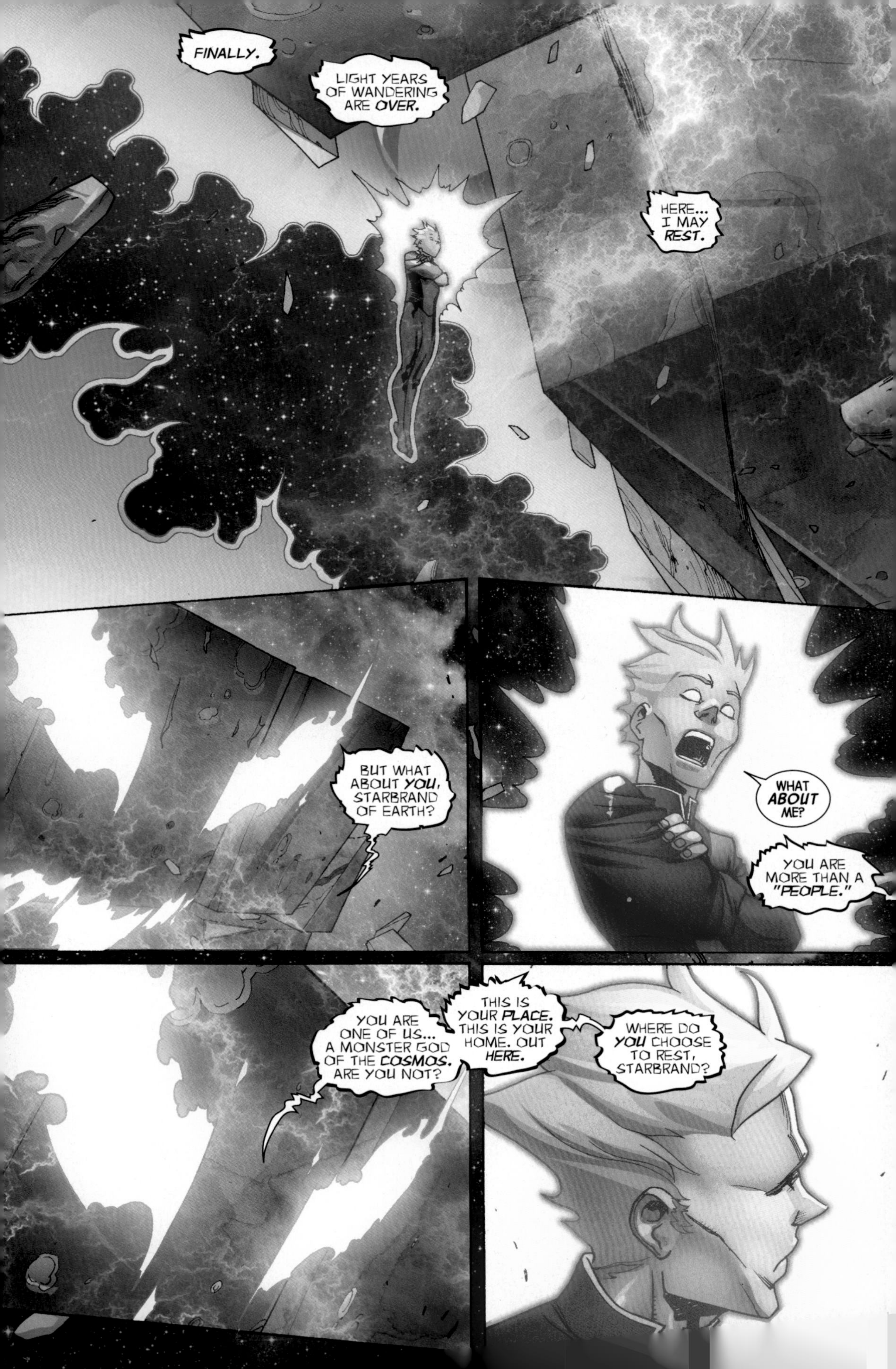
FINALLY.
LIGHT YEARS OF WANDERING ARE OVER.
HERE... I MAY REST.
BUT WHAT ABOUT YOU, STARBRAND OF EARTH?
WHAT ABOUT ME?
YOU ARE MORE THAN A "PEOPLE."
YOU ARE ONE OF US... A MONSTER GOD OF THE COSMOS. ARE YOU NOT?
THIS IS YOUR PLACE. THIS IS YOUR HOME. OUT HERE.
WHERE DO YOU CHOOSE TO REST, STARBRAND?

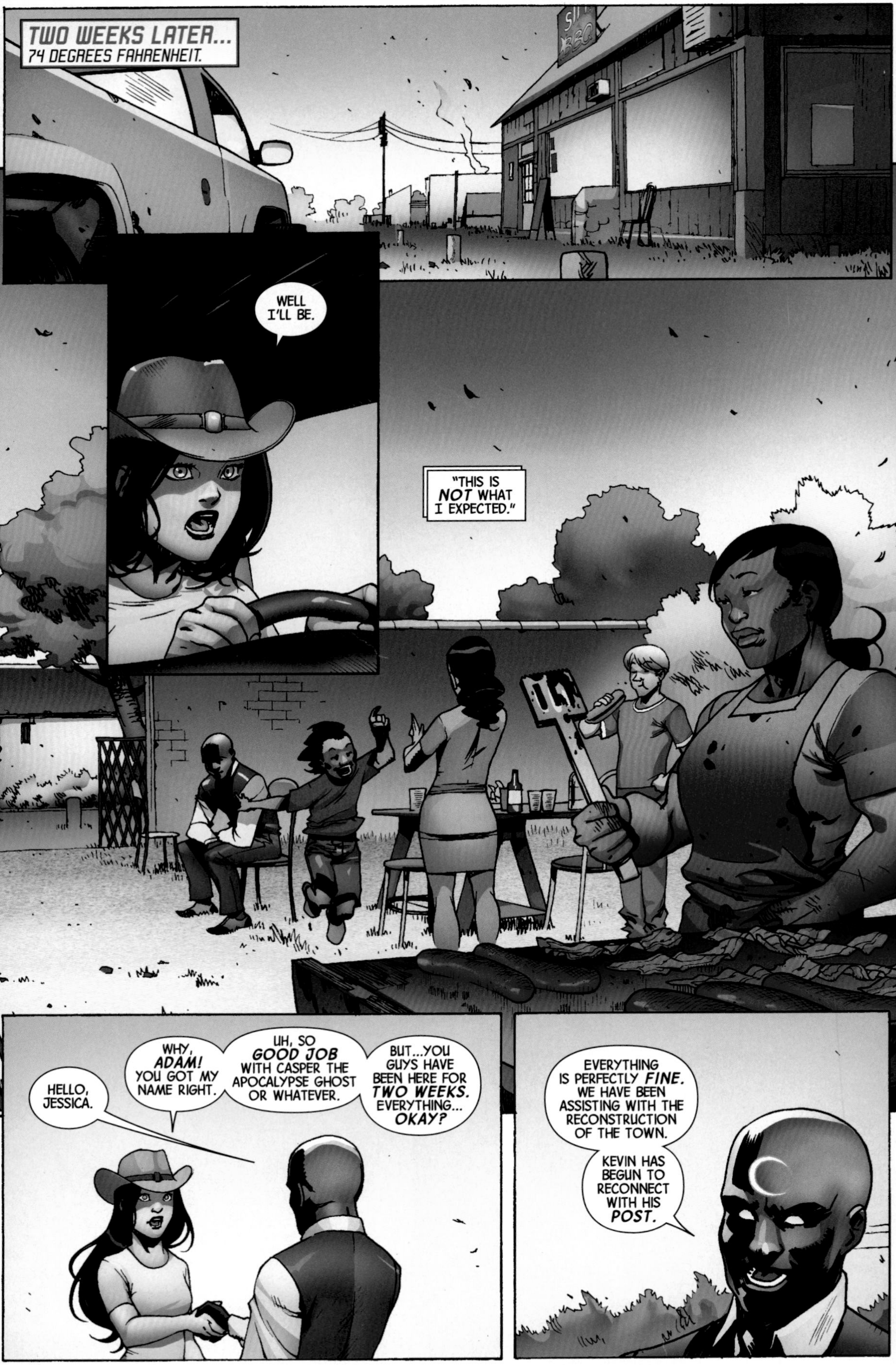
TWO WEEKS LATER... 74 DEGREES FAHRENHEIT.
WELL I'LL BE.
"THIS IS NOT WHAT I EXPECTED."
HELLO, JESSICA.
WHY, ADAM! YOU GOT MY NAME RIGHT.
UH, SO GOOD JOB WITH CASPER THE APOCALYPSE GHOST OR WHATEVER.
BUT...YOU GUYS HAVE BEEN HERE FOR TWO WEEKS. EVERYTHING... OKAY?
EVERYTHING IS PERFECTLY FINE. WE HAVE BEEN ASSISTING WITH THE RECONSTRUCTION OF THE TOWN.
KEVIN HAS BEGUN TO RECONNECT WITH HIS POST.

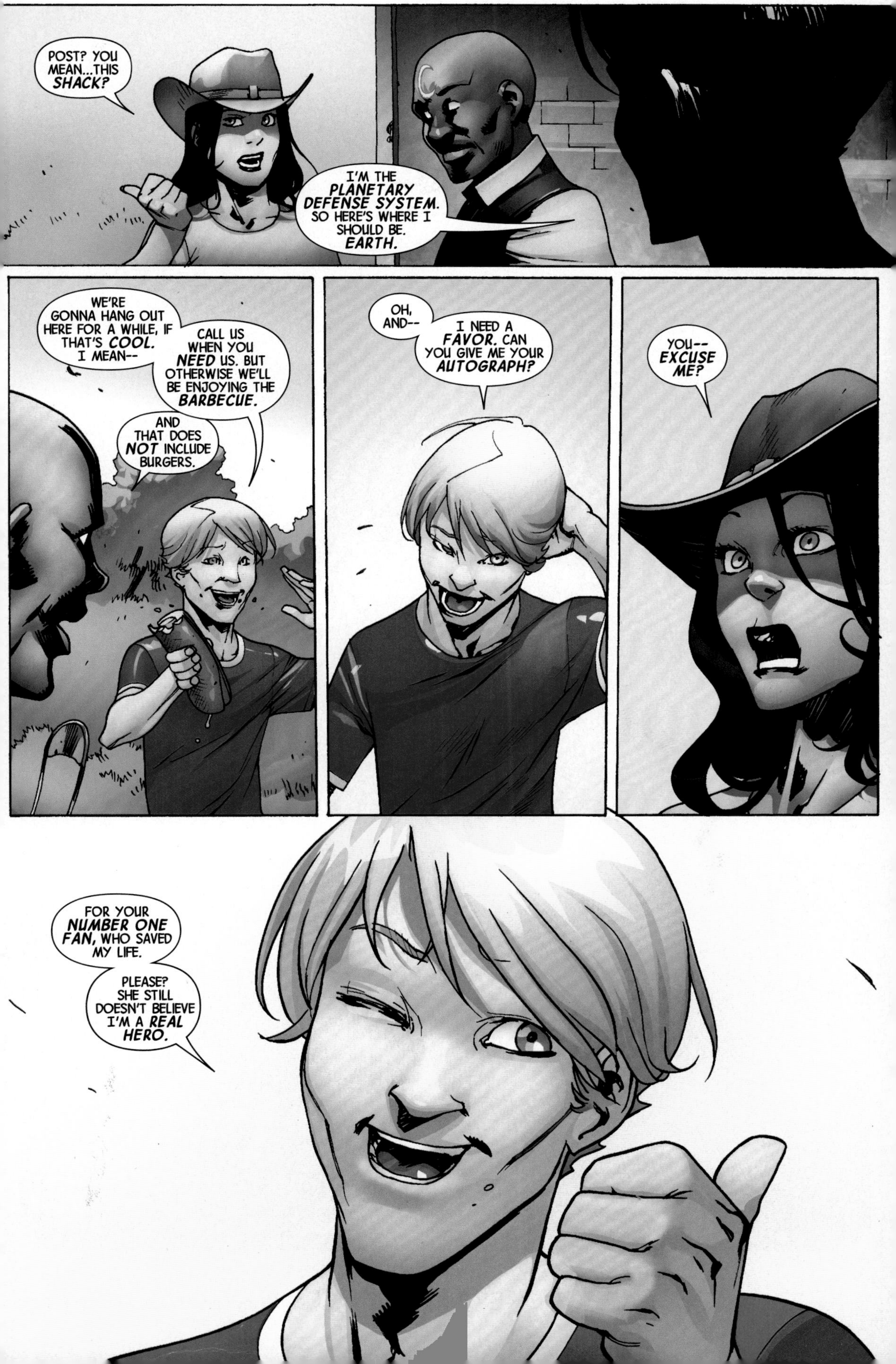
POST? YOU MEAN...THIS SHACK?
I'M THE PLANETARY DEFENSE SYSTEM. SO HERE'S WHERE I SHOULD BE. EARTH.
WE'RE GONNA HANG OUT HERE FOR A WHILE, IF THAT'S COOL. I MEAN--
CALL US WHEN YOU NEED US. BUT OTHERWISE WE'LL BE ENJOYING THE BARBECUE.
AND THAT DOES NOT INCLUDE BURGERS.
OH, AND--
I NEED A FAVOR. CAN YOU GIVE ME YOUR AUTOGRAPH?
YOU-- EXCUSE ME?
FOR YOUR NUMBER ONE FAN, WHO SAVED MY LIFE.
PLEASE? SHE STILL DOESN'T BELIEVE I'M A REAL HERO.

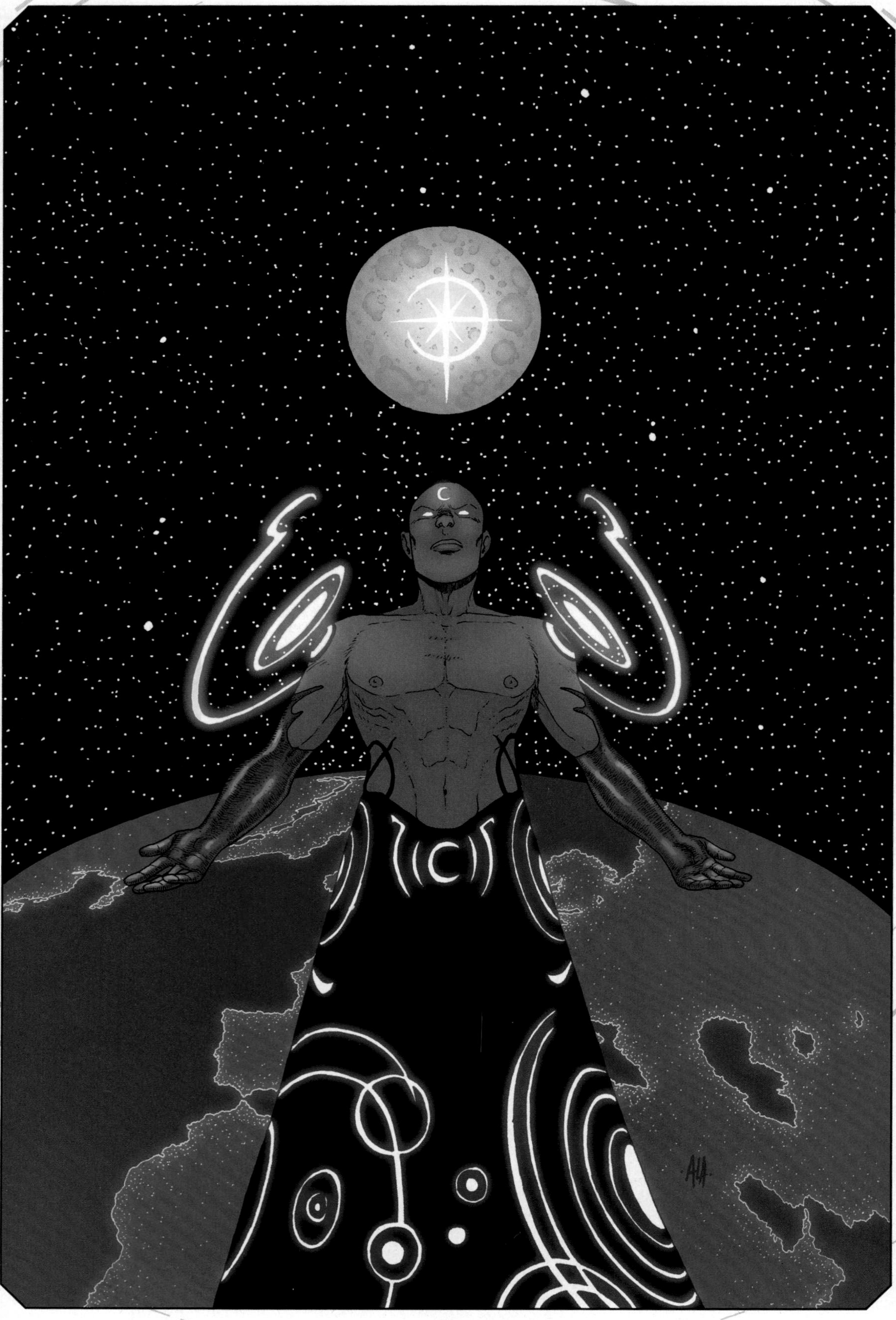

**AVENGERS 34.2 Variant Cover** by Andre Araujo & Jordie Bellaire

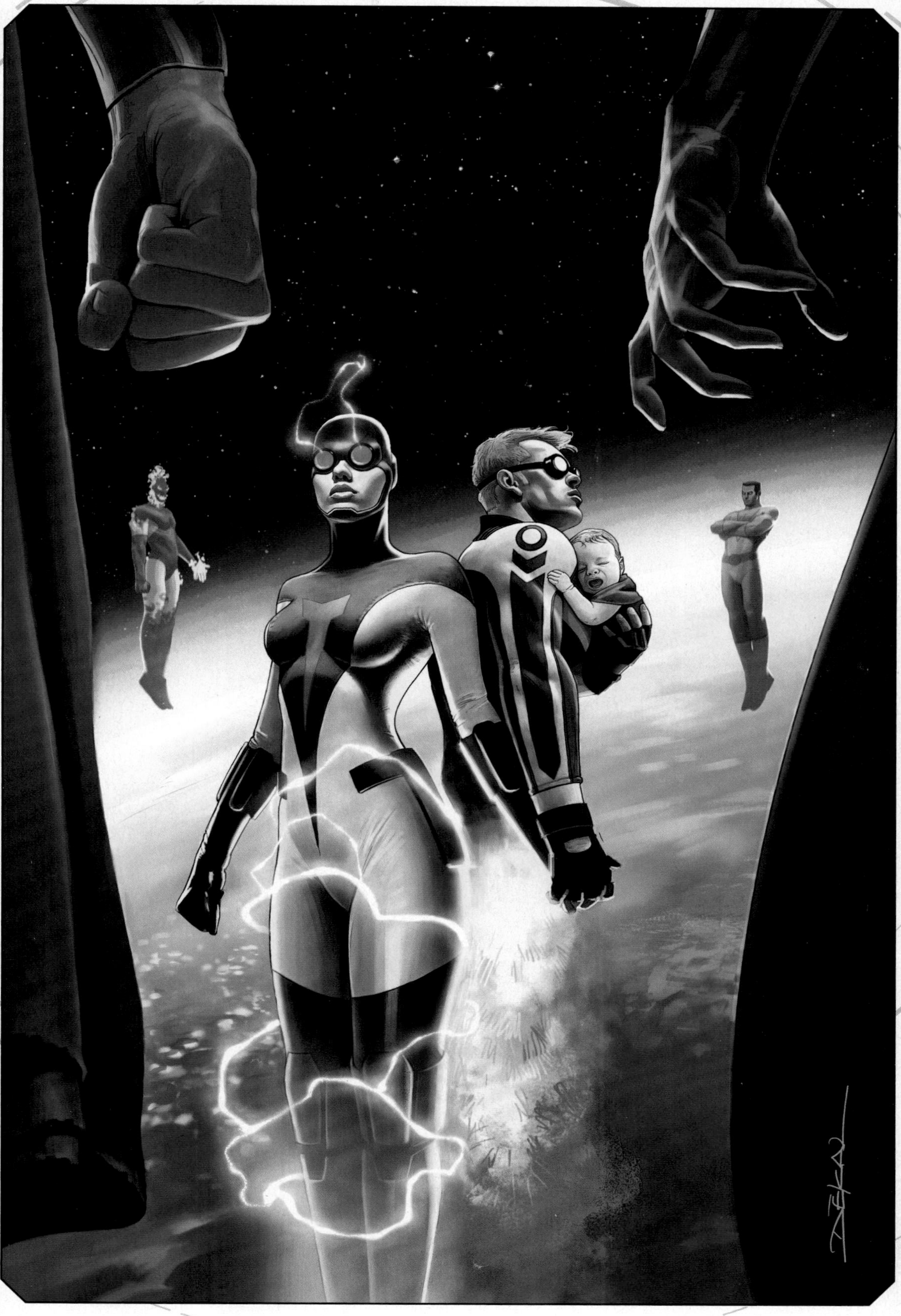

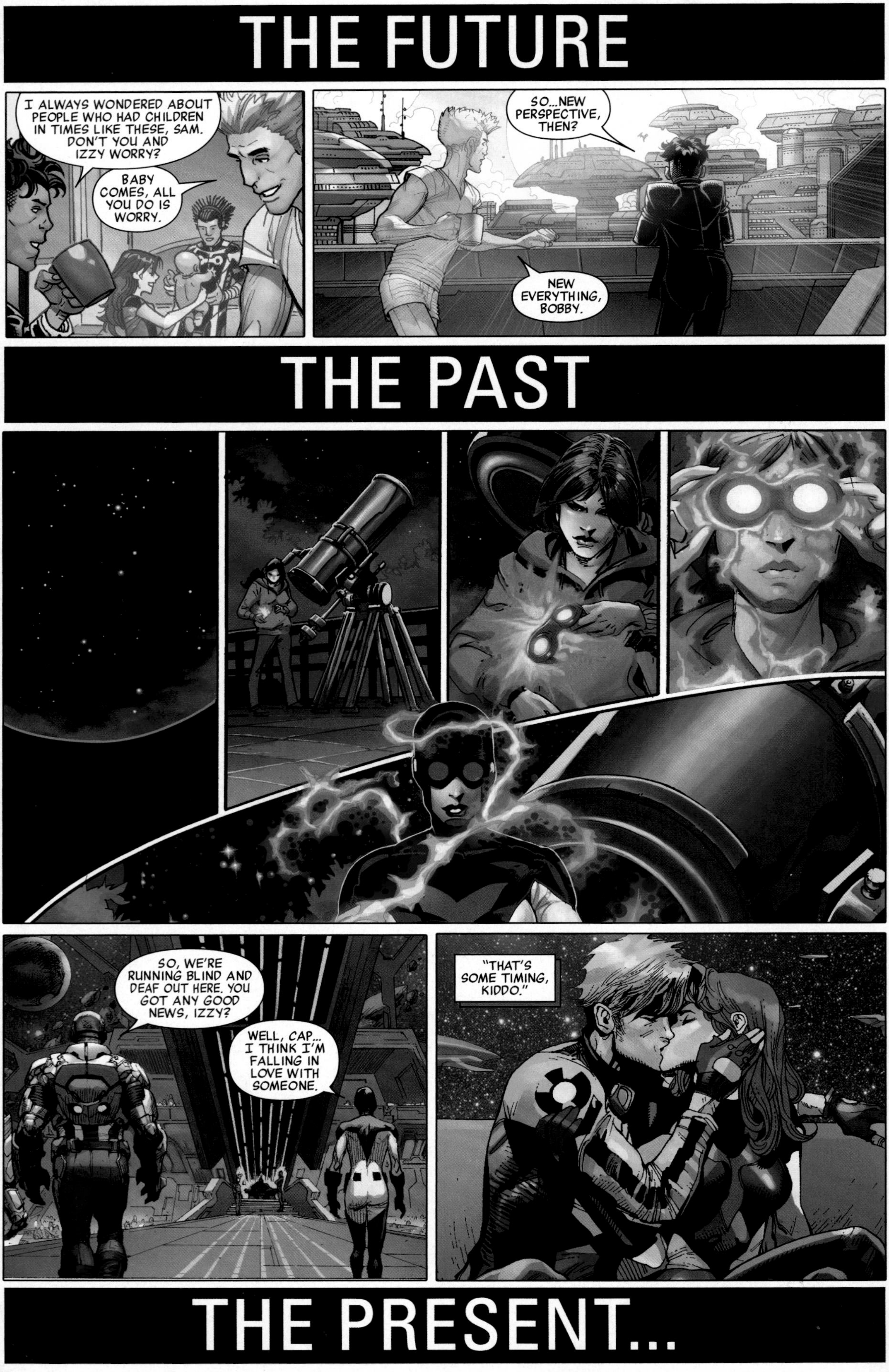
THE FUTURE
I ALWAYS WONDERED ABOUT PEOPLE WHO HAD CHILDREN IN TIMES LIKE THESE, SAM. DON'T YOU AND IZZY WORRY?
BABY COMES, ALL YOU DO IS WORRY.
SO...NEW PERSPECTIVE, THEN?
NEW EVERYTHING, BOBBY.
THE PAST
SO, WE'RE RUNNING BLIND AND DEAF OUT HERE. YOU GOT ANY GOOD NEWS, IZZY?
WELL, CAP... I THINK I'M FALLING IN LOVE WITH SOMEONE.
"THAT'S SOME TIMING, KIDDO."
THE PRESENT...

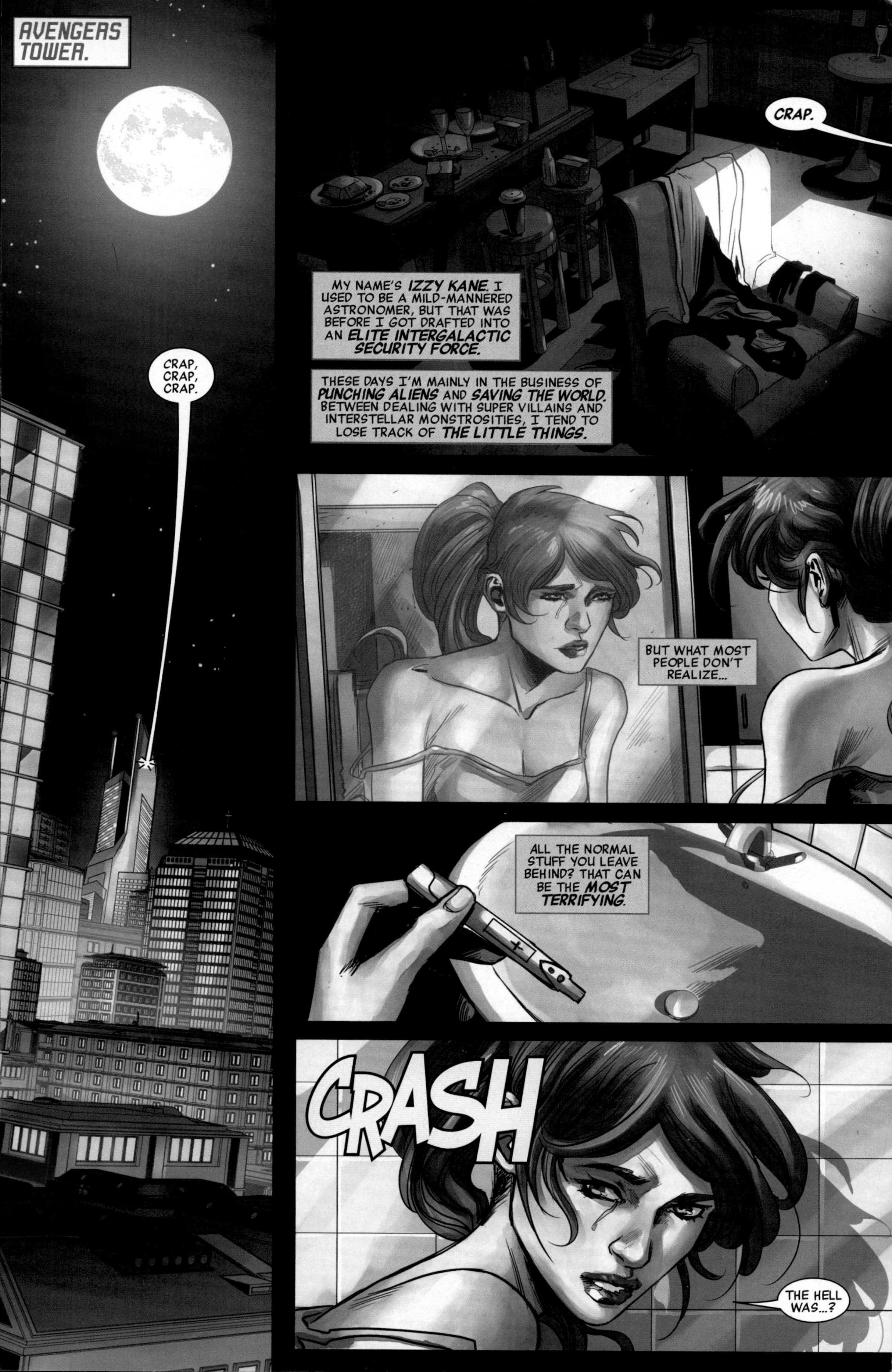
AVENGERS TOWER.
CRAP, CRAP, CRAP.
CRAP.
MY NAME'S IZZY KANE. I USED TO BE A MILD-MANNERED ASTRONOMER, BUT THAT WAS BEFORE I GOT DRAFTED INTO AN ELITE INTERGALACTIC SECURITY FORCE.
THESE DAYS I'M MAINLY IN THE BUSINESS OF PUNCHING ALIENS AND SAVING THE WORLD. BETWEEN DEALING WITH SUPER VILLAINS AND INTERSTELLAR MONSTROSITIES, I TEND TO LOSE TRACK OF THE LITTLE THINGS.
BUT WHAT MOST PEOPLE DON'T REALIZE...
ALL THE NORMAL STUFF YOU LEAVE BEHIND? THAT CAN BE THE MOST TERRIFYING.
CRASH
THE HELL WAS...?

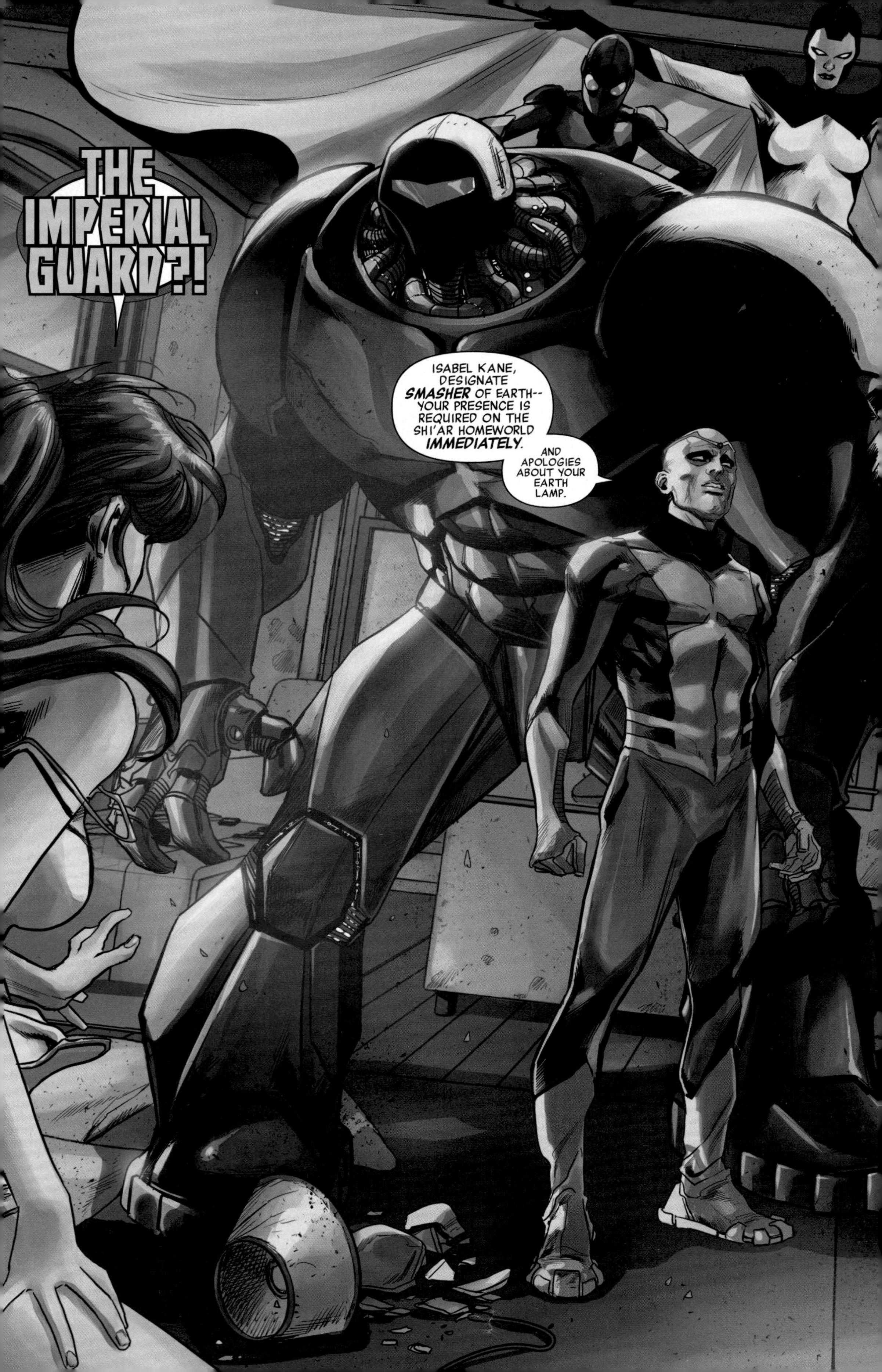
THE IMPERIAL GUARD?!
ISABEL KANE, DESIGNATE SMASHER OF EARTH-- YOUR PRESENCE IS REQUIRED ON THE SHI'AR HOMEWORLD IMMEDIATELY.
AND APOLOGIES ABOUT YOUR EARTH LAMP.

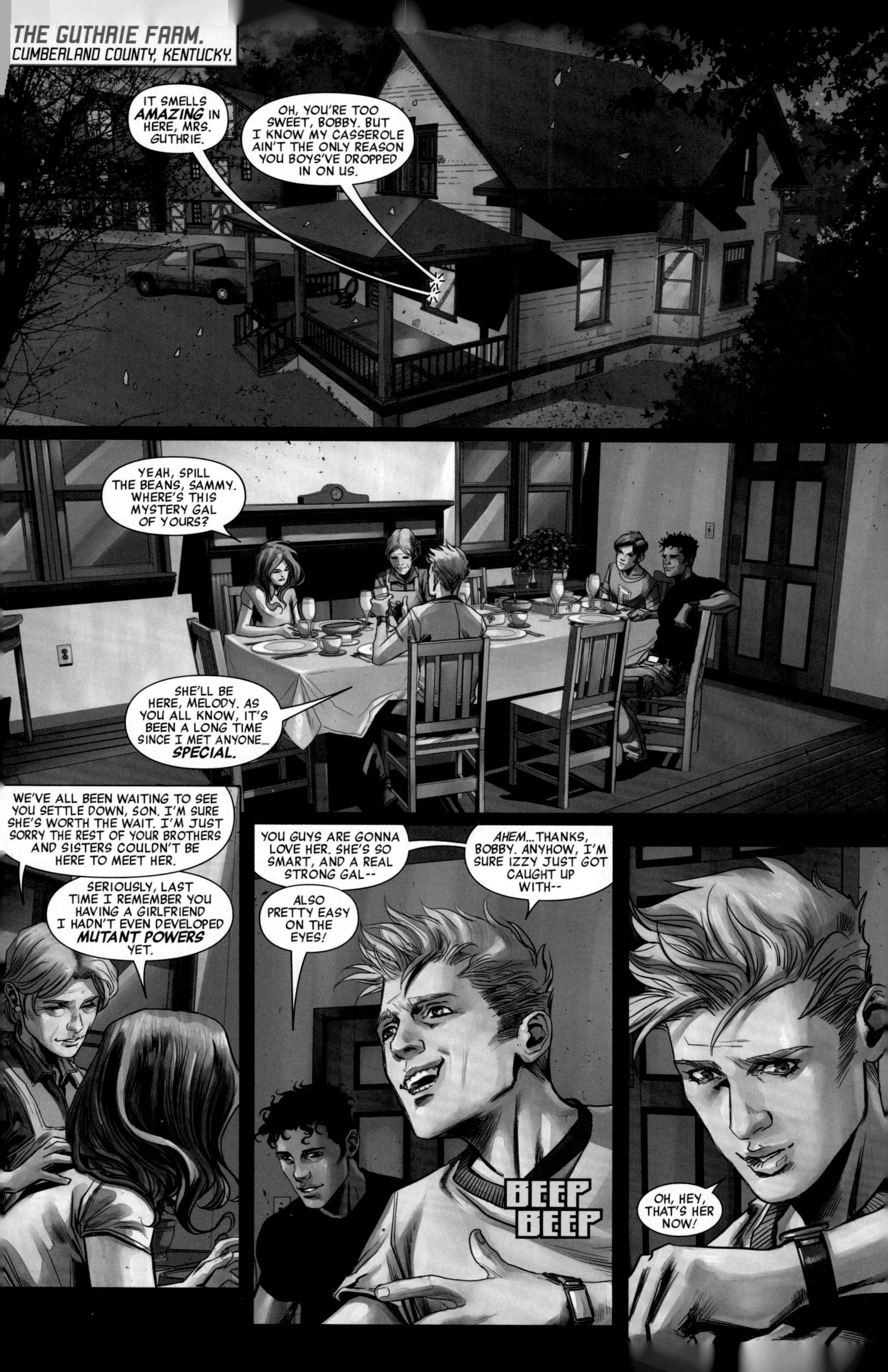
THE GUTHRIE FARM.
CUMBERLAND COUNTY, KENTUCKY.
IT SMELLS AMAZING IN HERE, MRS. GUTHRIE.
OH, YOU'RE TOO SWEET, BOBBY. BUT I KNOW MY CASSEROLE AIN'T THE ONLY REASON YOU BOYS'VE DROPPED IN ON US.
YEAH, SPILL THE BEANS, SAMMY. WHERE'S THIS MYSTERY GAL OF YOURS?
SHE'LL BE HERE, MELODY. AS YOU ALL KNOW, IT'S BEEN A LONG TIME SINCE I MET ANYONE... SPECIAL.
WE'VE ALL BEEN WAITING TO SEE YOU SETTLE DOWN, SON. I'M SURE SHE'S WORTH THE WAIT. I'M JUST SORRY THE REST OF YOUR BROTHERS AND SISTERS COULDN'T BE HERE TO MEET HER.
SERIOUSLY, LAST TIME I REMEMBER YOU HAVING A GIRLFRIEND I HADN'T EVEN DEVELOPED MUTANT POWERS YET.
YOU GUYS ARE GONNA LOVE HER. SHE'S SO SMART, AND A REAL STRONG GAL--
ALSO PRETTY EASY ON THE EYES!
AHEM...THANKS, BOBBY. ANYHOW, I'M SURE IZZY JUST GOT CAUGHT UP WITH--
BEEP BEEP
OH, HEY, THAT'S HER NOW!

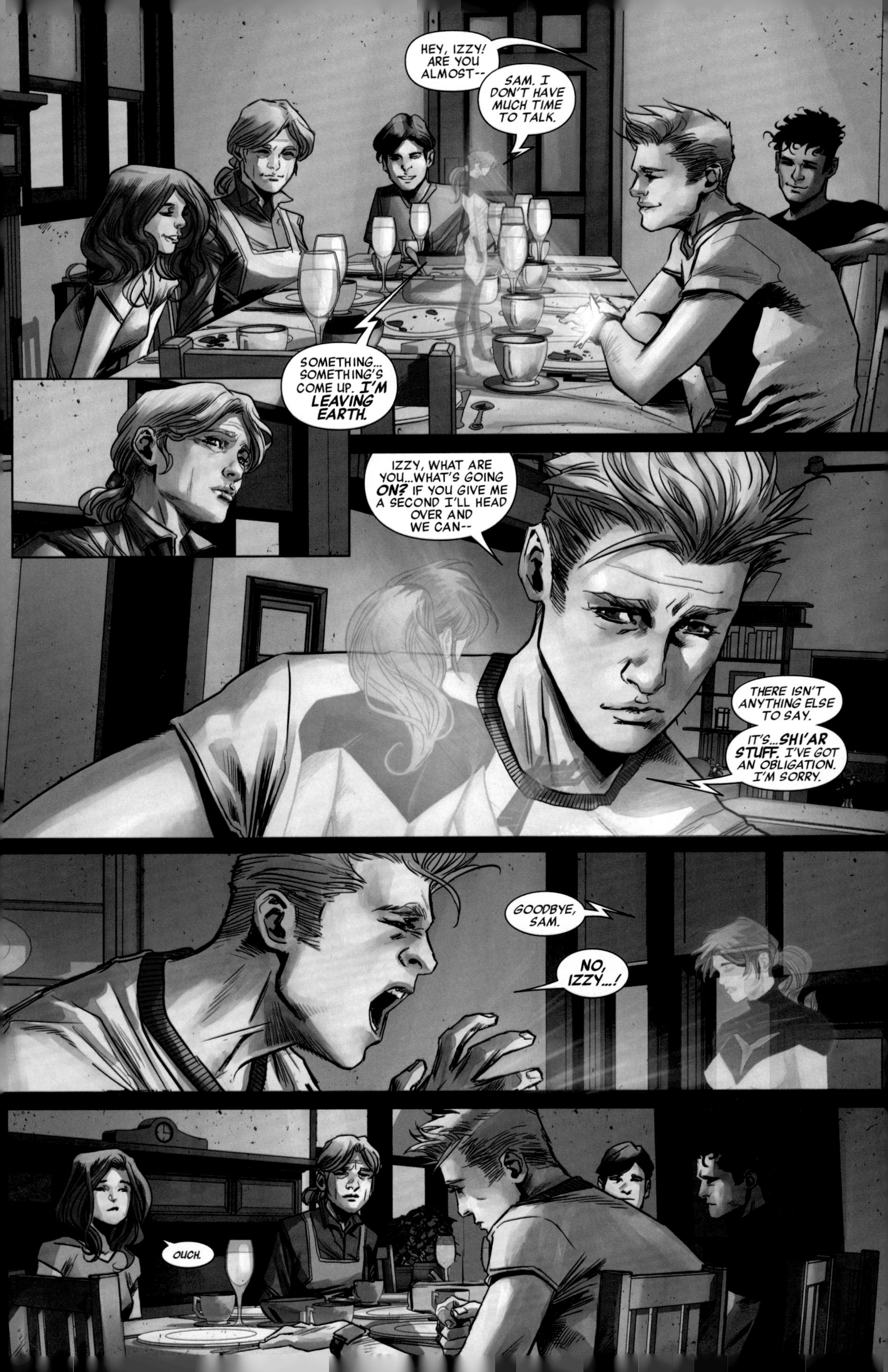
HEY, IZZY! ARE YOU ALMOST--
SAM. I DON'T HAVE MUCH TIME TO TALK.
SOMETHING... SOMETHING'S COME UP. I'M LEAVING EARTH.
IZZY, WHAT ARE YOU...WHAT'S GOING ON? IF YOU GIVE ME A SECOND I'LL HEAD OVER AND WE CAN--
THERE ISN'T ANYTHING ELSE TO SAY.
IT'S...SHI'AR STUFF. I'VE GOT AN OBLIGATION. I'M SORRY.
GOODBYE, SAM.
NO, IZZY...!
OUCH.

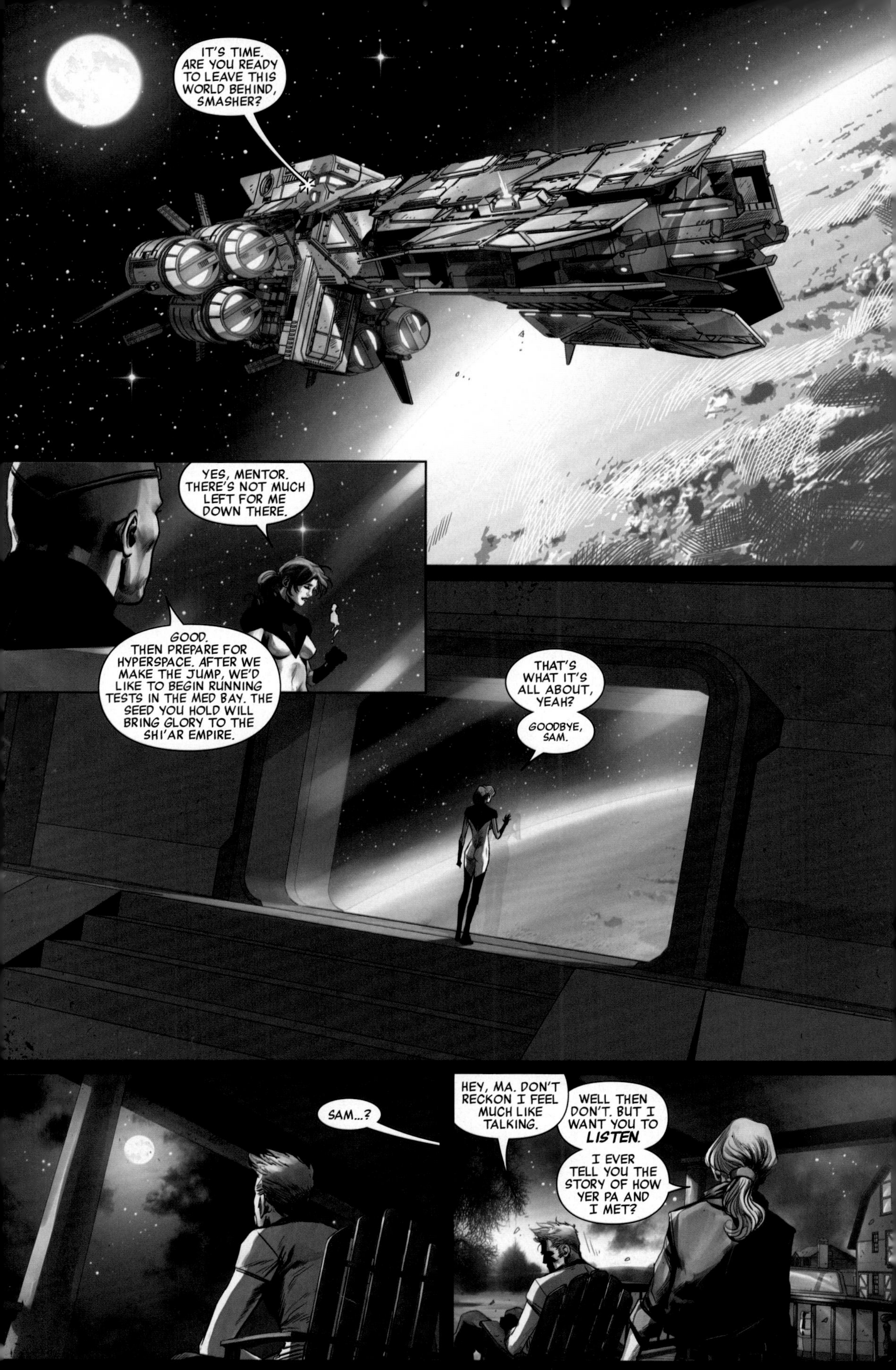
IT'S TIME. ARE YOU READY TO LEAVE THIS WORLD BEHIND, SMASHER?
YES, MENTOR. THERE'S NOT MUCH LEFT FOR ME DOWN THERE.
GOOD. THEN PREPARE FOR HYPERSPACE. AFTER WE MAKE THE JUMP, WE'D LIKE TO BEGIN RUNNING TESTS IN THE MED BAY. THE SEED YOU HOLD WILL BRING GLORY TO THE SHI'AR EMPIRE.
THAT'S WHAT IT'S ALL ABOUT, YEAH?
GOODBYE, SAM.
SAM...?
HEY, MA. DON'T RECKON I FEEL MUCH LIKE TALKING.
WELL THEN DON'T. BUT I WANT YOU TO LISTEN.
I EVER TELL YOU THE STORY OF HOW YER PA AND I MET?

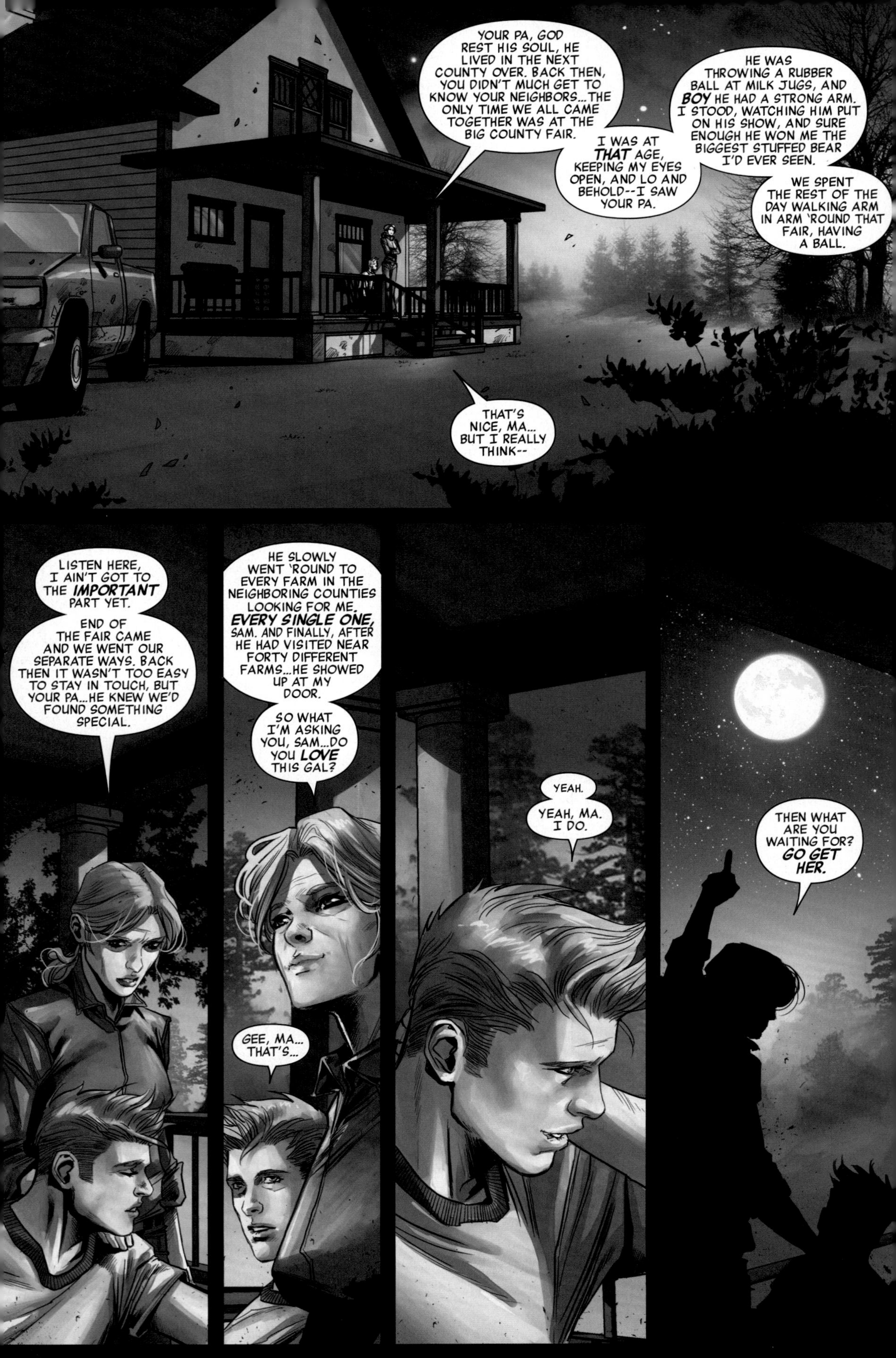
YOUR PA, GOD REST HIS SOUL, HE LIVED IN THE NEXT COUNTY OVER. BACK THEN, YOU DIDN'T MUCH GET TO KNOW YOUR NEIGHBORS...THE ONLY TIME WE ALL CAME TOGETHER WAS AT THE BIG COUNTY FAIR.
I WAS AT *THAT* AGE, KEEPING MY EYES OPEN, AND LO AND BEHOLD--I SAW YOUR PA.
HE WAS THROWING A RUBBER BALL AT MILK JUGS, AND *BOY* HE HAD A STRONG ARM. I STOOD, WATCHING HIM PUT ON HIS SHOW, AND SURE ENOUGH HE WON ME THE BIGGEST STUFFED BEAR I'D EVER SEEN.
WE SPENT THE REST OF THE DAY WALKING ARM IN ARM 'ROUND THAT FAIR, HAVING A BALL.
THAT'S NICE, MA... BUT I REALLY THINK--
LISTEN HERE, I AIN'T GOT TO THE *IMPORTANT* PART YET.
END OF THE FAIR CAME AND WE WENT OUR SEPARATE WAYS. BACK THEN IT WASN'T TOO EASY TO STAY IN TOUCH, BUT YOUR PA...HE KNEW WE'D FOUND SOMETHING SPECIAL.
HE SLOWLY WENT 'ROUND TO EVERY FARM IN THE NEIGHBORING COUNTIES LOOKING FOR ME. *EVERY SINGLE ONE,* SAM. AND FINALLY, AFTER HE HAD VISITED NEAR FORTY DIFFERENT FARMS...HE SHOWED UP AT MY DOOR.
GEE, MA... THAT'S...
SO WHAT I'M ASKING YOU, SAM...DO YOU *LOVE* THIS GAL?
YEAH.
YEAH, MA. I DO.
THEN WHAT ARE YOU WAITING FOR? *GO GET HER.*

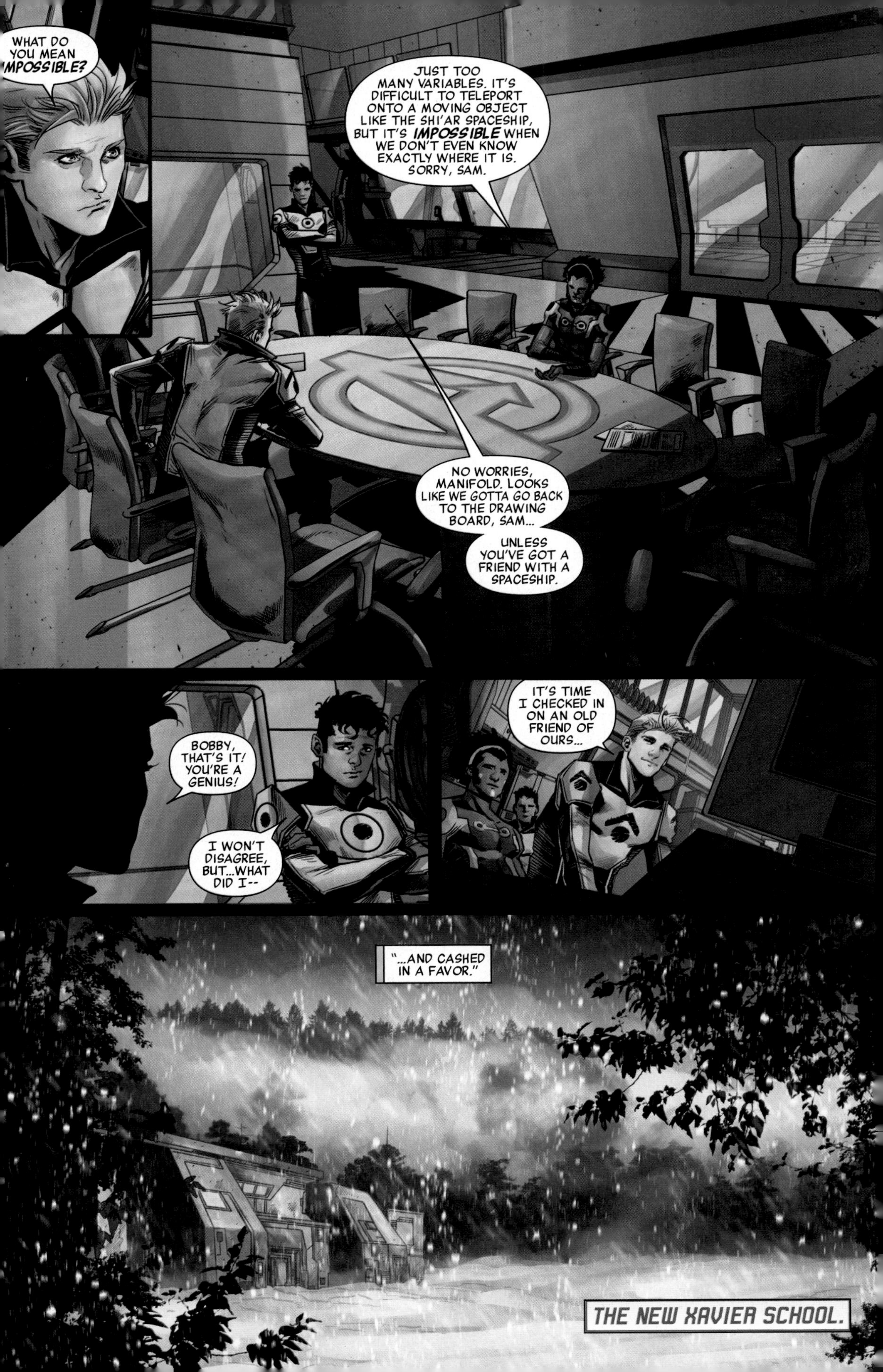
WHAT DO YOU MEAN IMPOSSIBLE?
JUST TOO MANY VARIABLES. IT'S DIFFICULT TO TELEPORT ONTO A MOVING OBJECT LIKE THE SHI'AR SPACESHIP, BUT IT'S IMPOSSIBLE WHEN WE DON'T EVEN KNOW EXACTLY WHERE IT IS. SORRY, SAM.
NO WORRIES, MANIFOLD. LOOKS LIKE WE GOTTA GO BACK TO THE DRAWING BOARD, SAM...
UNLESS YOU'VE GOT A FRIEND WITH A SPACESHIP.
BOBBY, THAT'S IT! YOU'RE A GENIUS!
I WON'T DISAGREE, BUT...WHAT DID I--
IT'S TIME I CHECKED IN ON AN OLD FRIEND OF OURS...
"...AND CASHED IN A FAVOR."
THE NEW XAVIER SCHOOL.

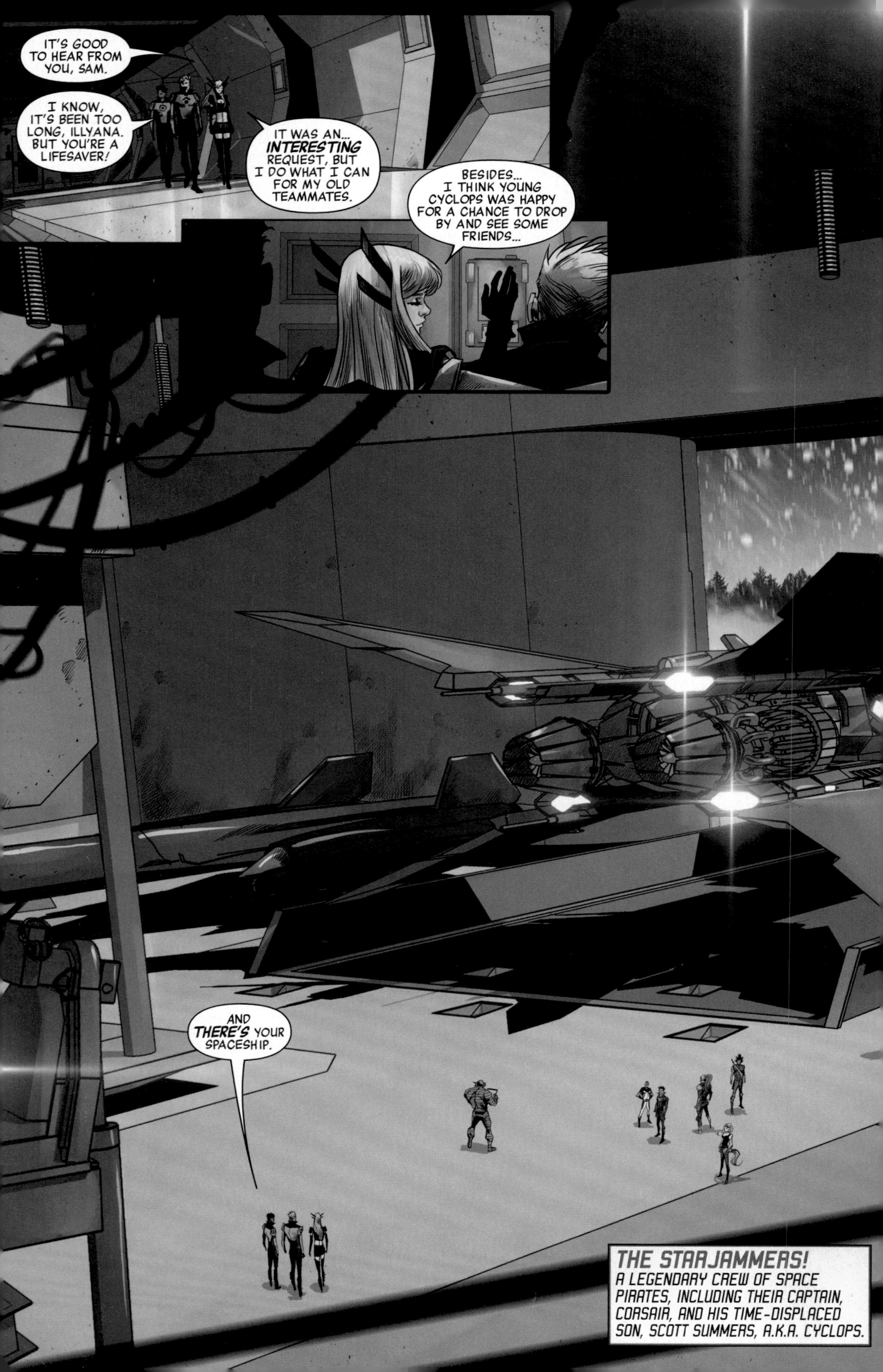

IT'S GOOD TO HEAR FROM YOU, SAM.
I KNOW, IT'S BEEN TOO LONG, ILLYANA. BUT YOU'RE A LIFESAVER!
IT WAS AN... INTERESTING REQUEST, BUT I DO WHAT I CAN FOR MY OLD TEAMMATES.
BESIDES... I THINK YOUNG CYCLOPS WAS HAPPY FOR A CHANCE TO DROP BY AND SEE SOME FRIENDS...
AND THERE'S YOUR SPACESHIP.
THE STARJAMMERS! A LEGENDARY CREW OF SPACE PIRATES, INCLUDING THEIR CAPTAIN, CORSAIR, AND HIS TIME-DISPLACED SON, SCOTT SUMMERS, A.K.A. CYCLOPS.

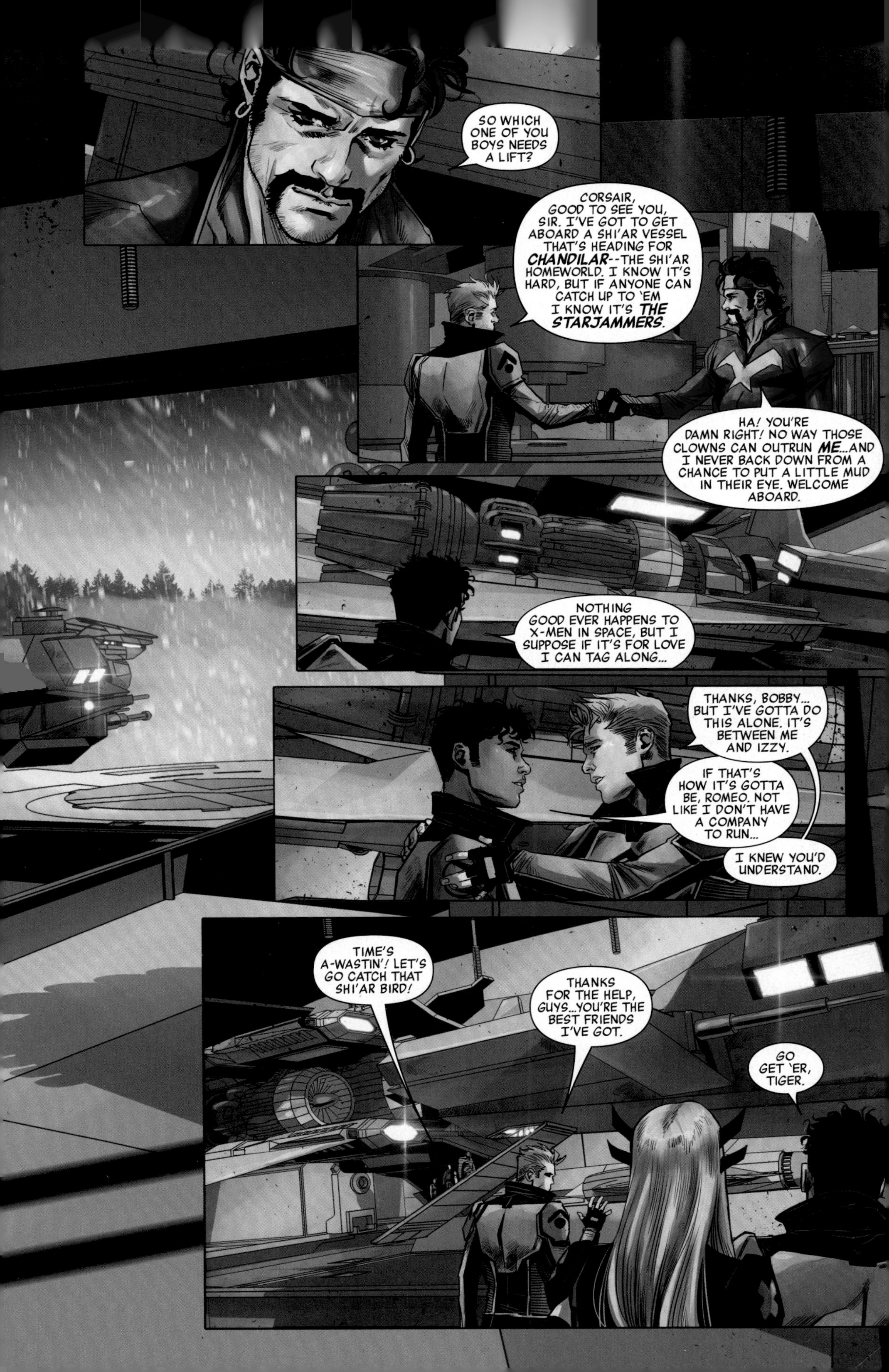
SO WHICH ONE OF YOU BOYS NEEDS A LIFT?
CORSAIR, GOOD TO SEE YOU, SIR. I'VE GOT TO GET ABOARD A SHI'AR VESSEL THAT'S HEADING FOR CHANDILAR--THE SHI'AR HOMEWORLD. I KNOW IT'S HARD, BUT IF ANYONE CAN CATCH UP TO 'EM I KNOW IT'S THE STARJAMMERS.
HA! YOU'RE DAMN RIGHT! NO WAY THOSE CLOWNS CAN OUTRUN ME...AND I NEVER BACK DOWN FROM A CHANCE TO PUT A LITTLE MUD IN THEIR EYE. WELCOME ABOARD.
NOTHING GOOD EVER HAPPENS TO X-MEN IN SPACE, BUT I SUPPOSE IF IT'S FOR LOVE I CAN TAG ALONG...
THANKS, BOBBY... BUT I'VE GOTTA DO THIS ALONE. IT'S BETWEEN ME AND IZZY.
IF THAT'S HOW IT'S GOTTA BE, ROMEO. NOT LIKE I DON'T HAVE A COMPANY TO RUN...
I KNEW YOU'D UNDERSTAND.
TIME'S A-WASTIN'! LET'S GO CATCH THAT SHI'AR BIRD!
THANKS FOR THE HELP, GUYS...YOU'RE THE BEST FRIENDS I'VE GOT.
GO GET 'ER, TIGER.

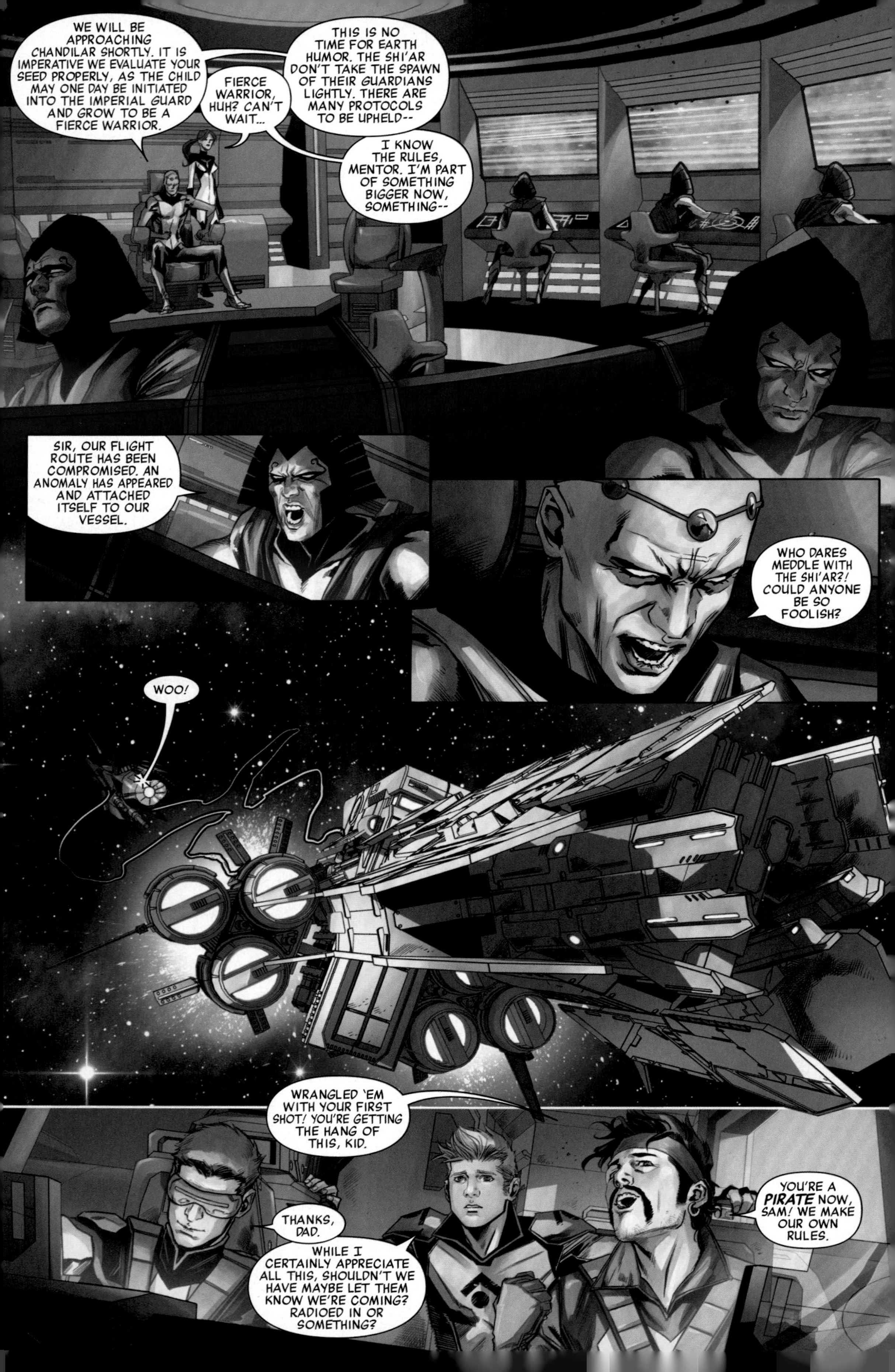
WE WILL BE APPROACHING CHANDILAR SHORTLY. IT IS IMPERATIVE WE EVALUATE YOUR SEED PROPERLY, AS THE CHILD MAY ONE DAY BE INITIATED INTO THE IMPERIAL GUARD AND GROW TO BE A FIERCE WARRIOR.
FIERCE WARRIOR, HUH? CAN'T WAIT...
THIS IS NO TIME FOR EARTH HUMOR. THE SHI'AR DON'T TAKE THE SPAWN OF THEIR GUARDIANS LIGHTLY. THERE ARE MANY PROTOCOLS TO BE UPHELD--
I KNOW THE RULES, MENTOR. I'M PART OF SOMETHING BIGGER NOW, SOMETHING--
SIR, OUR FLIGHT ROUTE HAS BEEN COMPROMISED. AN ANOMALY HAS APPEARED AND ATTACHED ITSELF TO OUR VESSEL.
WHO DARES MEDDLE WITH THE SHI'AR?! COULD ANYONE BE SO FOOLISH?
WOO!
WRANGLED 'EM WITH YOUR FIRST SHOT! YOU'RE GETTING THE HANG OF THIS, KID.
THANKS, DAD.
YOU'RE A *PIRATE* NOW, SAM! WE MAKE OUR OWN RULES.
WHILE I CERTAINLY APPRECIATE ALL THIS, SHOULDN'T WE HAVE MAYBE LET THEM KNOW WE'RE COMING? RADIOED IN OR SOMETHING?

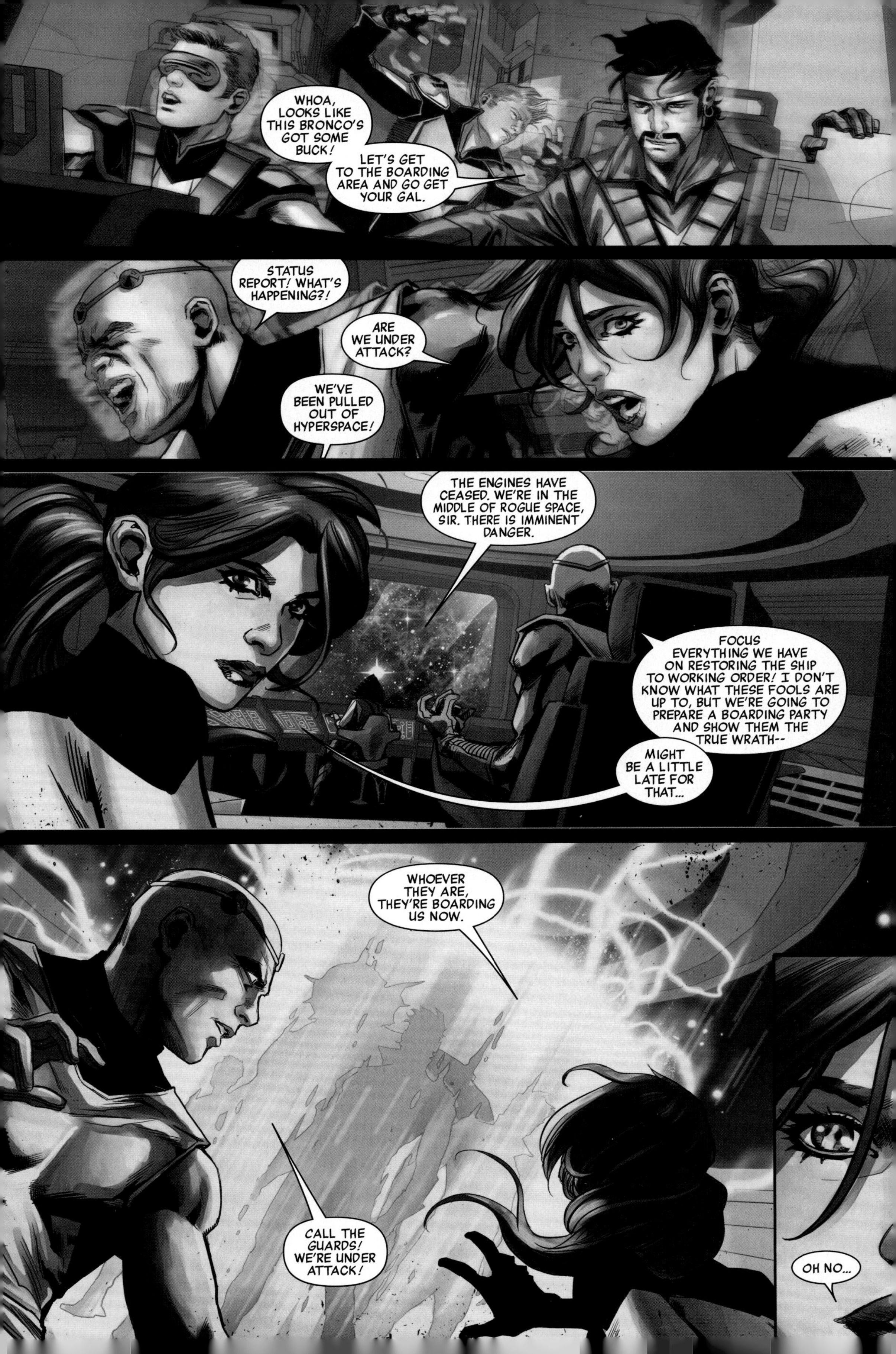
WHOA, LOOKS LIKE THIS BRONCO'S GOT SOME BUCK!
LET'S GET TO THE BOARDING AREA AND GO GET YOUR GAL.
STATUS REPORT! WHAT'S HAPPENING?!
ARE WE UNDER ATTACK?
WE'VE BEEN PULLED OUT OF HYPERSPACE!
THE ENGINES HAVE CEASED. WE'RE IN THE MIDDLE OF ROGUE SPACE, SIR. THERE IS IMMINENT DANGER.
FOCUS EVERYTHING WE HAVE ON RESTORING THE SHIP TO WORKING ORDER! I DON'T KNOW WHAT THESE FOOLS ARE UP TO, BUT WE'RE GOING TO PREPARE A BOARDING PARTY AND SHOW THEM THE TRUE WRATH--
MIGHT BE A LITTLE LATE FOR THAT...
WHOEVER THEY ARE, THEY'RE BOARDING US NOW.
CALL THE GUARDS! WE'RE UNDER ATTACK!
OH NO...

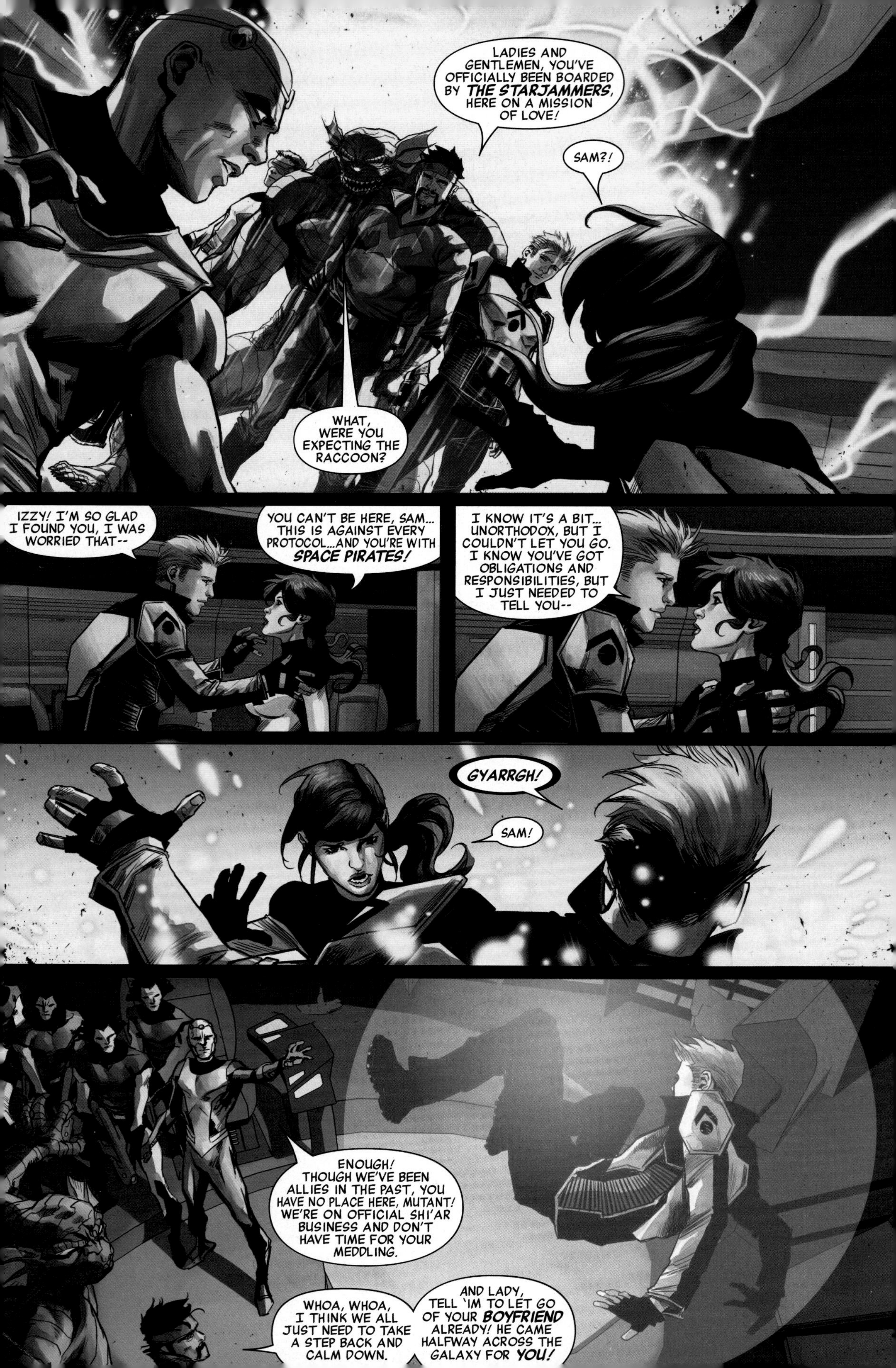
LADIES AND GENTLEMEN, YOU'VE OFFICIALLY BEEN BOARDED BY ***THE STARJAMMERS***, HERE ON A MISSION OF LOVE!
SAM?!
WHAT, WERE YOU EXPECTING THE RACCOON?
IZZY! I'M SO GLAD I FOUND YOU, I WAS WORRIED THAT--
YOU CAN'T BE HERE, SAM... THIS IS AGAINST EVERY PROTOCOL...AND YOU'RE WITH ***SPACE PIRATES!***
I KNOW IT'S A BIT... UNORTHODOX, BUT I COULDN'T LET YOU GO. I KNOW YOU'VE GOT OBLIGATIONS AND RESPONSIBILITIES, BUT I JUST NEEDED TO TELL YOU--
GYARRGH!
SAM!
ENOUGH! THOUGH WE'VE BEEN ALLIES IN THE PAST, YOU HAVE NO PLACE HERE, MUTANT! WE'RE ON OFFICIAL SHI'AR BUSINESS AND DON'T HAVE TIME FOR YOUR MEDDLING.
WHOA, WHOA, I THINK WE ALL JUST NEED TO TAKE A STEP BACK AND CALM DOWN.
AND LADY, TELL 'IM TO LET GO OF YOUR ***BOYFRIEND*** ALREADY! HE CAME HALFWAY ACROSS THE GALAXY FOR ***YOU!***

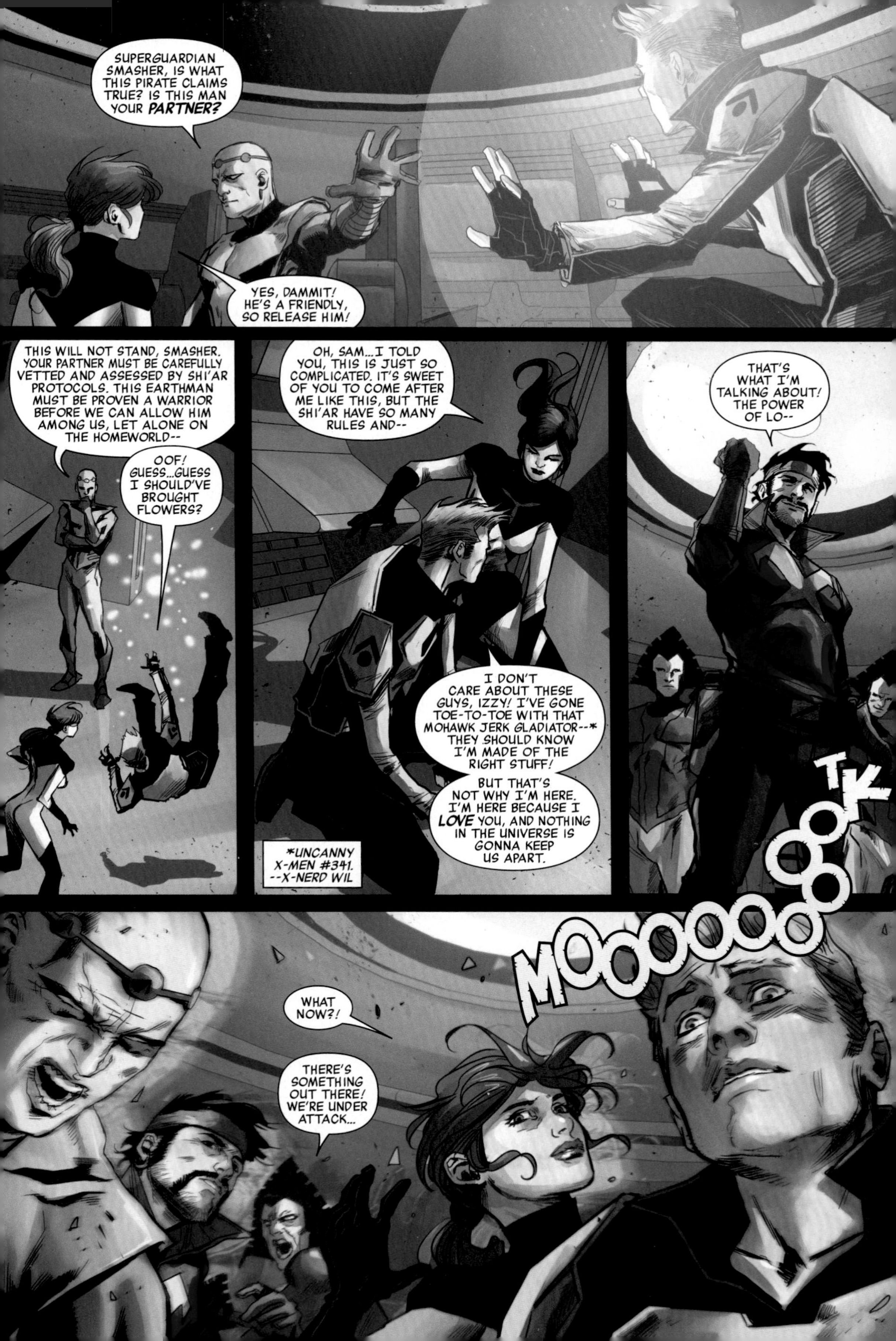
SUPERGUARDIAN SMASHER, IS WHAT THIS PIRATE CLAIMS TRUE? IS THIS MAN YOUR PARTNER?
YES, DAMMIT! HE'S A FRIENDLY, SO RELEASE HIM!
THIS WILL NOT STAND, SMASHER. YOUR PARTNER MUST BE CAREFULLY VETTED AND ASSESSED BY SHI'AR PROTOCOLS. THIS EARTHMAN MUST BE PROVEN A WARRIOR BEFORE WE CAN ALLOW HIM AMONG US, LET ALONE ON THE HOMEWORLD--
OOF! GUESS...GUESS I SHOULD'VE BROUGHT FLOWERS?
OH, SAM...I TOLD YOU, THIS IS JUST SO COMPLICATED. IT'S SWEET OF YOU TO COME AFTER ME LIKE THIS, BUT THE SHI'AR HAVE SO MANY RULES AND--
I DON'T CARE ABOUT THESE GUYS, IZZY! I'VE GONE TOE-TO-TOE WITH THAT MOHAWK JERK GLADIATOR--* THEY SHOULD KNOW I'M MADE OF THE RIGHT STUFF!
BUT THAT'S NOT WHY I'M HERE. I'M HERE BECAUSE I LOVE YOU, AND NOTHING IN THE UNIVERSE IS GONNA KEEP US APART.
*UNCANNY X-MEN #341. --X-NERD WIL
THAT'S WHAT I'M TALKING ABOUT! THE POWER OF LO--
TK
MOOOOOOOOOO
WHAT NOW?!
THERE'S SOMETHING OUT THERE! WE'RE UNDER ATTACK...

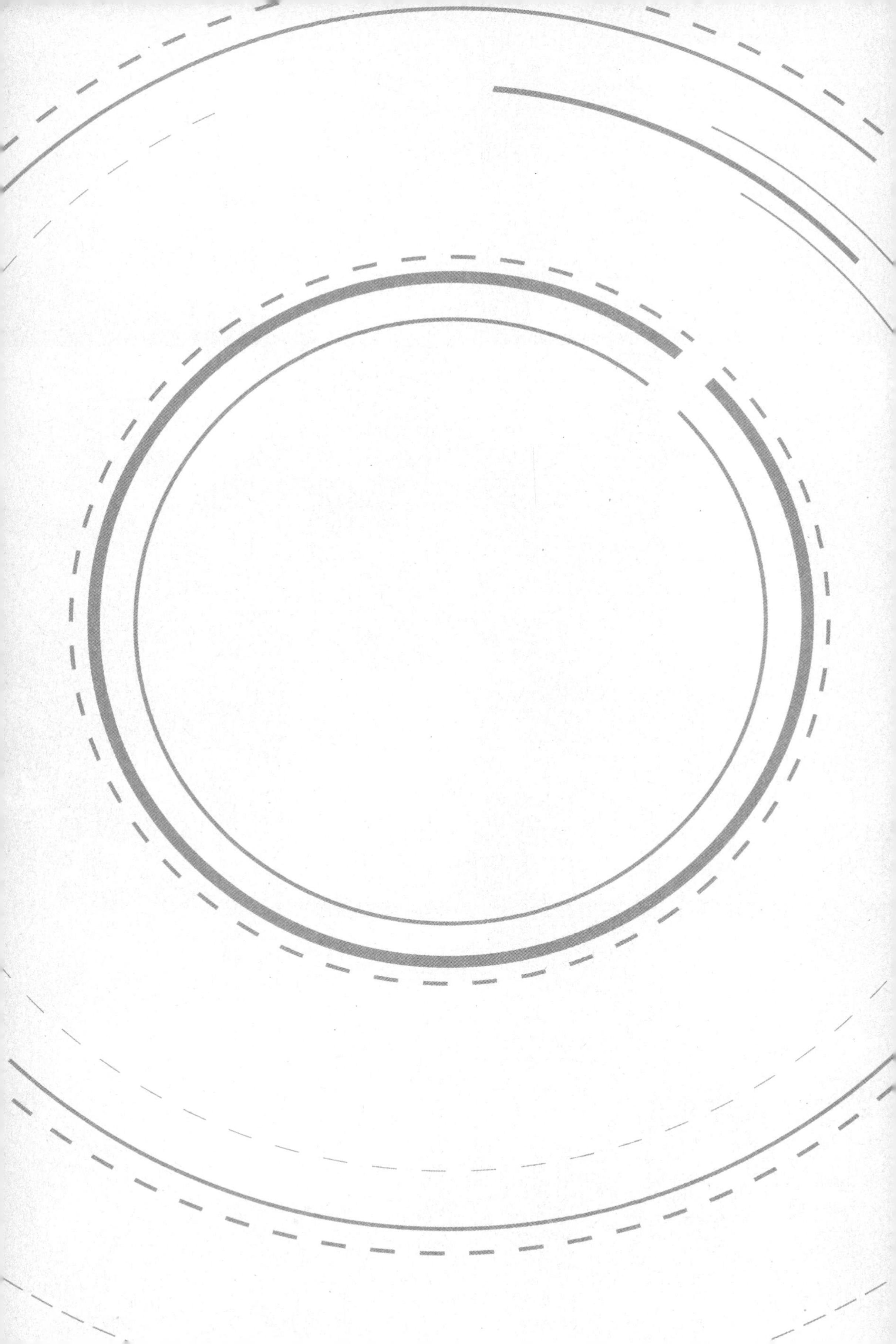

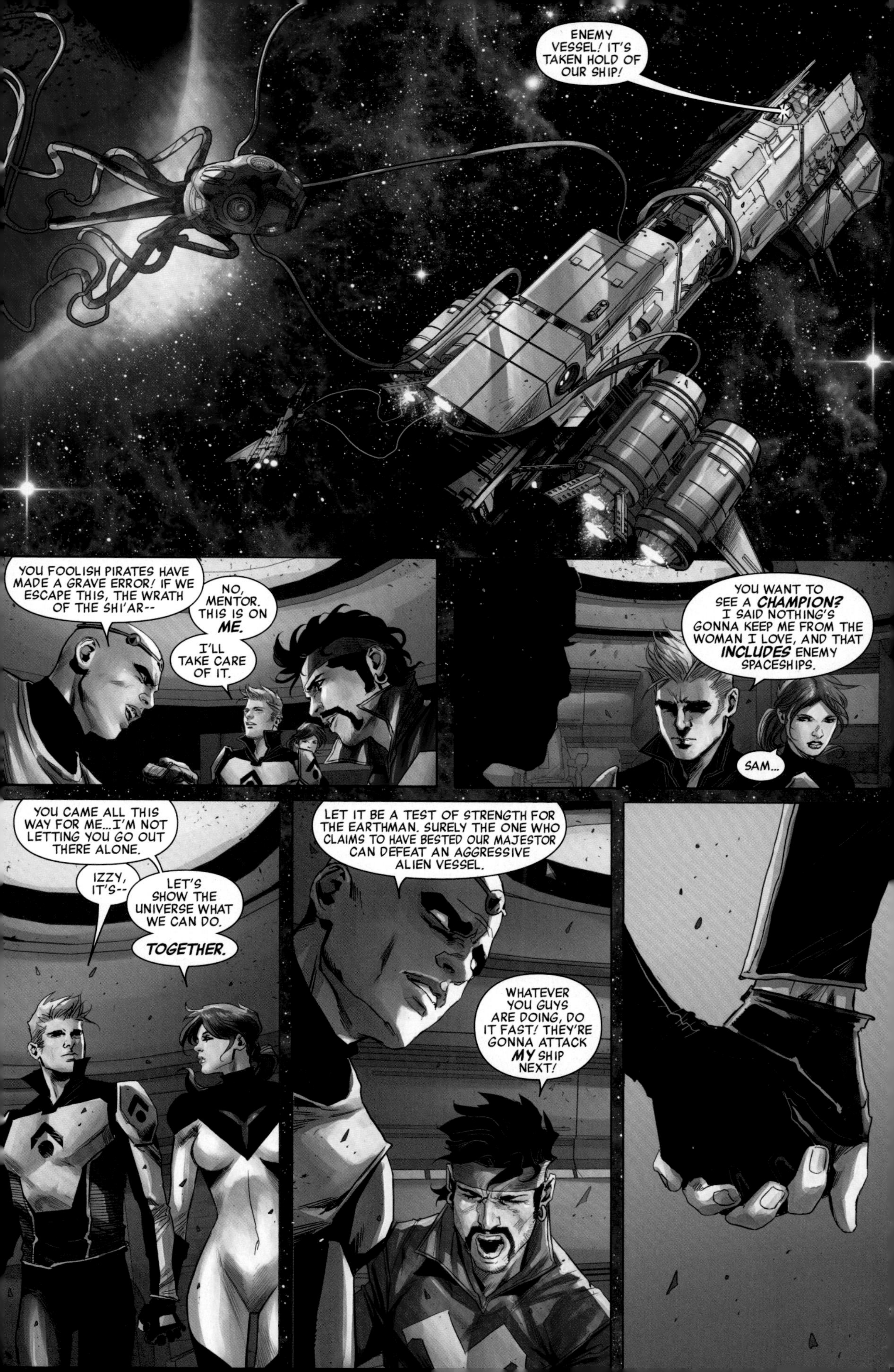
ENEMY VESSEL! IT'S TAKEN HOLD OF OUR SHIP!
YOU FOOLISH PIRATES HAVE MADE A GRAVE ERROR! IF WE ESCAPE THIS, THE WRATH OF THE SHI'AR--
NO, MENTOR. THIS IS ON ME.
I'LL TAKE CARE OF IT.
YOU WANT TO SEE A CHAMPION? I SAID NOTHING'S GONNA KEEP ME FROM THE WOMAN I LOVE, AND THAT INCLUDES ENEMY SPACESHIPS.
SAM...
YOU CAME ALL THIS WAY FOR ME... I'M NOT LETTING YOU GO OUT THERE ALONE.
IZZY, IT'S--
LET'S SHOW THE UNIVERSE WHAT WE CAN DO.
TOGETHER.
LET IT BE A TEST OF STRENGTH FOR THE EARTHMAN. SURELY THE ONE WHO CLAIMS TO HAVE BESTED OUR MAJESTOR CAN DEFEAT AN AGGRESSIVE ALIEN VESSEL.
WHATEVER YOU GUYS ARE DOING, DO IT FAST! THEY'RE GONNA ATTACK MY SHIP NEXT!

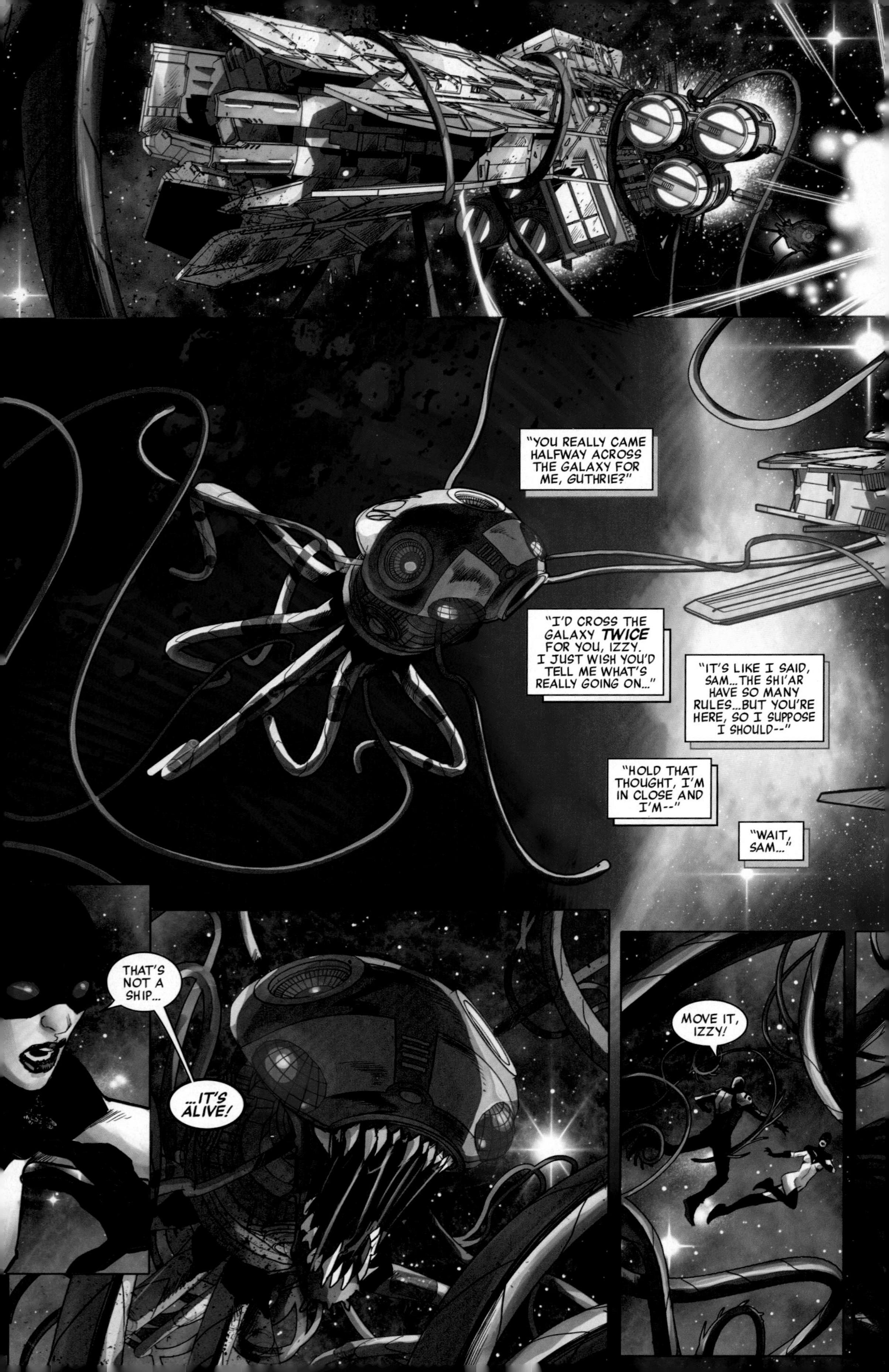
"YOU REALLY CAME HALFWAY ACROSS THE GALAXY FOR ME, GUTHRIE?"
"I'D CROSS THE GALAXY TWICE FOR YOU, IZZY. I JUST WISH YOU'D TELL ME WHAT'S REALLY GOING ON..."
"IT'S LIKE I SAID, SAM...THE SHI'AR HAVE SO MANY RULES...BUT YOU'RE HERE, SO I SUPPOSE I SHOULD--"
"HOLD THAT THOUGHT, I'M IN CLOSE AND I'M--"
"WAIT, SAM..."
THAT'S NOT A SHIP...
...IT'S ALIVE!
MOVE IT, IZZY!

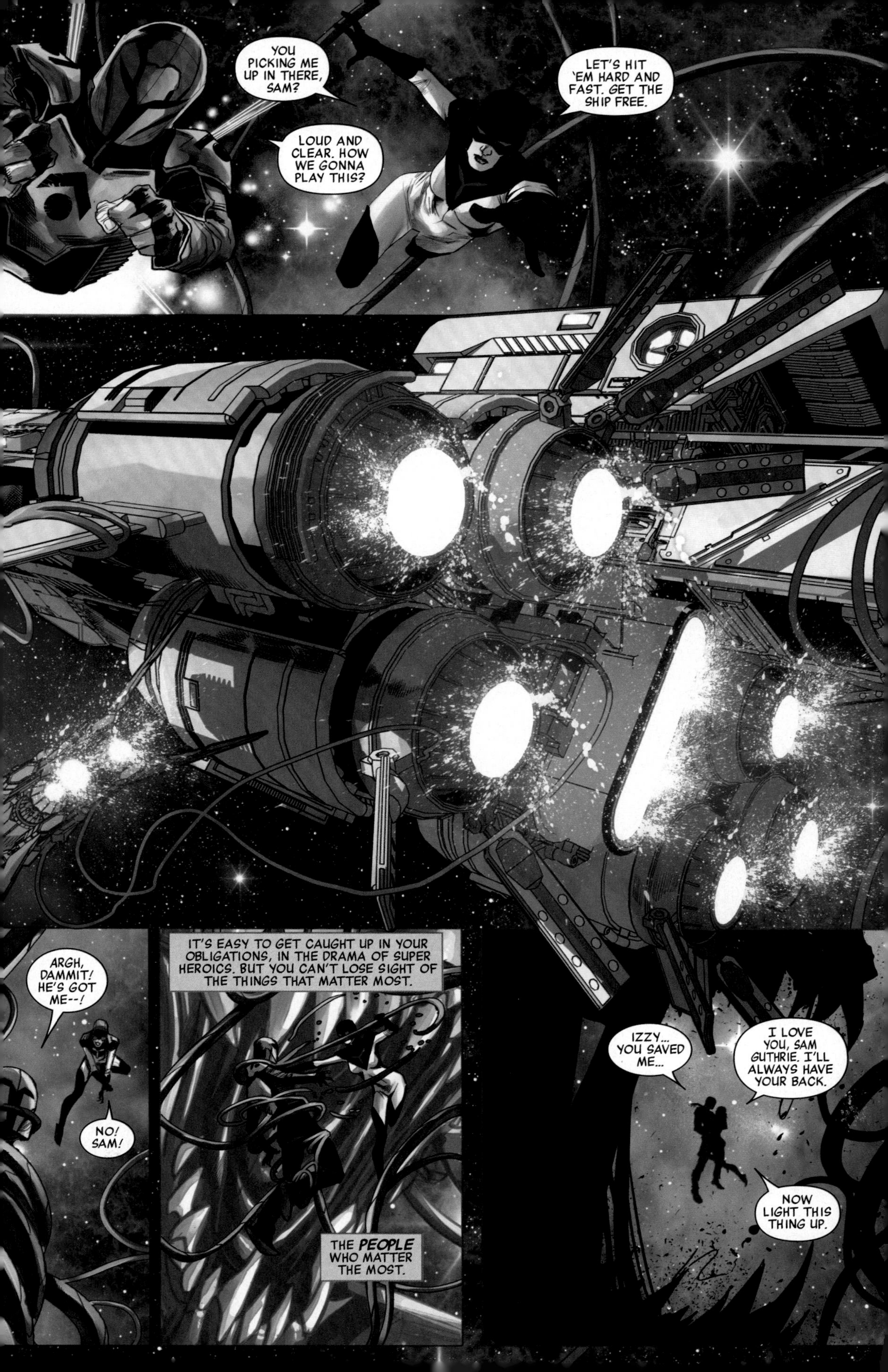
YOU PICKING ME UP IN THERE, SAM?
LOUD AND CLEAR. HOW WE GONNA PLAY THIS?
LET'S HIT 'EM HARD AND FAST. GET THE SHIP FREE.
ARGH, DAMMIT! HE'S GOT ME--!
NO! SAM!
IT'S EASY TO GET CAUGHT UP IN YOUR OBLIGATIONS, IN THE DRAMA OF SUPER HEROICS. BUT YOU CAN'T LOSE SIGHT OF THE THINGS THAT MATTER MOST.
THE PEOPLE WHO MATTER THE MOST.
IZZY... YOU SAVED ME...
I LOVE YOU, SAM GUTHRIE. I'LL ALWAYS HAVE YOUR BACK.
NOW LIGHT THIS THING UP.

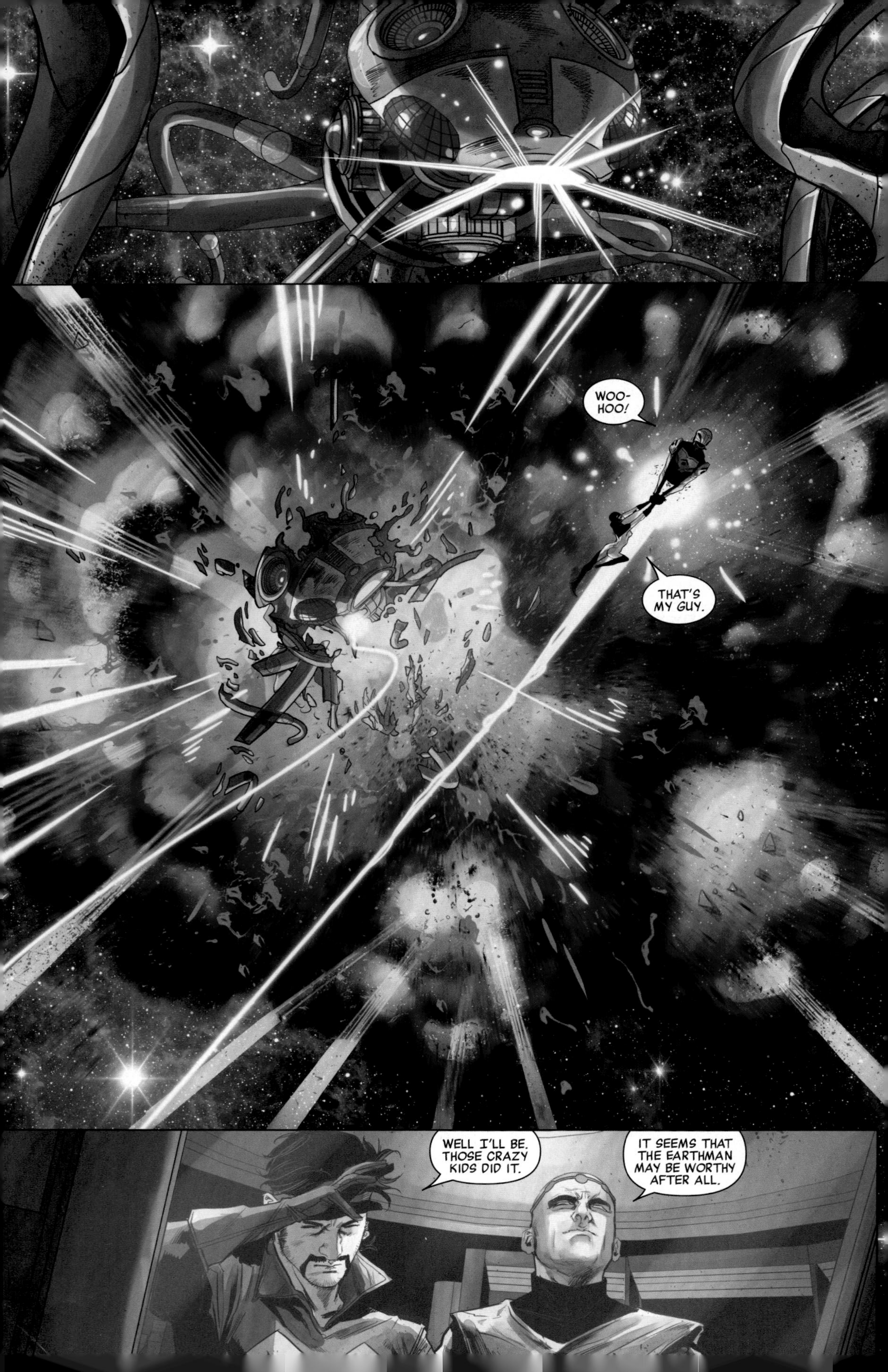
WOO-HOO!
THAT'S MY GUY.
WELL I'LL BE. THOSE CRAZY KIDS DID IT.
IT SEEMS THAT THE EARTHMAN MAY BE WORTHY AFTER ALL.

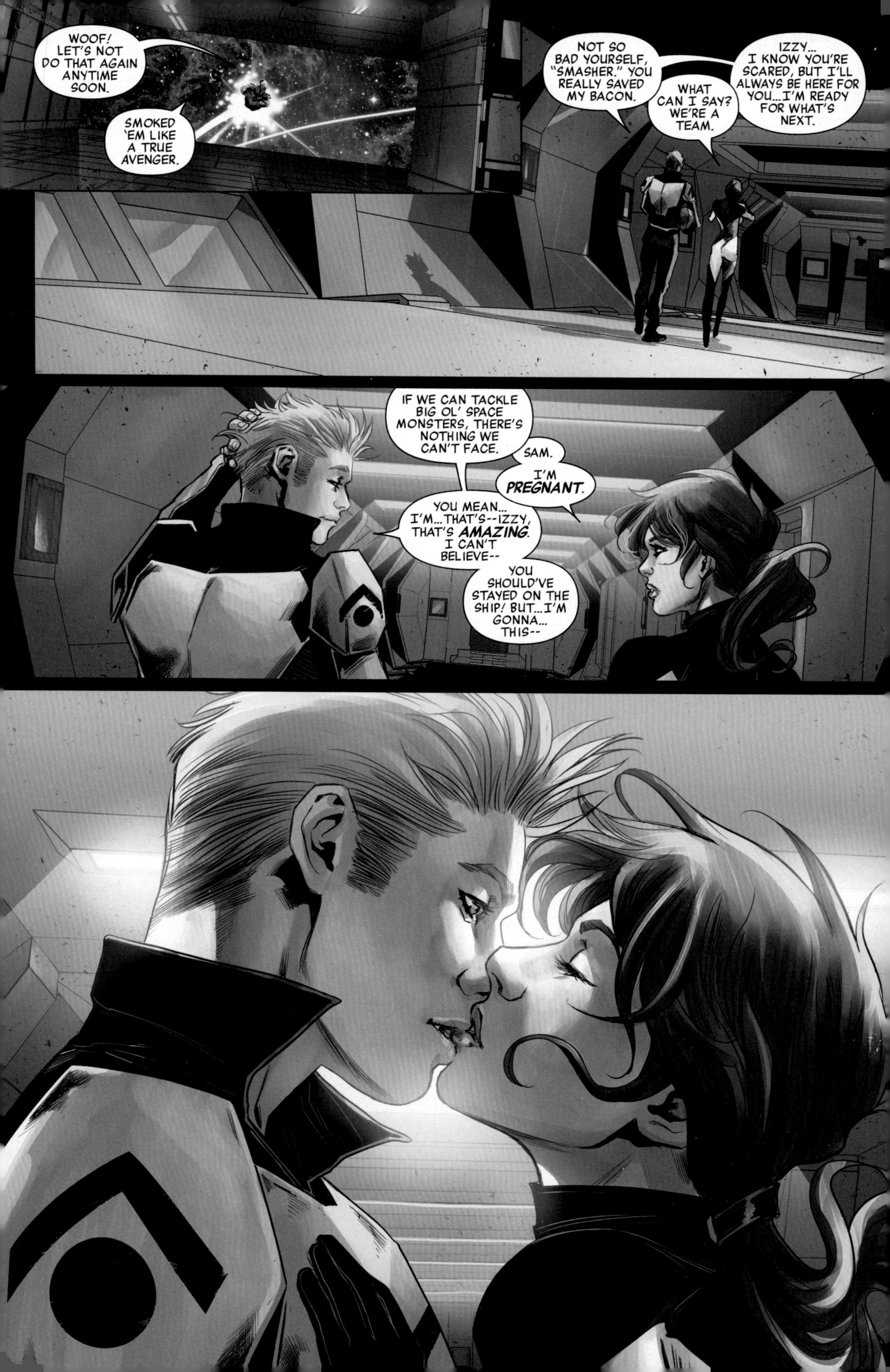
WOOF! LET'S NOT DO THAT AGAIN ANYTIME SOON.
SMOKED 'EM LIKE A TRUE AVENGER.
NOT SO BAD YOURSELF, "SMASHER." YOU REALLY SAVED MY BACON.
WHAT CAN I SAY? WE'RE A TEAM.
IZZY... I KNOW YOU'RE SCARED, BUT I'LL ALWAYS BE HERE FOR YOU...I'M READY FOR WHAT'S NEXT.
IF WE CAN TACKLE BIG OL' SPACE MONSTERS, THERE'S NOTHING WE CAN'T FACE.
SAM.
I'M PREGNANT.
YOU MEAN... I'M...THAT'S--IZZY, THAT'S AMAZING. I CAN'T BELIEVE--
YOU SHOULD'VE STAYED ON THE SHIP! BUT...I'M GONNA... THIS--

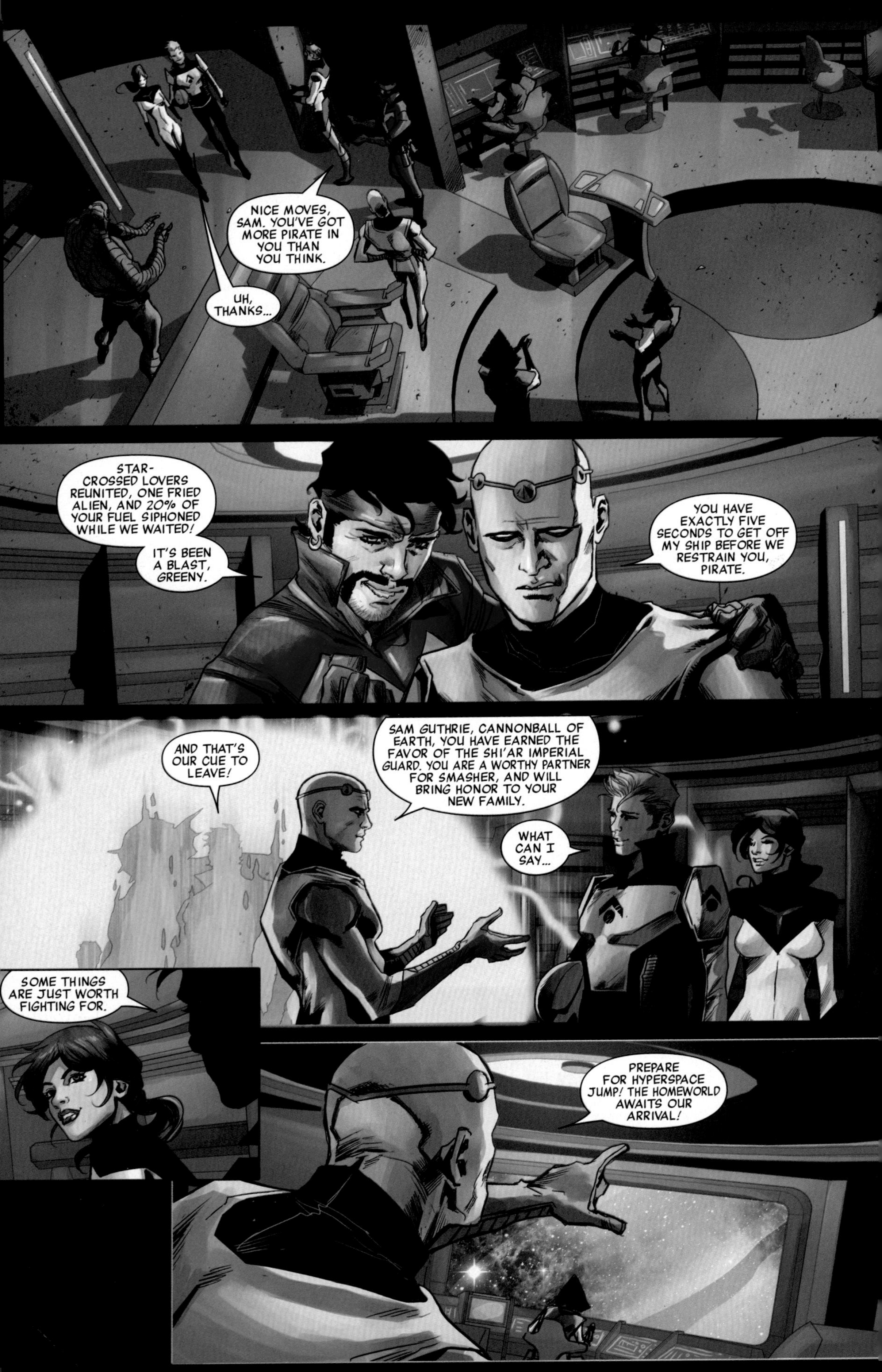
NICE MOVES, SAM. YOU'VE GOT MORE PIRATE IN YOU THAN YOU THINK.
UH, THANKS...
STAR-CROSSED LOVERS REUNITED, ONE FRIED ALIEN, AND 20% OF YOUR FUEL SIPHONED WHILE WE WAITED!
IT'S BEEN A BLAST, GREENY.
YOU HAVE EXACTLY FIVE SECONDS TO GET OFF MY SHIP BEFORE WE RESTRAIN YOU, PIRATE.
AND THAT'S OUR CUE TO LEAVE!
SAM GUTHRIE, CANNONBALL OF EARTH, YOU HAVE EARNED THE FAVOR OF THE SHI'AR IMPERIAL GUARD. YOU ARE A WORTHY PARTNER FOR SMASHER, AND WILL BRING HONOR TO YOUR NEW FAMILY.
WHAT CAN I SAY...
SOME THINGS ARE JUST WORTH FIGHTING FOR.
PREPARE FOR HYPERSPACE JUMP! THE HOMEWORLD AWAITS OUR ARRIVAL!

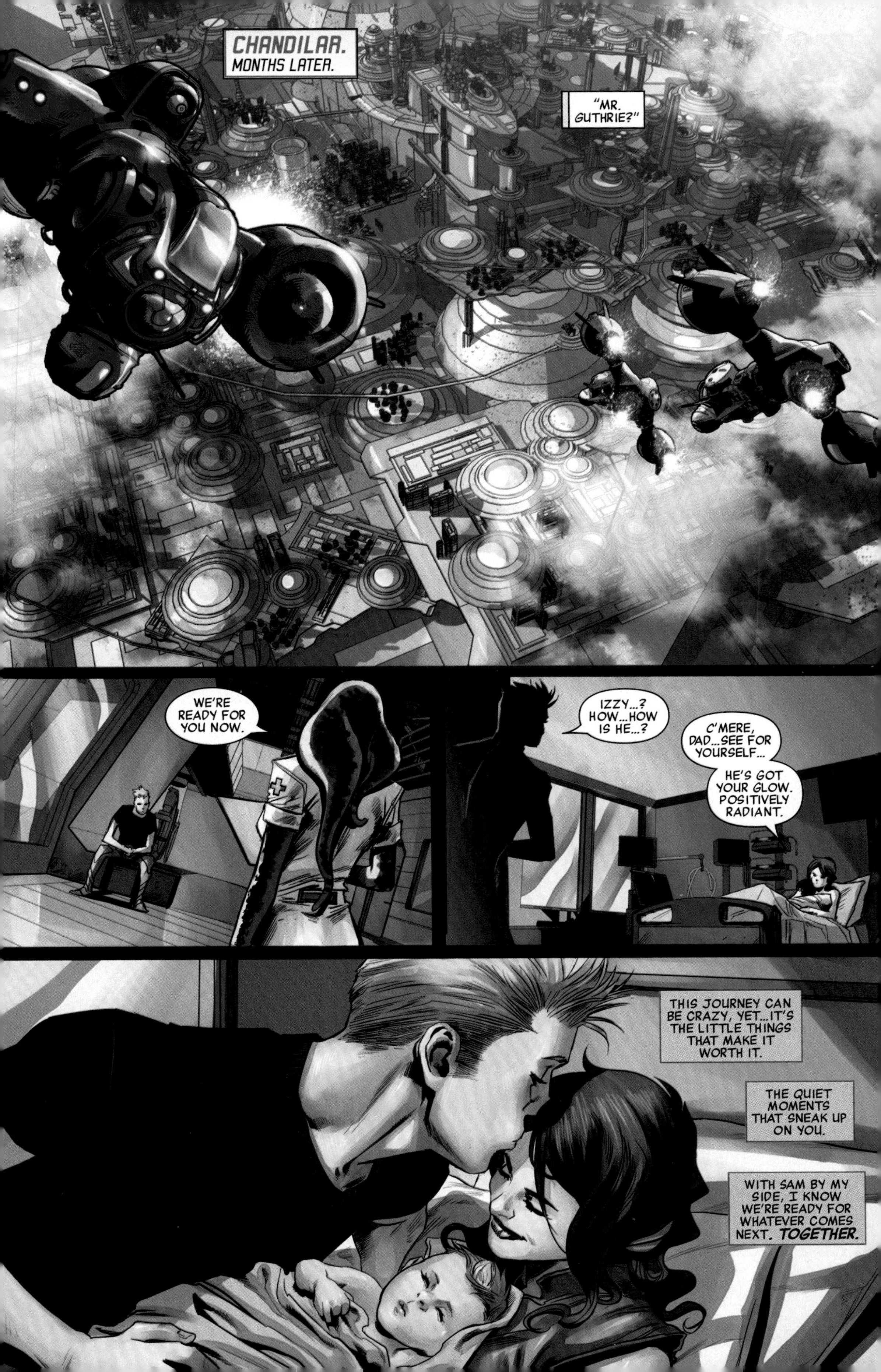
CHANDILAR.
MONTHS LATER.
"MR. GUTHRIE?"
WE'RE READY FOR YOU NOW.
IZZY...? HOW...HOW IS HE...?
C'MERE, DAD...SEE FOR YOURSELF...
HE'S GOT YOUR GLOW. POSITIVELY RADIANT.
THIS JOURNEY CAN BE CRAZY, YET...IT'S THE LITTLE THINGS THAT MAKE IT WORTH IT.
THE QUIET MOMENTS THAT SNEAK UP ON YOU.
WITH SAM BY MY SIDE, I KNOW WE'RE READY FOR WHATEVER COMES NEXT. TOGETHER.

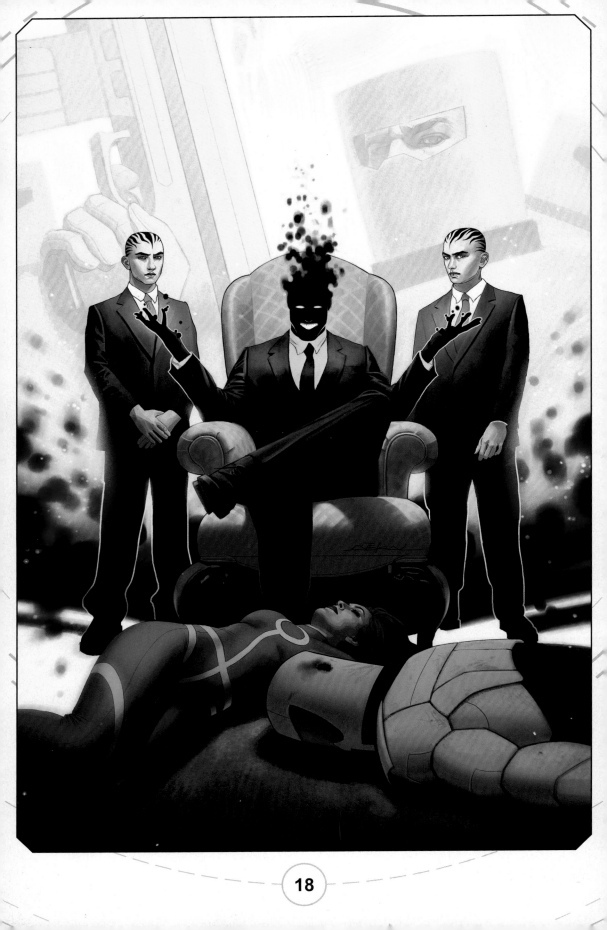

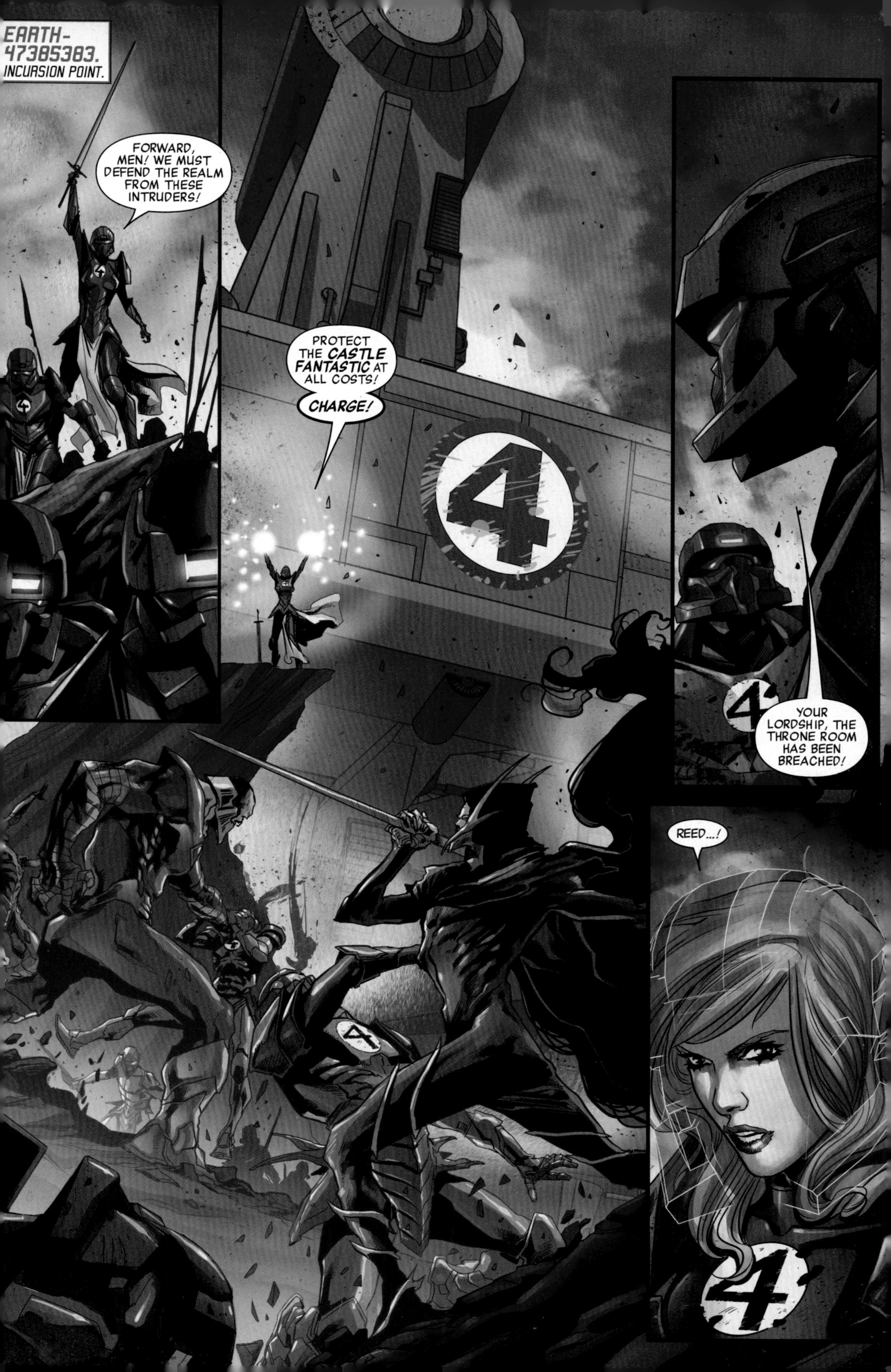
EARTH-47385383. INCURSION POINT.
FORWARD, MEN! WE MUST DEFEND THE REALM FROM THESE INTRUDERS!
PROTECT THE CASTLE FANTASTIC AT ALL COSTS!
CHARGE!
YOUR LORDSHIP, THE THRONE ROOM HAS BEEN BREACHED!
REED...!

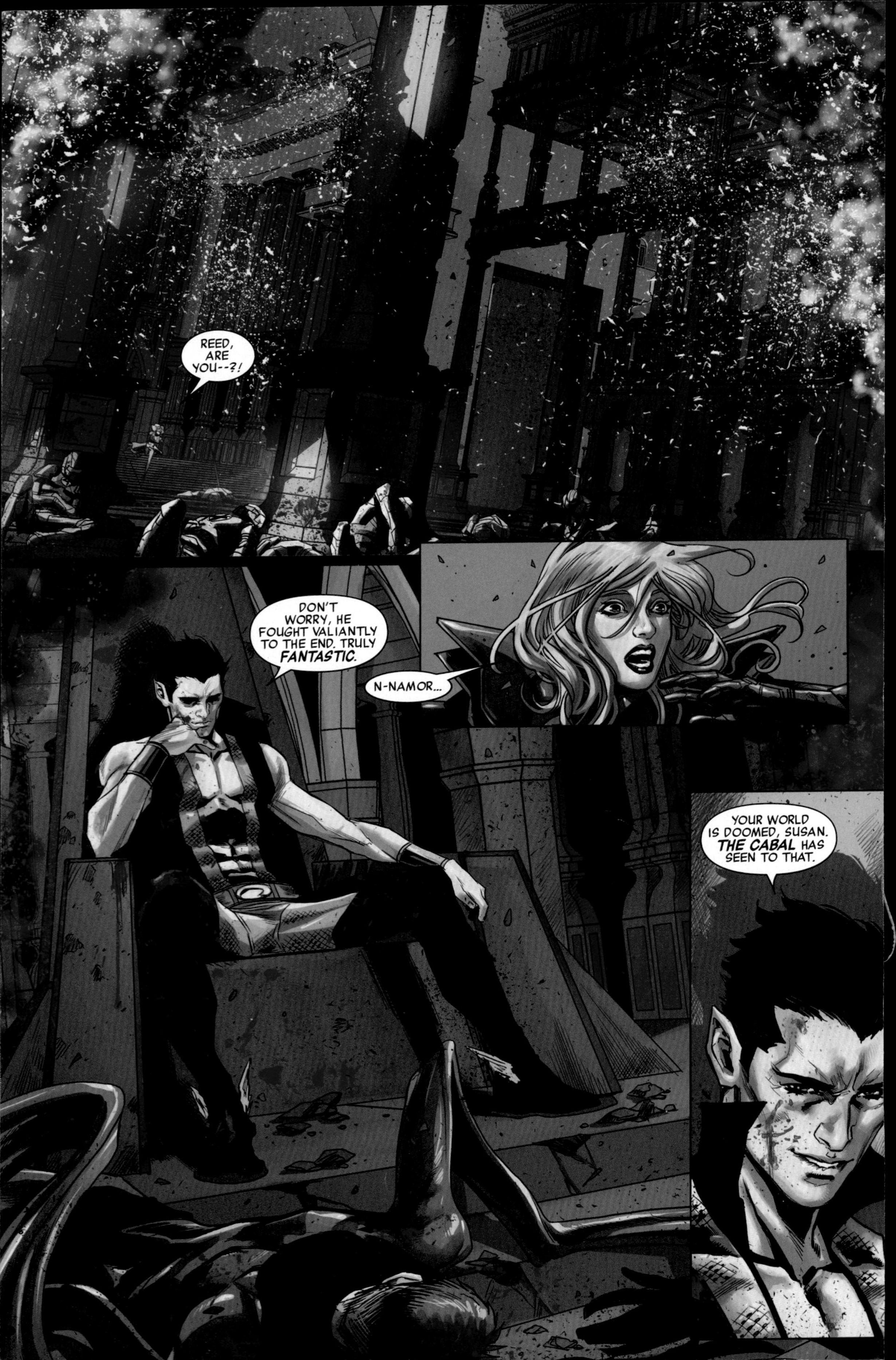
REED, ARE YOU--?!
DON'T WORRY, HE FOUGHT VALIANTLY TO THE END. TRULY FANTASTIC.
N-NAMOR...
YOUR WORLD IS DOOMED, SUSAN. THE CABAL HAS SEEN TO THAT.

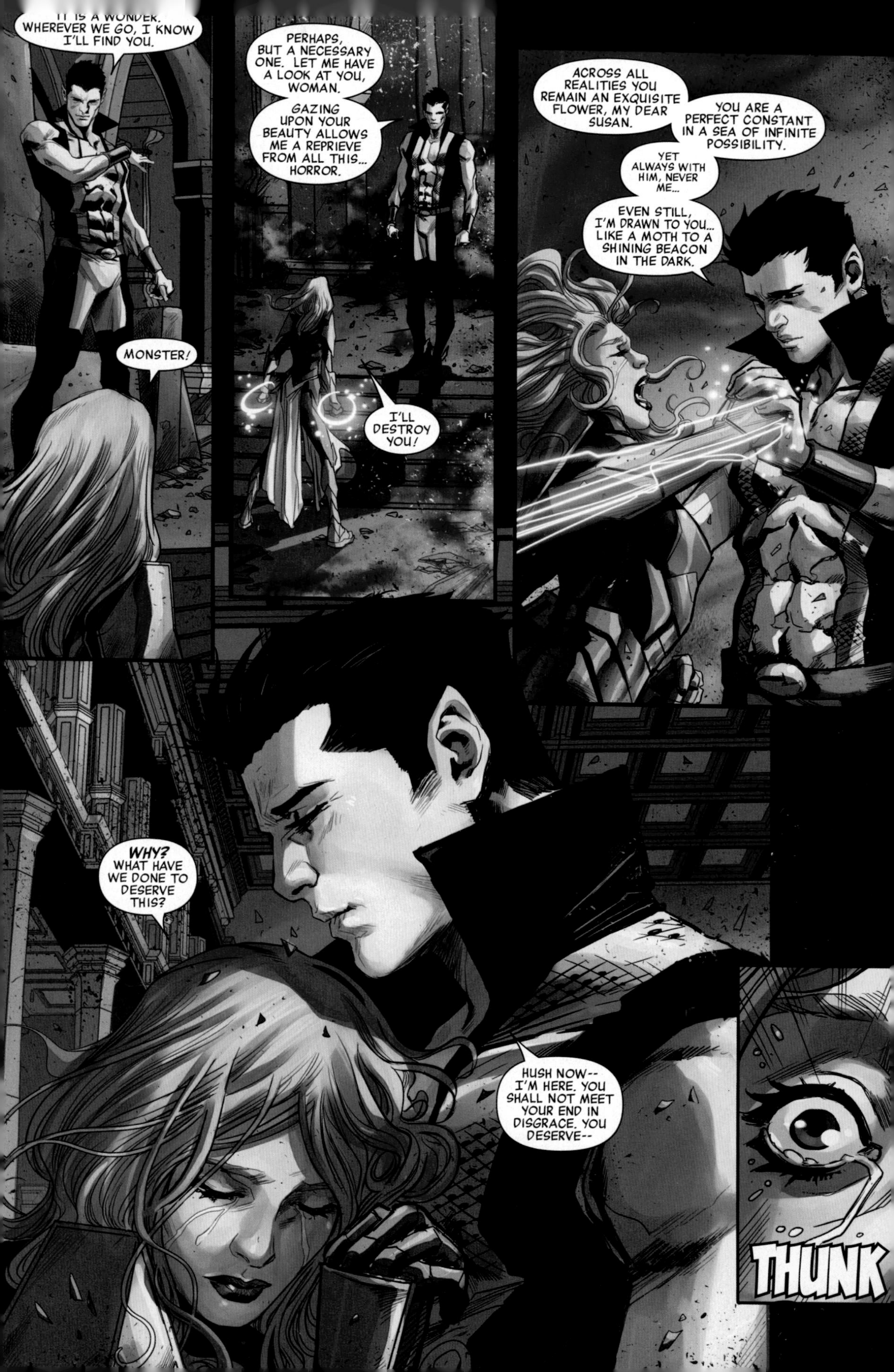
IT IS A WONDER. WHEREVER WE GO, I KNOW I'LL FIND YOU.
MONSTER!
PERHAPS, BUT A NECESSARY ONE. LET ME HAVE A LOOK AT YOU, WOMAN.
GAZING UPON YOUR BEAUTY ALLOWS ME A REPRIEVE FROM ALL THIS... HORROR.
I'LL DESTROY YOU!
ACROSS ALL REALITIES YOU REMAIN AN EXQUISITE FLOWER, MY DEAR SUSAN.
YOU ARE A PERFECT CONSTANT IN A SEA OF INFINITE POSSIBILITY.
YET ALWAYS WITH HIM, NEVER ME...
EVEN STILL, I'M DRAWN TO YOU... LIKE A MOTH TO A SHINING BEACON IN THE DARK.
WHY? WHAT HAVE WE DONE TO DESERVE THIS?
HUSH NOW-- I'M HERE. YOU SHALL NOT MEET YOUR END IN DISGRACE. YOU DESERVE--
THUNK

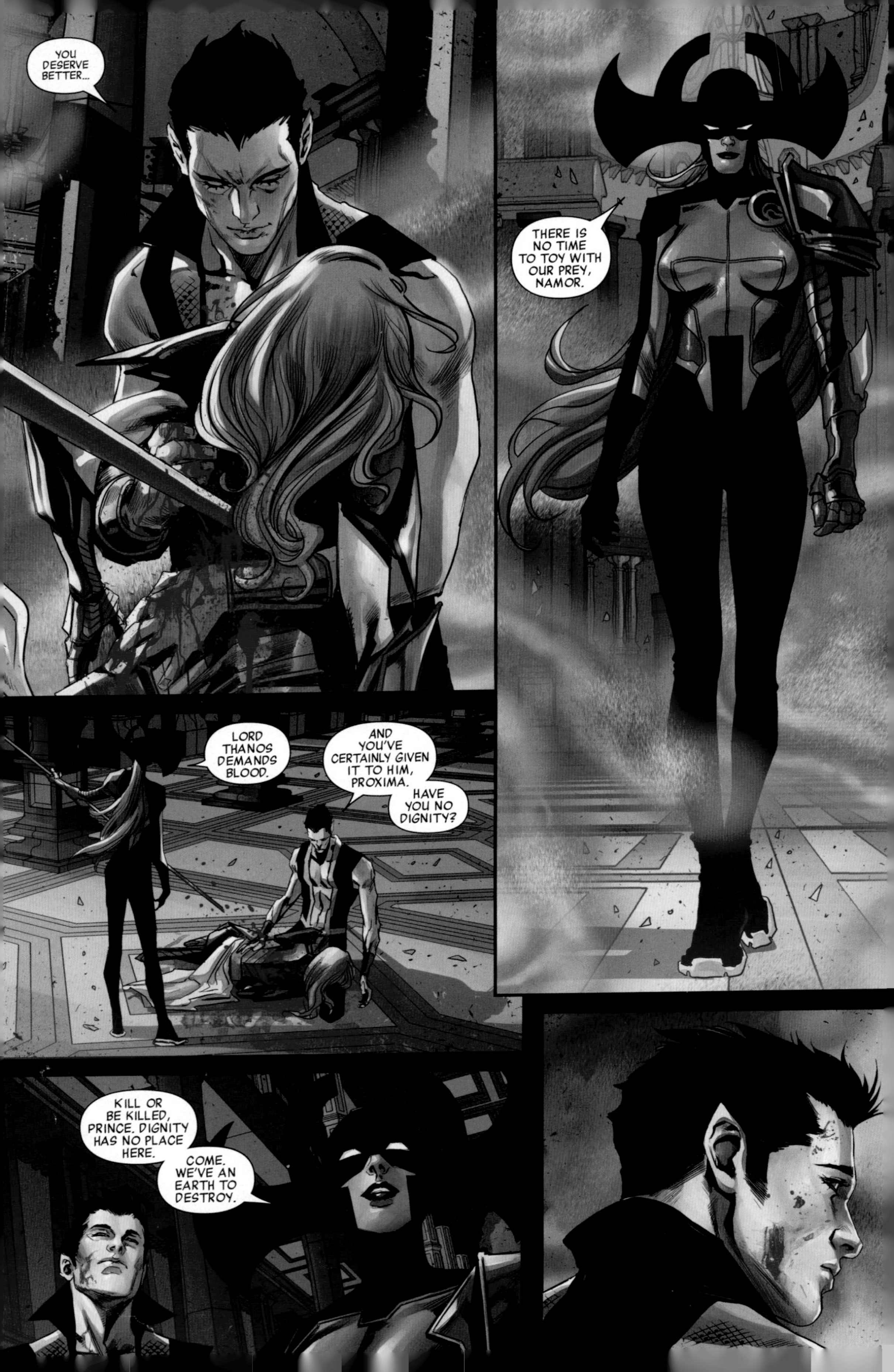
YOU DESERVE BETTER...
THERE IS NO TIME TO TOY WITH OUR PREY, NAMOR.
LORD THANOS DEMANDS BLOOD.
AND YOU'VE CERTAINLY GIVEN IT TO HIM, PROXIMA.
HAVE YOU NO DIGNITY?
KILL OR BE KILLED, PRINCE. DIGNITY HAS NO PLACE HERE.
COME. WE'VE AN EARTH TO DESTROY.

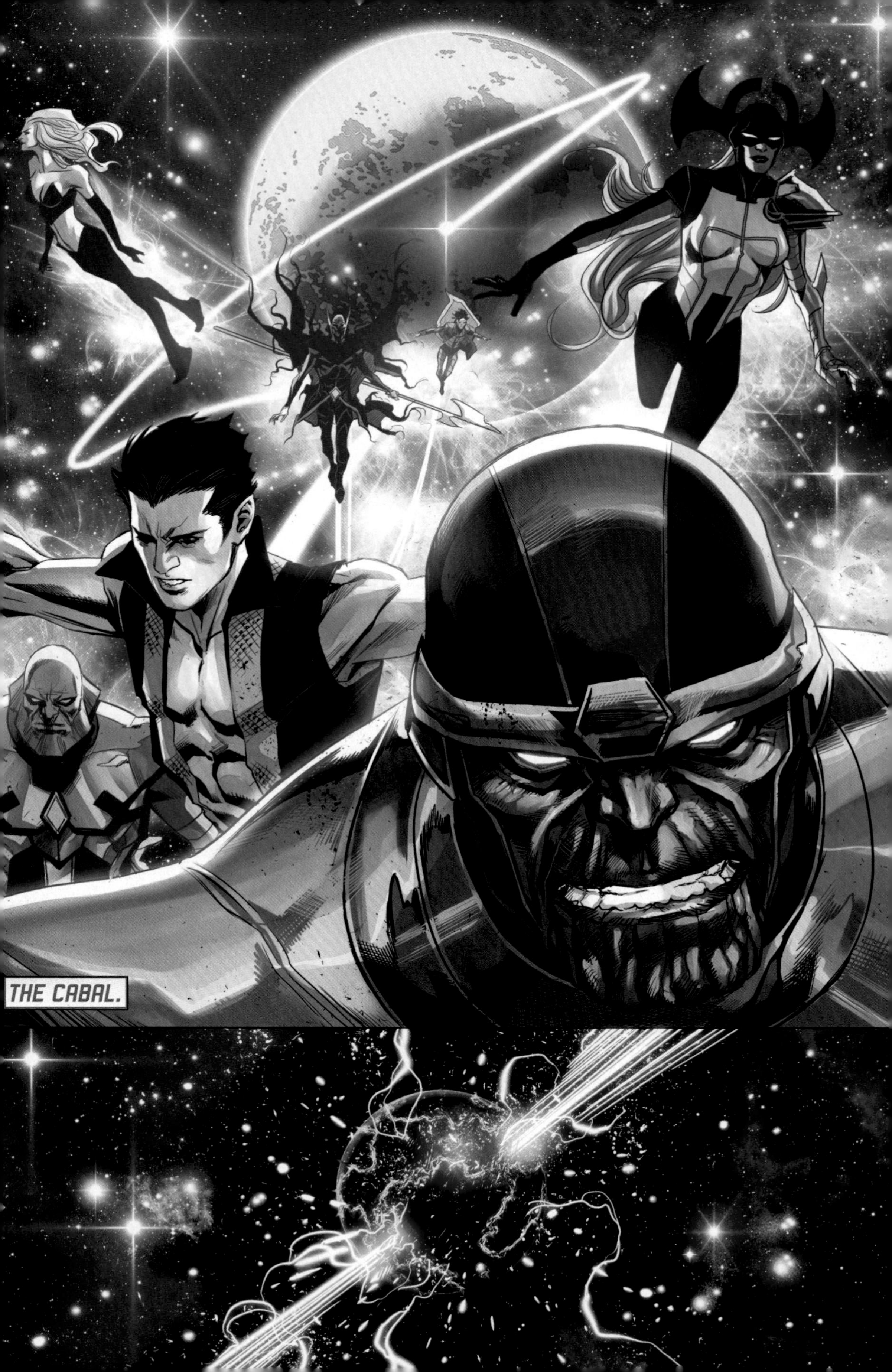
THE CABAL.

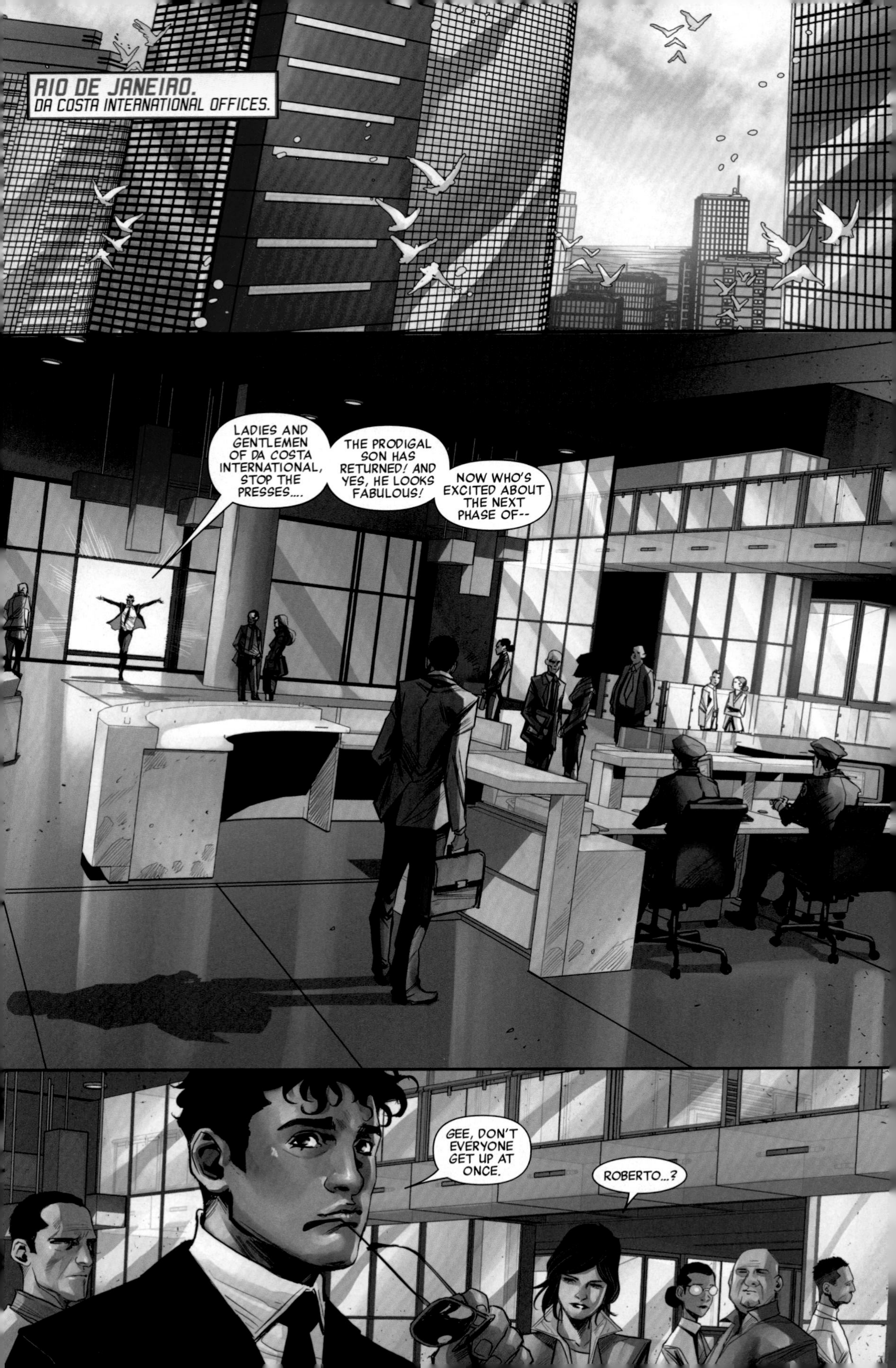
RIO DE JANEIRO.
DA COSTA INTERNATIONAL OFFICES.
LADIES AND GENTLEMEN OF DA COSTA INTERNATIONAL, STOP THE PRESSES....
THE PRODIGAL SON HAS RETURNED! AND YES, HE LOOKS FABULOUS!
NOW WHO'S EXCITED ABOUT THE NEXT PHASE OF--
GEE, DON'T EVERYONE GET UP AT ONCE.
ROBERTO...?

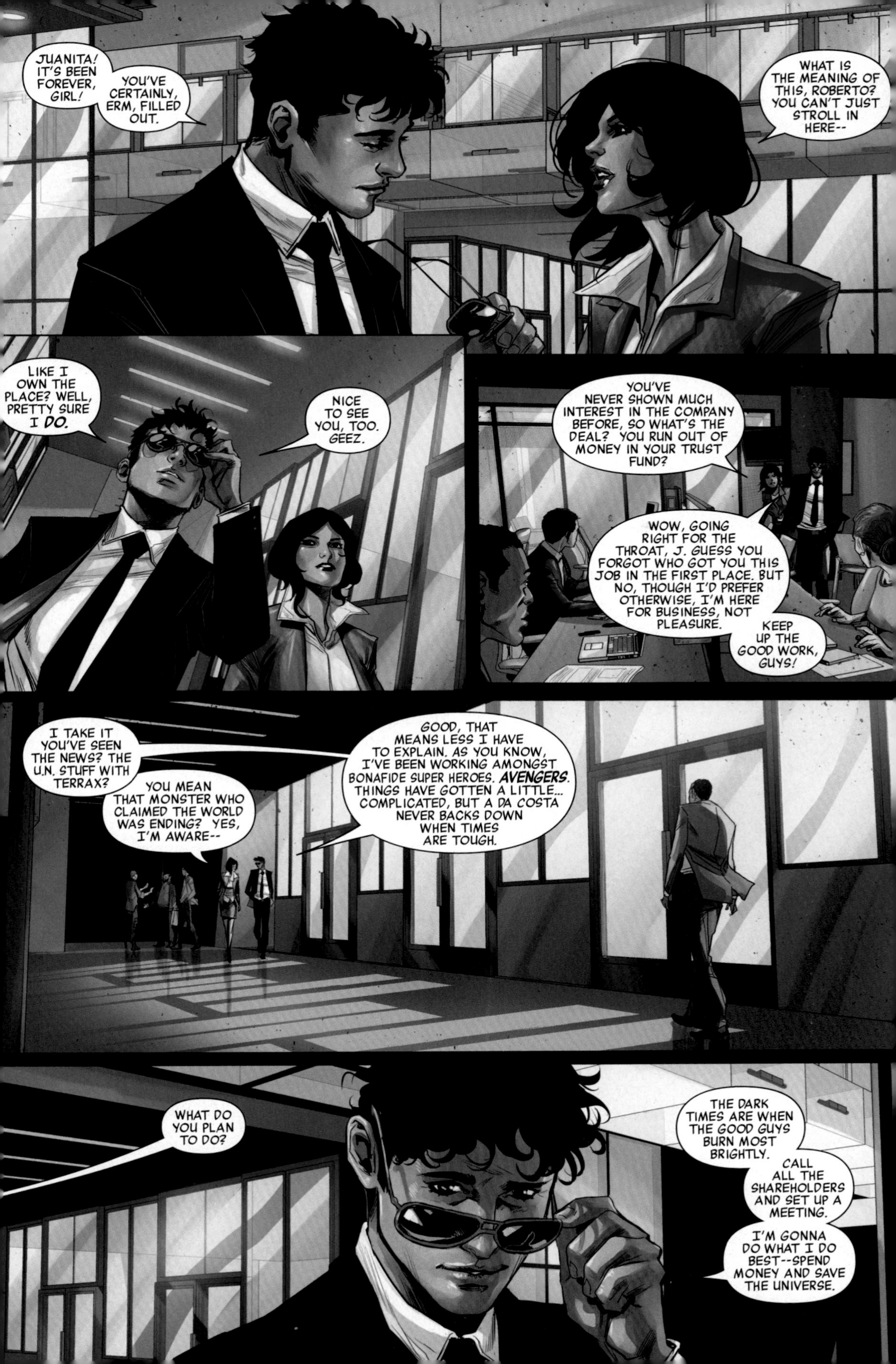

JUANITA! IT'S BEEN FOREVER, GIRL!
YOU'VE CERTAINLY, ERM, FILLED OUT.
WHAT IS THE MEANING OF THIS, ROBERTO? YOU CAN'T JUST STROLL IN HERE--
LIKE I OWN THE PLACE? WELL, PRETTY SURE I DO.
NICE TO SEE YOU, TOO. GEEZ.
YOU'VE NEVER SHOWN MUCH INTEREST IN THE COMPANY BEFORE, SO WHAT'S THE DEAL? YOU RUN OUT OF MONEY IN YOUR TRUST FUND?
WOW, GOING RIGHT FOR THE THROAT, J. GUESS YOU FORGOT WHO GOT YOU THIS JOB IN THE FIRST PLACE. BUT NO, THOUGH I'D PREFER OTHERWISE, I'M HERE FOR BUSINESS, NOT PLEASURE.
KEEP UP THE GOOD WORK, GUYS!
I TAKE IT YOU'VE SEEN THE NEWS? THE U.N. STUFF WITH TERRAX?
YOU MEAN THAT MONSTER WHO CLAIMED THE WORLD WAS ENDING? YES, I'M AWARE--
GOOD, THAT MEANS LESS I HAVE TO EXPLAIN. AS YOU KNOW, I'VE BEEN WORKING AMONGST BONAFIDE SUPER HEROES. AVENGERS. THINGS HAVE GOTTEN A LITTLE... COMPLICATED, BUT A DA COSTA NEVER BACKS DOWN WHEN TIMES ARE TOUGH.
WHAT DO YOU PLAN TO DO?
THE DARK TIMES ARE WHEN THE GOOD GUYS BURN MOST BRIGHTLY.
CALL ALL THE SHAREHOLDERS AND SET UP A MEETING.
I'M GONNA DO WHAT I DO BEST--SPEND MONEY AND SAVE THE UNIVERSE.

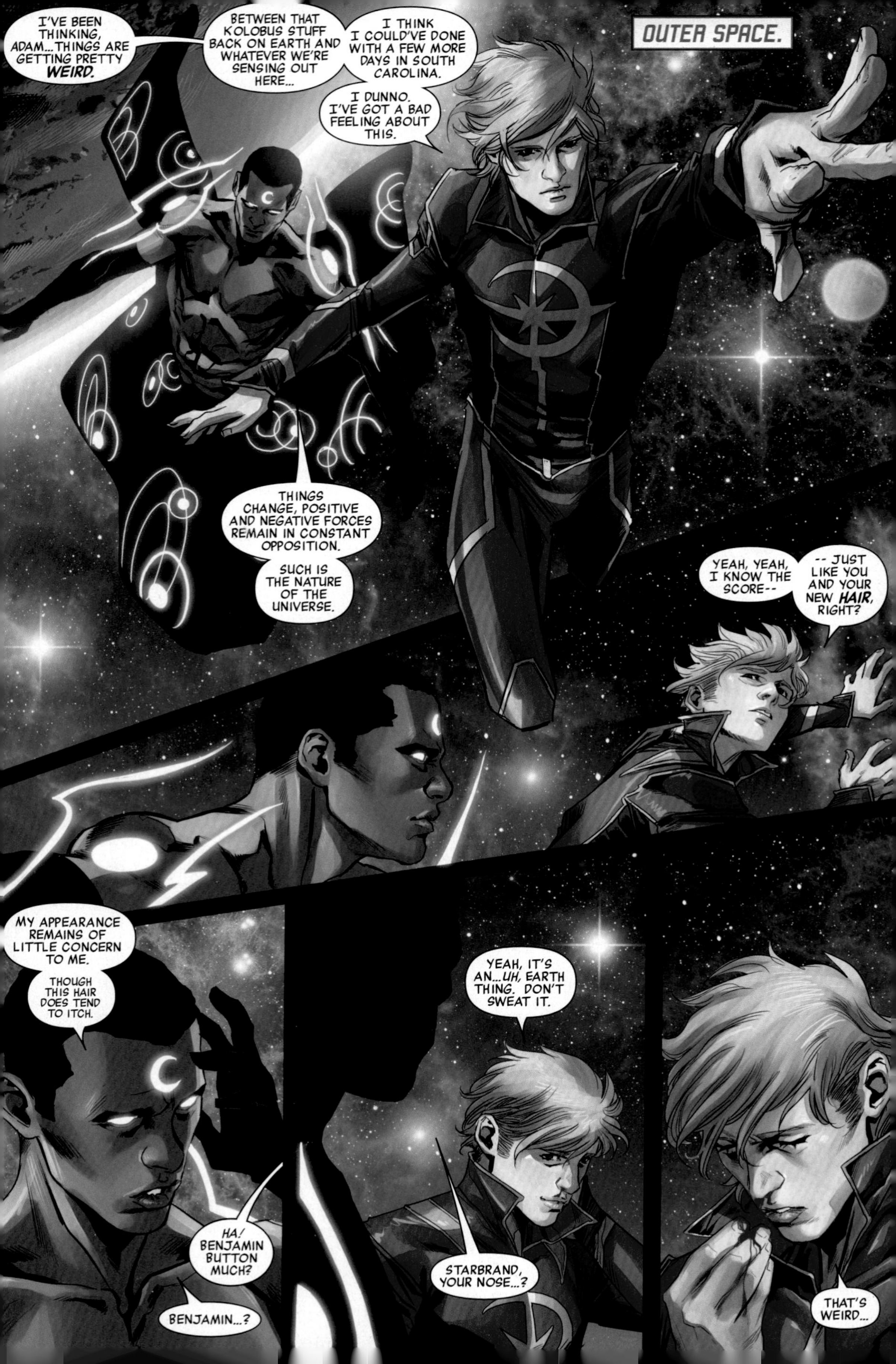
OUTER SPACE.
I'VE BEEN THINKING, ADAM...THINGS ARE GETTING PRETTY WEIRD.
BETWEEN THAT KOLOBUS STUFF BACK ON EARTH AND WHATEVER WE'RE SENSING OUT HERE...
I THINK I COULD'VE DONE WITH A FEW MORE DAYS IN SOUTH CAROLINA.
I DUNNO. I'VE GOT A BAD FEELING ABOUT THIS.
THINGS CHANGE, POSITIVE AND NEGATIVE FORCES REMAIN IN CONSTANT OPPOSITION.
SUCH IS THE NATURE OF THE UNIVERSE.
YEAH, YEAH, I KNOW THE SCORE--
-- JUST LIKE YOU AND YOUR NEW HAIR, RIGHT?
MY APPEARANCE REMAINS OF LITTLE CONCERN TO ME.
THOUGH THIS HAIR DOES TEND TO ITCH.
HA! BENJAMIN BUTTON MUCH?
BENJAMIN...?
YEAH, IT'S AN...UH, EARTH THING. DON'T SWEAT IT.
STARBRAND, YOUR NOSE...?
THAT'S WEIRD...

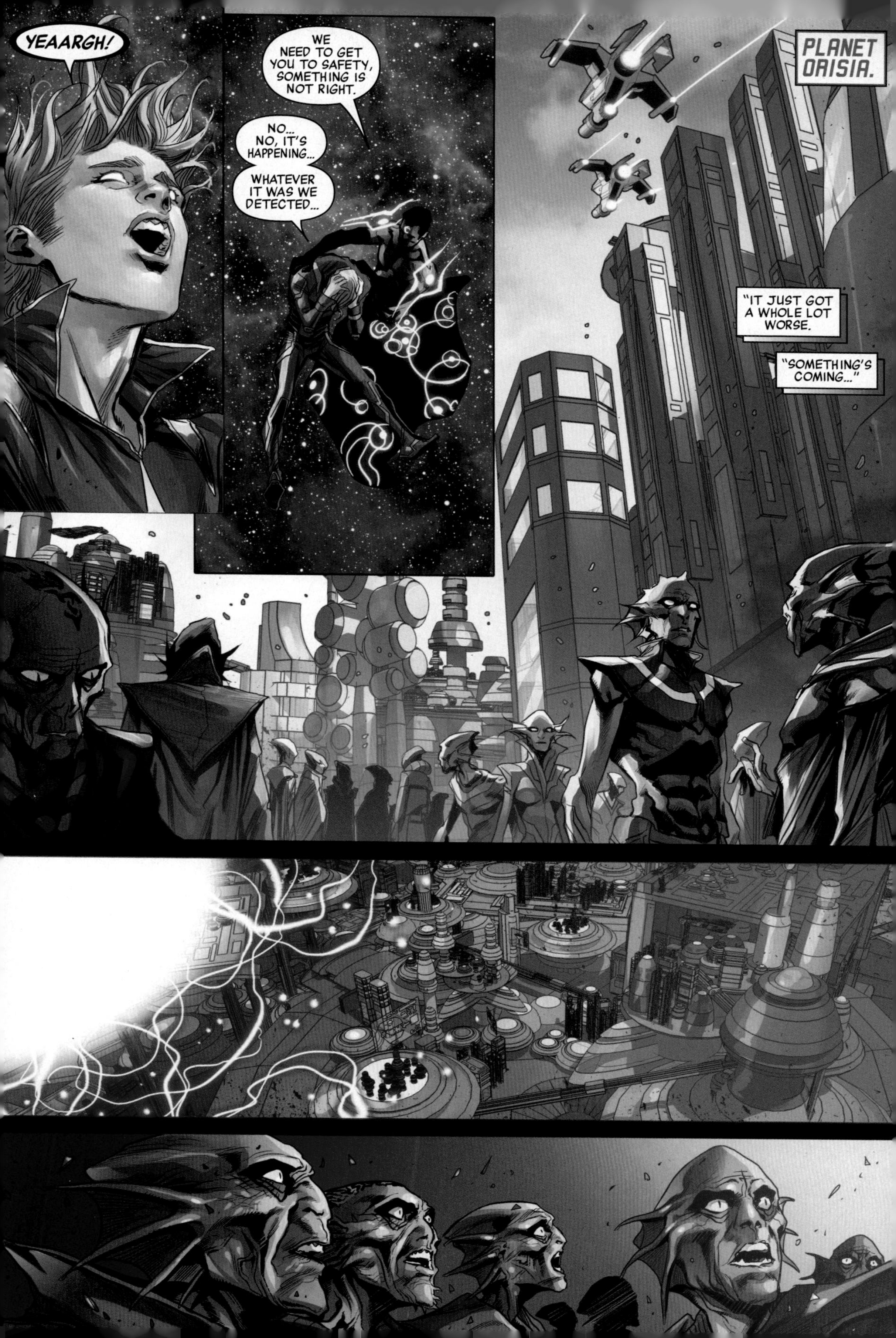
YEAARGH!
WE NEED TO GET YOU TO SAFETY, SOMETHING IS NOT RIGHT.
NO... NO, IT'S HAPPENING...
WHATEVER IT WAS WE DETECTED...
PLANET ORISIA.
"IT JUST GOT A WHOLE LOT WORSE.
"SOMETHING'S COMING..."

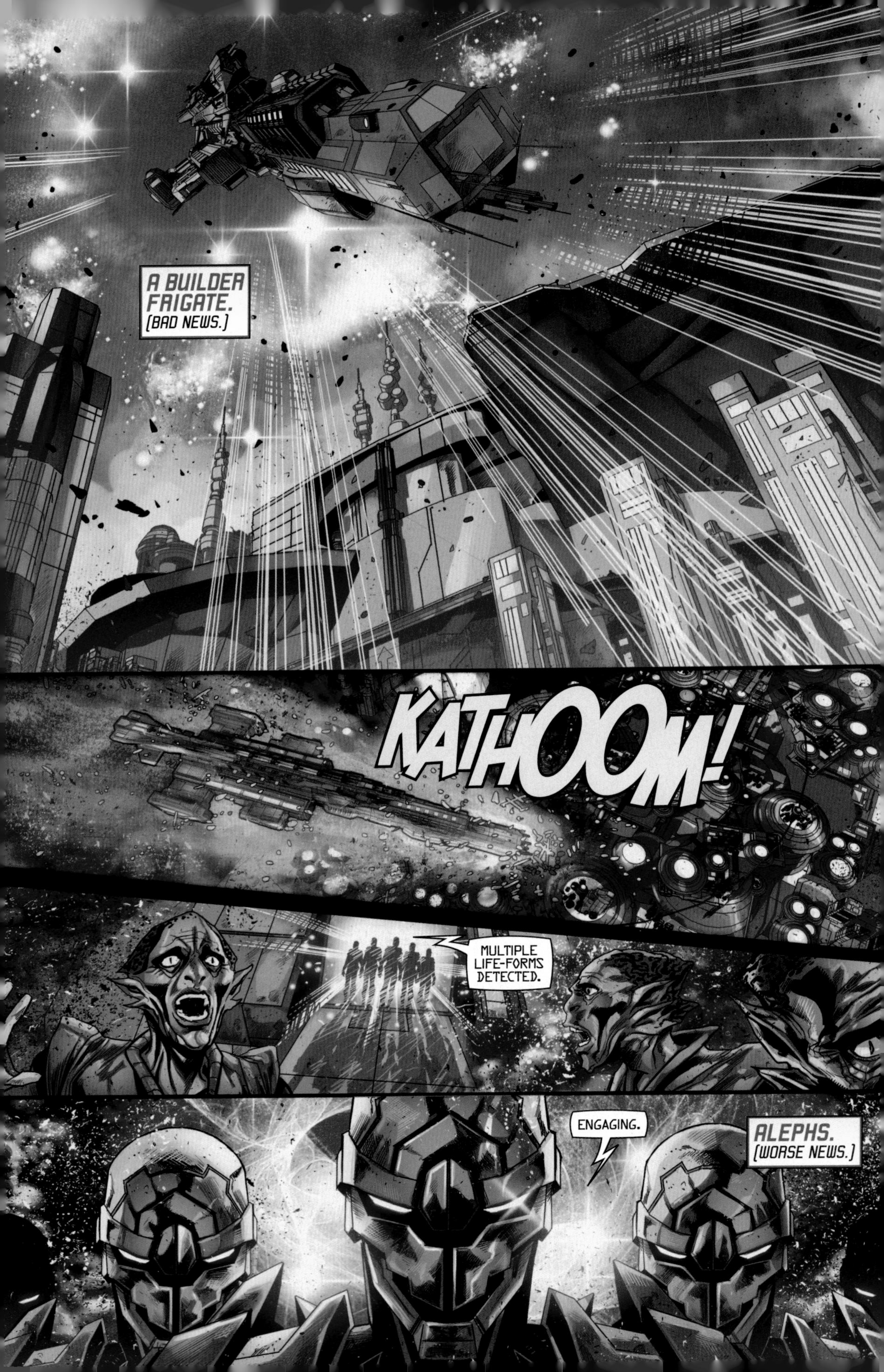
A BUILDER FRIGATE. (BAD NEWS.)
KATHOOM!
MULTIPLE LIFE-FORMS DETECTED.
ENGAGING.
ALEPHS. (WORSE NEWS.)

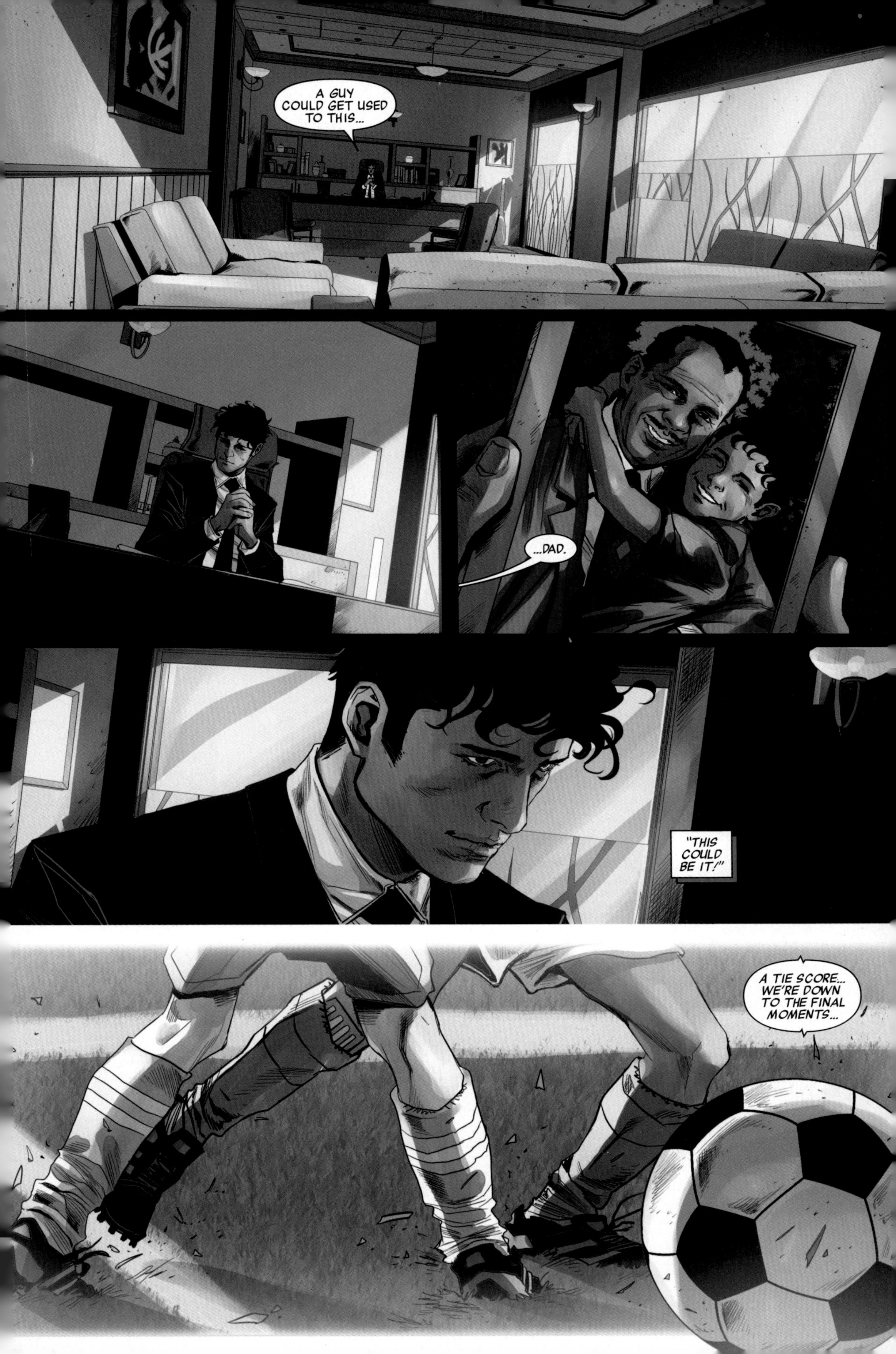
A GUY COULD GET USED TO THIS...
...DAD.
"THIS COULD BE IT!"
A TIE SCORE... WE'RE DOWN TO THE FINAL MOMENTS...

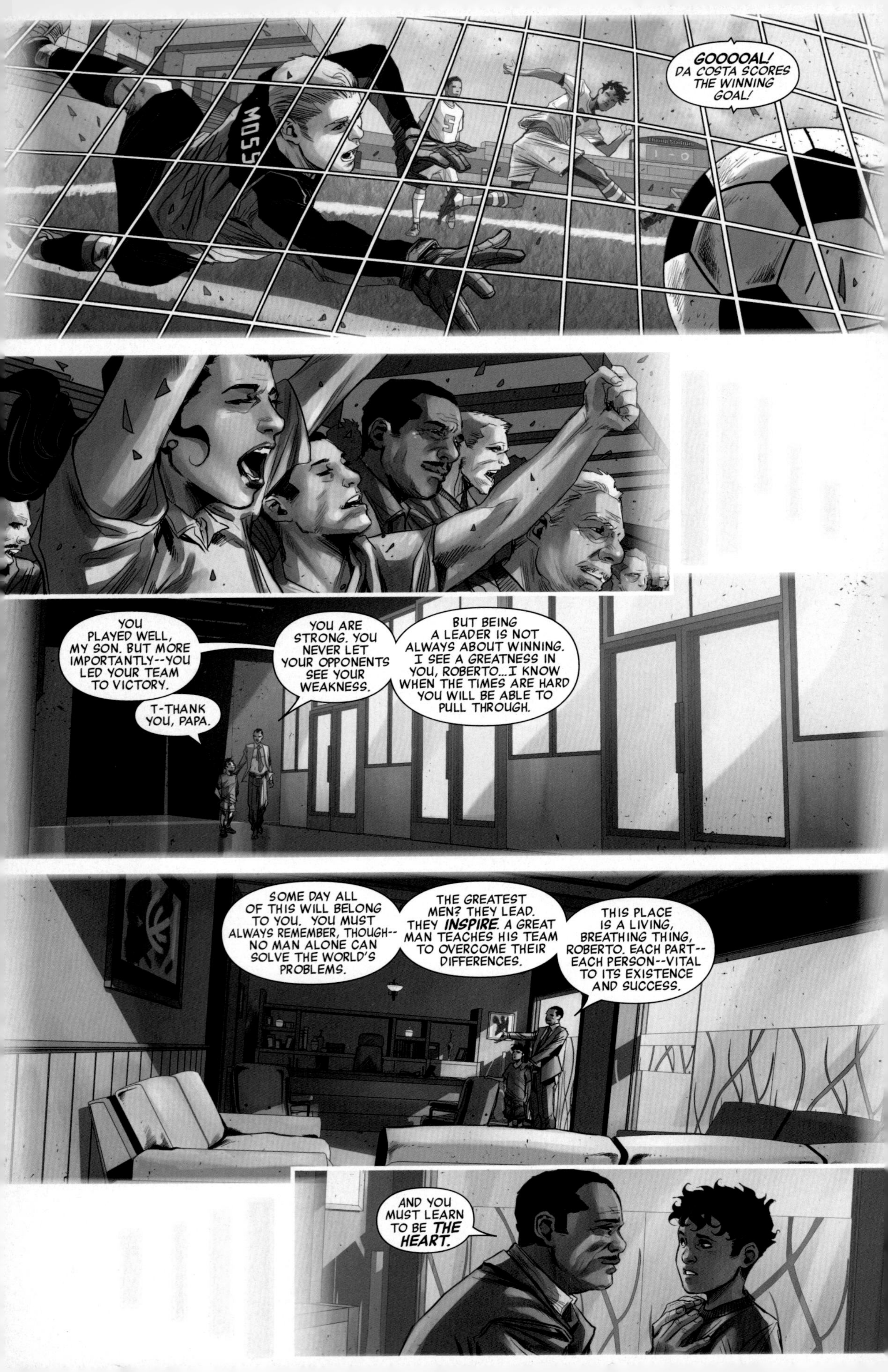
GOOOOAL! DA COSTA SCORES THE WINNING GOAL!
YOU PLAYED WELL, MY SON. BUT MORE IMPORTANTLY--YOU LED YOUR TEAM TO VICTORY.
T-THANK YOU, PAPA.
YOU ARE STRONG. YOU NEVER LET YOUR OPPONENTS SEE YOUR WEAKNESS.
BUT BEING A LEADER IS NOT ALWAYS ABOUT WINNING. I SEE A GREATNESS IN YOU, ROBERTO...I KNOW WHEN THE TIMES ARE HARD YOU WILL BE ABLE TO PULL THROUGH.
SOME DAY ALL OF THIS WILL BELONG TO YOU. YOU MUST ALWAYS REMEMBER, THOUGH--NO MAN ALONE CAN SOLVE THE WORLD'S PROBLEMS.
THE GREATEST MEN? THEY LEAD. THEY INSPIRE. A GREAT MAN TEACHES HIS TEAM TO OVERCOME THEIR DIFFERENCES.
THIS PLACE IS A LIVING, BREATHING THING, ROBERTO. EACH PART--EACH PERSON--VITAL TO ITS EXISTENCE AND SUCCESS.
AND YOU MUST LEARN TO BE THE HEART.

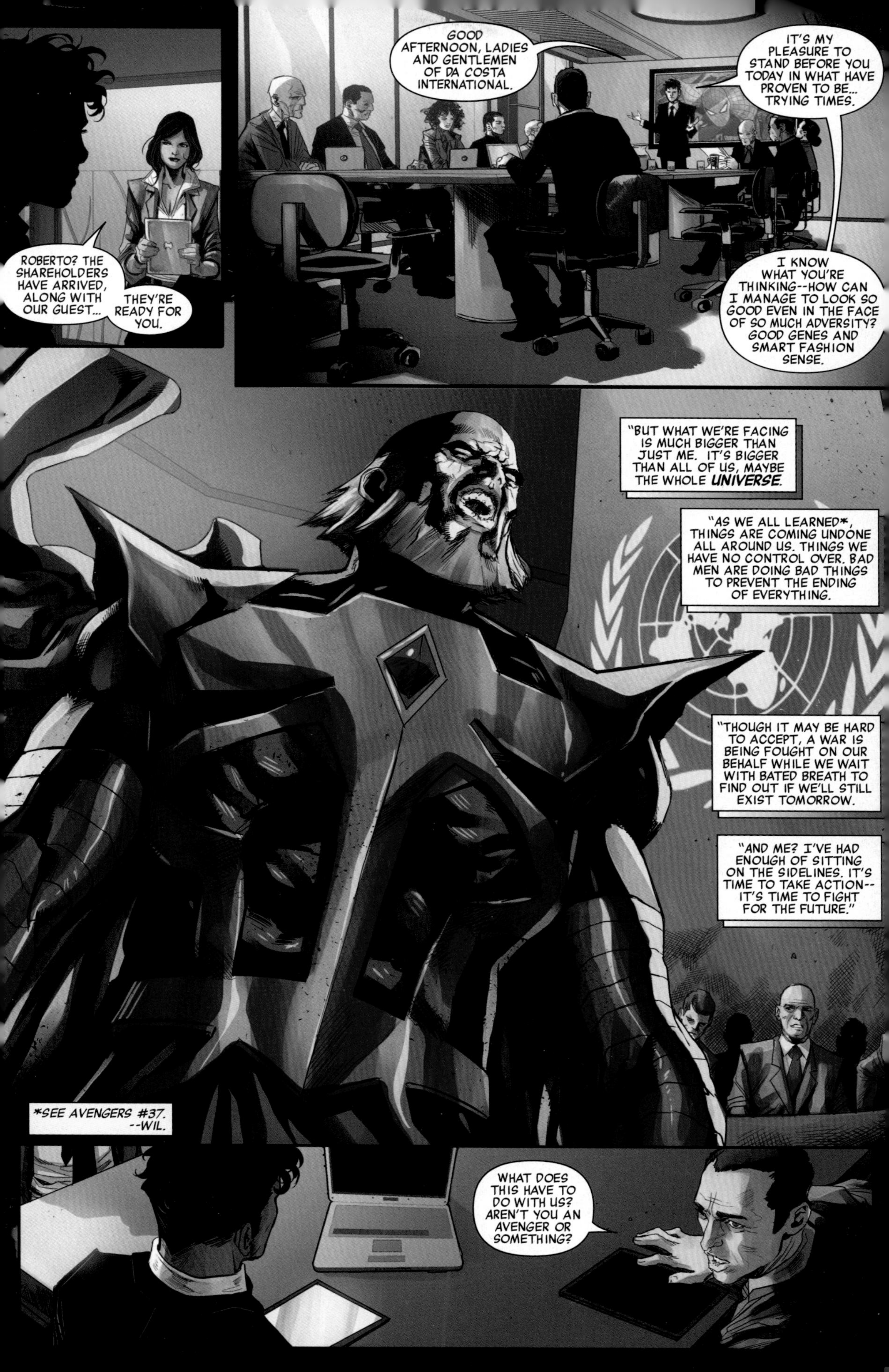
ROBERTO? THE SHAREHOLDERS HAVE ARRIVED, ALONG WITH OUR GUEST...
THEY'RE READY FOR YOU.
GOOD AFTERNOON, LADIES AND GENTLEMEN OF DA COSTA INTERNATIONAL.
IT'S MY PLEASURE TO STAND BEFORE YOU TODAY IN WHAT HAVE PROVEN TO BE... TRYING TIMES.
I KNOW WHAT YOU'RE THINKING--HOW CAN I MANAGE TO LOOK SO GOOD EVEN IN THE FACE OF SO MUCH ADVERSITY? GOOD GENES AND SMART FASHION SENSE.
"BUT WHAT WE'RE FACING IS MUCH BIGGER THAN JUST ME. IT'S BIGGER THAN ALL OF US, MAYBE THE WHOLE UNIVERSE.
"AS WE ALL LEARNED*, THINGS ARE COMING UNDONE ALL AROUND US. THINGS WE HAVE NO CONTROL OVER. BAD MEN ARE DOING BAD THINGS TO PREVENT THE ENDING OF EVERYTHING.
"THOUGH IT MAY BE HARD TO ACCEPT, A WAR IS BEING FOUGHT ON OUR BEHALF WHILE WE WAIT WITH BATED BREATH TO FIND OUT IF WE'LL STILL EXIST TOMORROW.
"AND ME? I'VE HAD ENOUGH OF SITTING ON THE SIDELINES. IT'S TIME TO TAKE ACTION-- IT'S TIME TO FIGHT FOR THE FUTURE."
*SEE AVENGERS #37. --WIL.
WHAT DOES THIS HAVE TO DO WITH US? AREN'T YOU AN AVENGER OR SOMETHING?

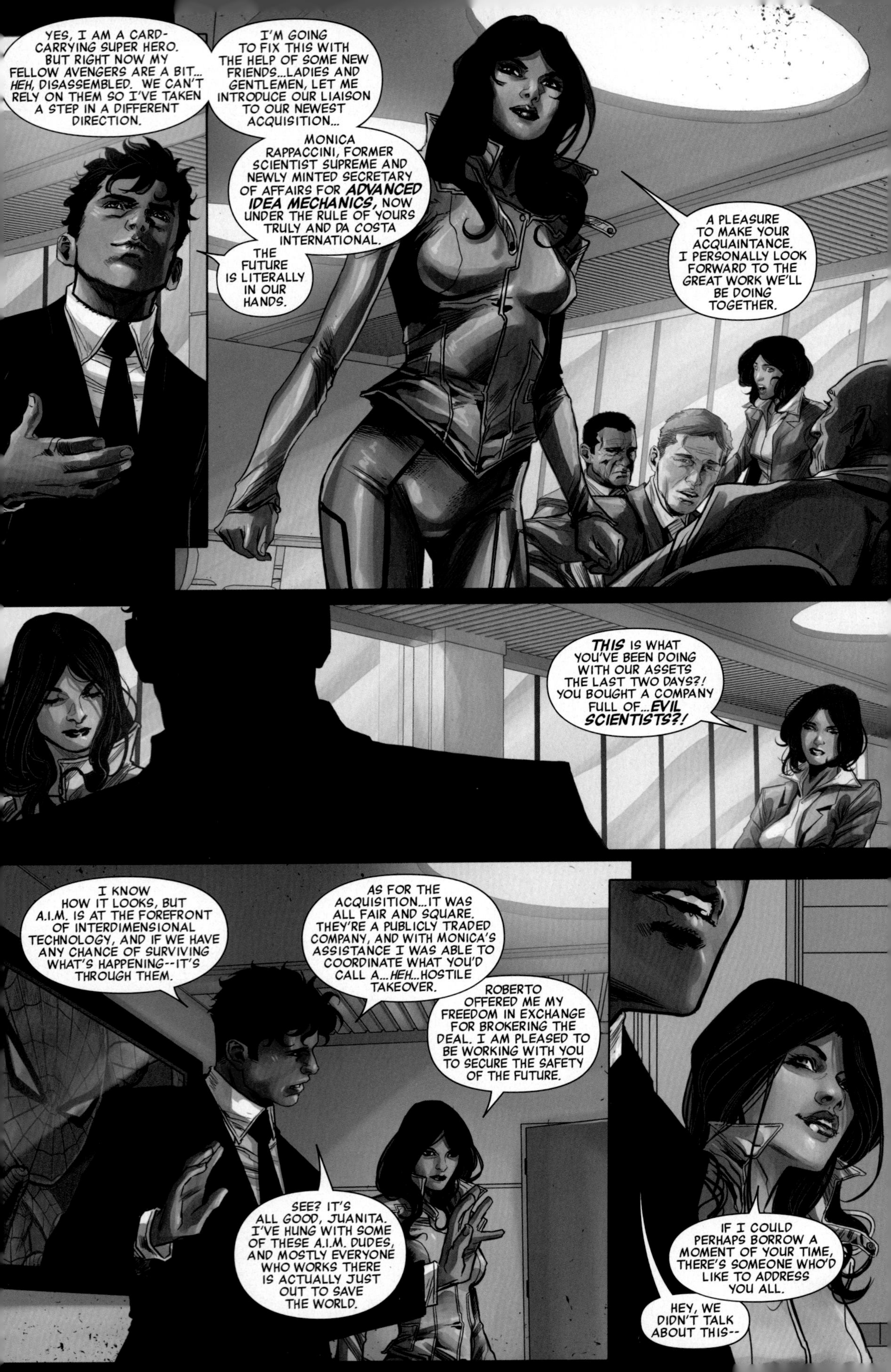

YES, I AM A CARD-CARRYING SUPER HERO. BUT RIGHT NOW MY FELLOW AVENGERS ARE A BIT... HEH, DISASSEMBLED. WE CAN'T RELY ON THEM SO I'VE TAKEN A STEP IN A DIFFERENT DIRECTION.
I'M GOING TO FIX THIS WITH THE HELP OF SOME NEW FRIENDS...LADIES AND GENTLEMEN, LET ME INTRODUCE OUR LIAISON TO OUR NEWEST ACQUISITION...
MONICA RAPPACCINI, FORMER SCIENTIST SUPREME AND NEWLY MINTED SECRETARY OF AFFAIRS FOR ADVANCED IDEA MECHANICS, NOW UNDER THE RULE OF YOURS TRULY AND DA COSTA INTERNATIONAL.
THE FUTURE IS LITERALLY IN OUR HANDS.
A PLEASURE TO MAKE YOUR ACQUAINTANCE. I PERSONALLY LOOK FORWARD TO THE GREAT WORK WE'LL BE DOING TOGETHER.
THIS IS WHAT YOU'VE BEEN DOING WITH OUR ASSETS THE LAST TWO DAYS?! YOU BOUGHT A COMPANY FULL OF...EVIL SCIENTISTS?!
I KNOW HOW IT LOOKS, BUT A.I.M. IS AT THE FOREFRONT OF INTERDIMENSIONAL TECHNOLOGY, AND IF WE HAVE ANY CHANCE OF SURVIVING WHAT'S HAPPENING--IT'S THROUGH THEM.
AS FOR THE ACQUISITION...IT WAS ALL FAIR AND SQUARE. THEY'RE A PUBLICLY TRADED COMPANY, AND WITH MONICA'S ASSISTANCE I WAS ABLE TO COORDINATE WHAT YOU'D CALL A...HEH...HOSTILE TAKEOVER.
ROBERTO OFFERED ME MY FREEDOM IN EXCHANGE FOR BROKERING THE DEAL. I AM PLEASED TO BE WORKING WITH YOU TO SECURE THE SAFETY OF THE FUTURE.
SEE? IT'S ALL GOOD, JUANITA. I'VE HUNG WITH SOME OF THESE A.I.M. DUDES, AND MOSTLY EVERYONE WHO WORKS THERE IS ACTUALLY JUST OUT TO SAVE THE WORLD.
IF I COULD PERHAPS BORROW A MOMENT OF YOUR TIME, THERE'S SOMEONE WHO'D LIKE TO ADDRESS YOU ALL.
HEY, WE DIDN'T TALK ABOUT THIS--

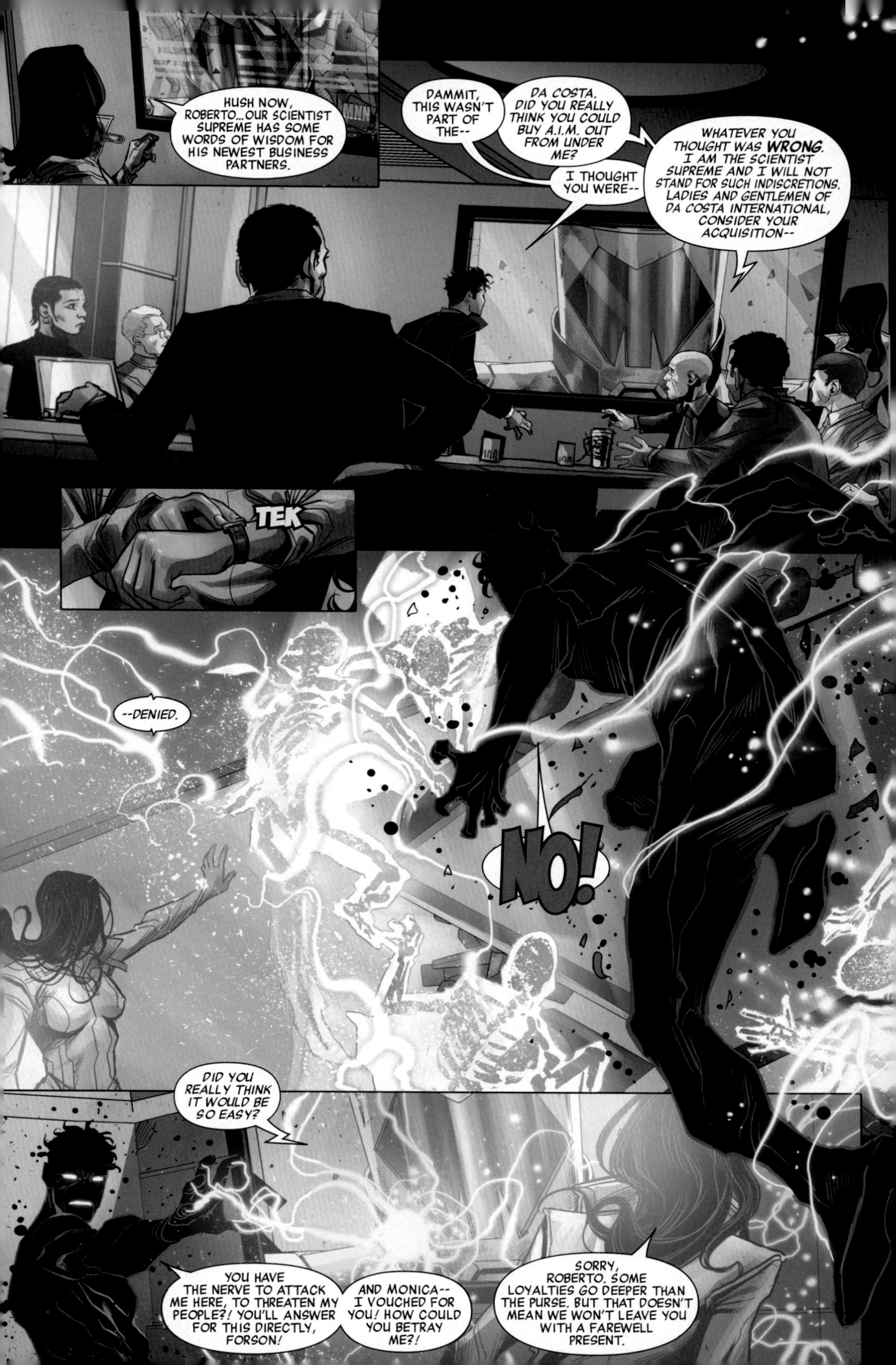
HUSH NOW, ROBERTO...OUR SCIENTIST SUPREME HAS SOME WORDS OF WISDOM FOR HIS NEWEST BUSINESS PARTNERS.
DAMMIT, THIS WASN'T PART OF THE--
DA COSTA. DID YOU REALLY THINK YOU COULD BUY A.I.M. OUT FROM UNDER ME?
I THOUGHT YOU WERE--
WHATEVER YOU THOUGHT WAS WRONG. I AM THE SCIENTIST SUPREME AND I WILL NOT STAND FOR SUCH INDISCRETIONS. LADIES AND GENTLEMEN OF DA COSTA INTERNATIONAL, CONSIDER YOUR ACQUISITION--
TEK
--DENIED.
NO!
DID YOU REALLY THINK IT WOULD BE SO EASY?
YOU HAVE THE NERVE TO ATTACK ME HERE, TO THREATEN MY PEOPLE?! YOU'LL ANSWER FOR THIS DIRECTLY, FORSON!
AND MONICA-- I VOUCHED FOR YOU! HOW COULD YOU BETRAY ME?!
SORRY, ROBERTO. SOME LOYALTIES GO DEEPER THAN THE PURSE. BUT THAT DOESN'T MEAN WE WON'T LEAVE YOU WITH A FAREWELL PRESENT.

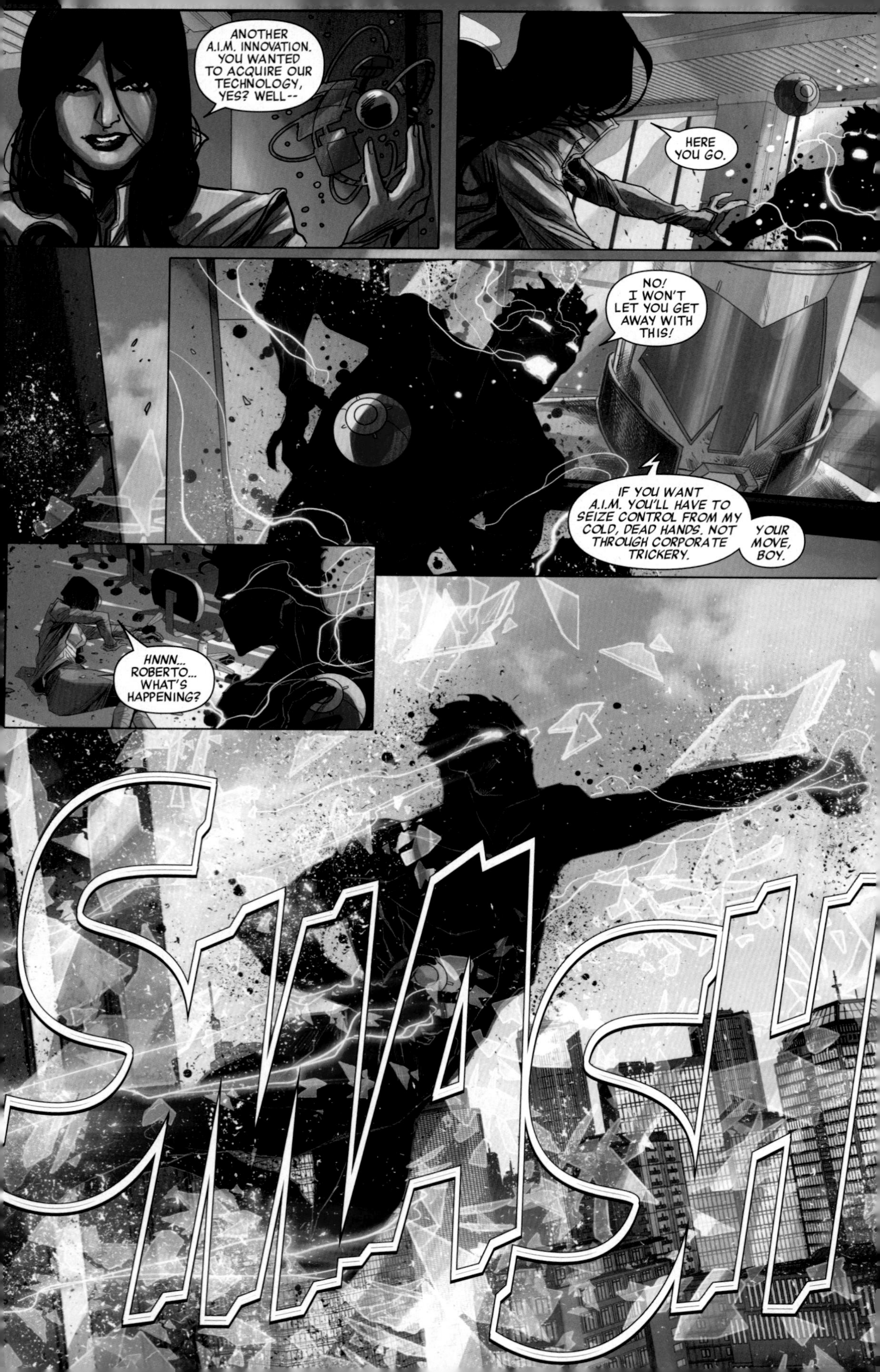

ANOTHER A.I.M. INNOVATION. YOU WANTED TO ACQUIRE OUR TECHNOLOGY, YES? WELL--
HERE YOU GO.
NO! I WON'T LET YOU GET AWAY WITH THIS!
IF YOU WANT A.I.M. YOU'LL HAVE TO SEIZE CONTROL FROM MY COLD, DEAD HANDS. NOT THROUGH CORPORATE TRICKERY.
YOUR MOVE, BOY.
HNNN... ROBERTO... WHAT'S HAPPENING?
SMASH!

"YOU MUST BE THE HEART."

THE HEART DOES NOT FALTER. YOU ALONE MUST BEAR THE SUFFERING. YOU MUST BE STRONG.

ARE YOU WITH US, BOBBY? WILL YOU HELP US HUNT DOWN THESE ILLUMINATI TRAITORS?

YOU'VE GOT IT ALL WRONG, STEVE. THIS ISN'T WHAT THE AVENGERS ARE.

I WON'T HUNT DOWN OUR FRIENDS... NO MATTER *WHAT* THEY'VE DONE.

SO WHAT WILL YOU DO WHILE I'M GONE?

I'M GOING TO DO WHAT WE'VE ALWAYS DONE, SAM...

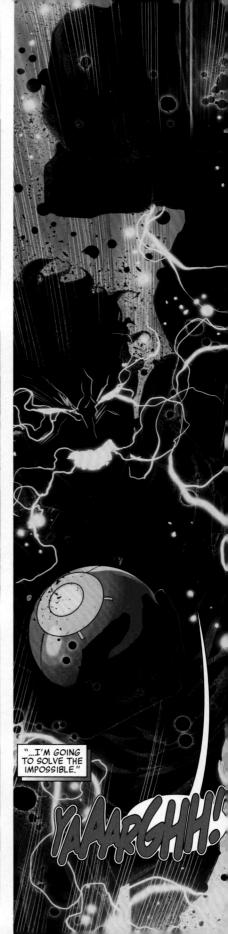

"...I'M GOING TO SOLVE THE IMPOSSIBLE."

YAAARGHH!!

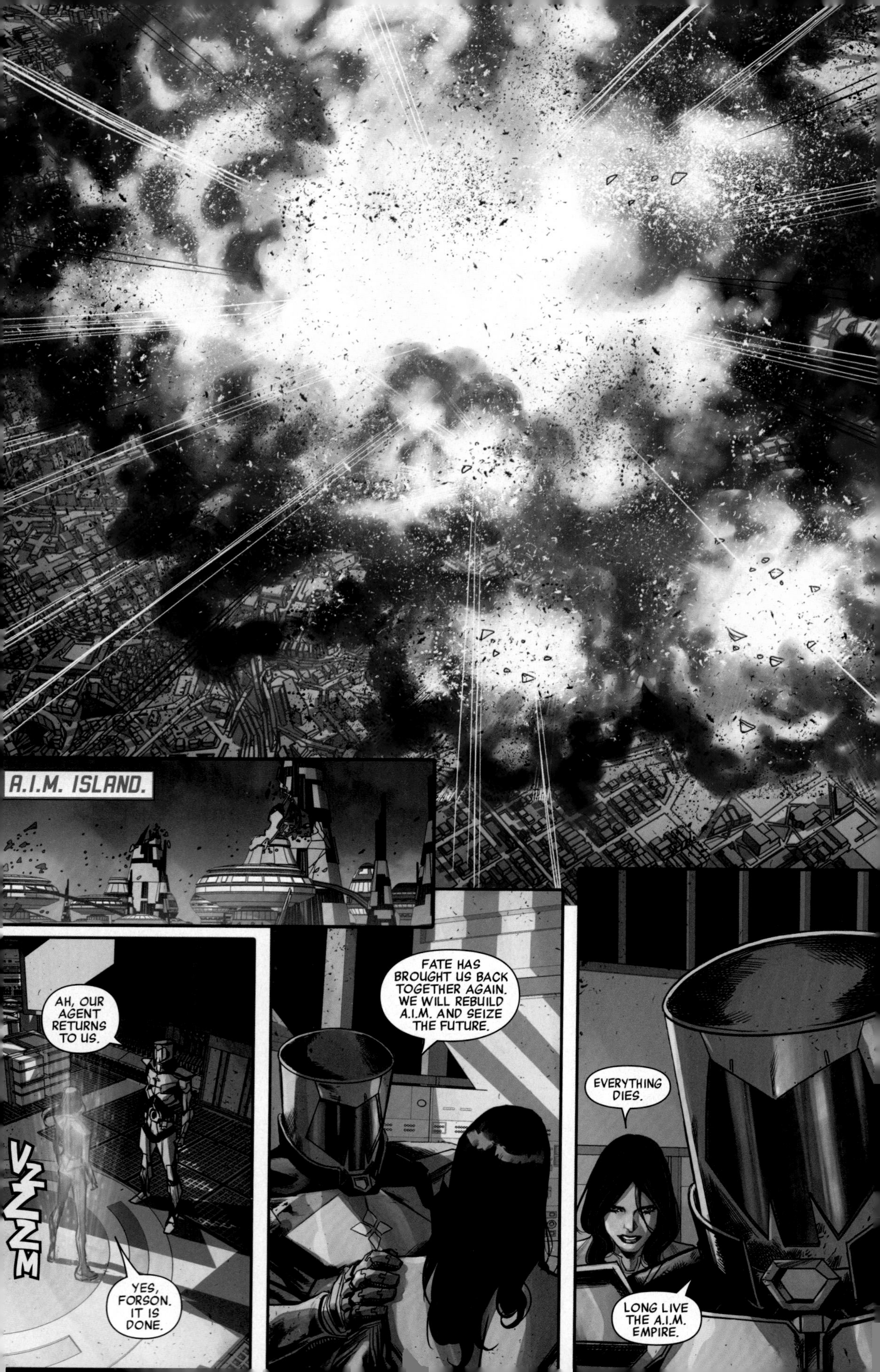
A.I.M. ISLAND.
AH, OUR AGENT RETURNS TO US.
VZZZM
YES, FORSON. IT IS DONE.
FATE HAS BROUGHT US BACK TOGETHER AGAIN. WE WILL REBUILD A.I.M. AND SEIZE THE FUTURE.
EVERYTHING DIES.
LONG LIVE THE A.I.M. EMPIRE.

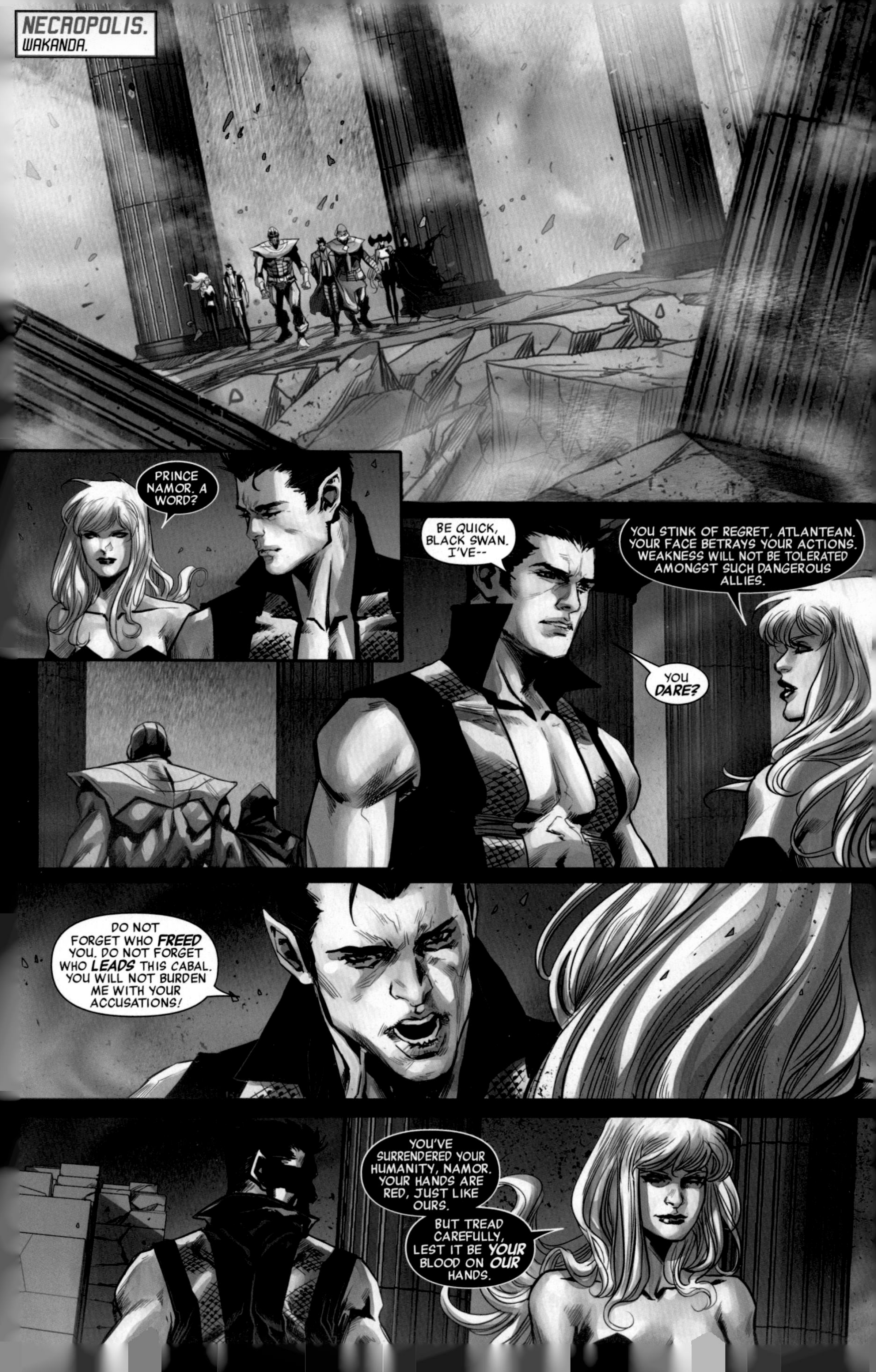
NECROPOLIS.
WAKANDA.
PRINCE NAMOR. A WORD?
BE QUICK, BLACK SWAN. I'VE--
YOU STINK OF REGRET, ATLANTEAN. YOUR FACE BETRAYS YOUR ACTIONS. WEAKNESS WILL NOT BE TOLERATED AMONGST SUCH DANGEROUS ALLIES.
YOU DARE?
DO NOT FORGET WHO FREED YOU. DO NOT FORGET WHO LEADS THIS CABAL. YOU WILL NOT BURDEN ME WITH YOUR ACCUSATIONS!
YOU'VE SURRENDERED YOUR HUMANITY, NAMOR. YOUR HANDS ARE RED, JUST LIKE OURS.
BUT TREAD CAREFULLY, LEST IT BE YOUR BLOOD ON OUR HANDS.

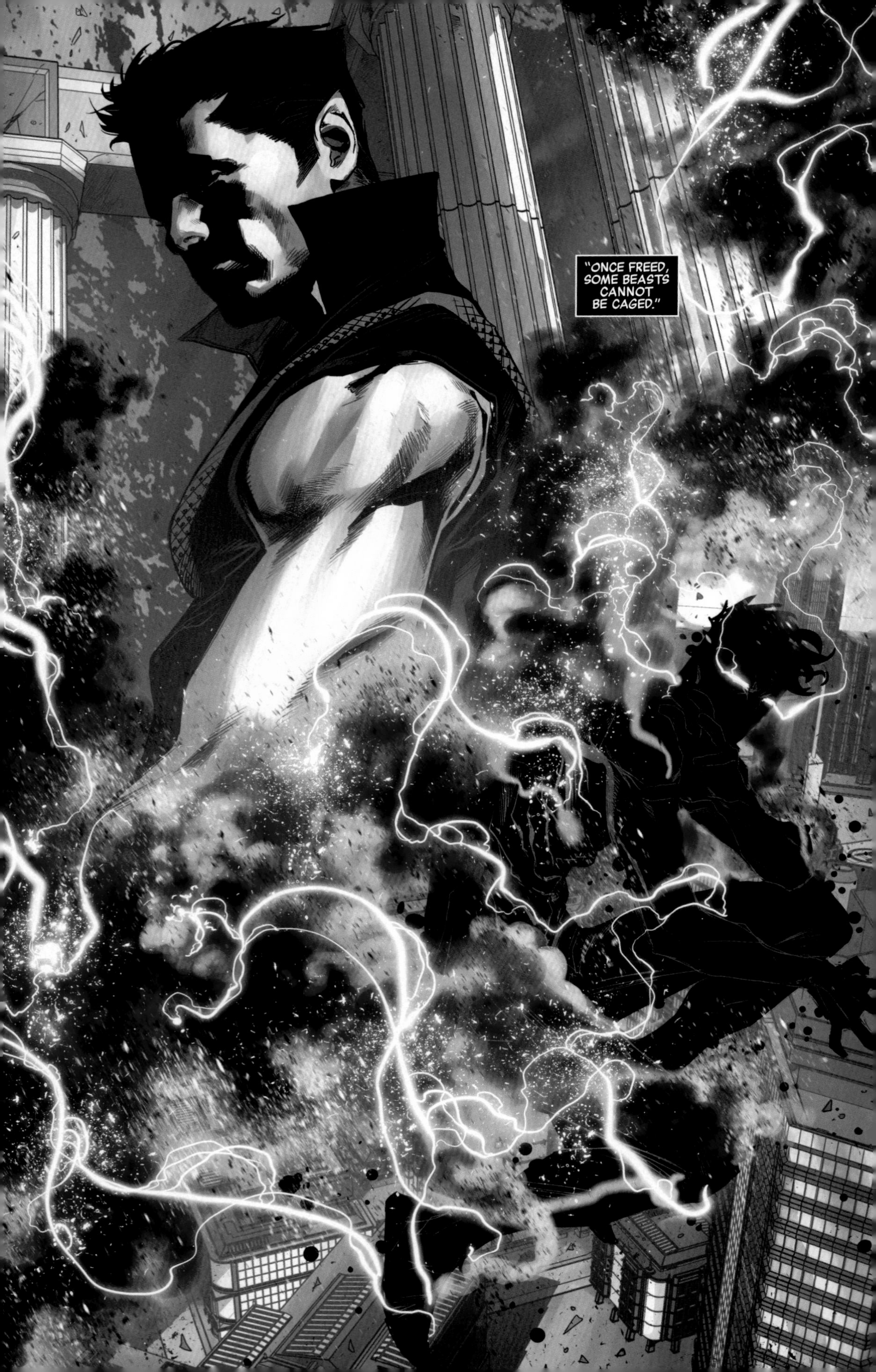
"ONCE FREED, SOME BEASTS CANNOT BE CAGED."

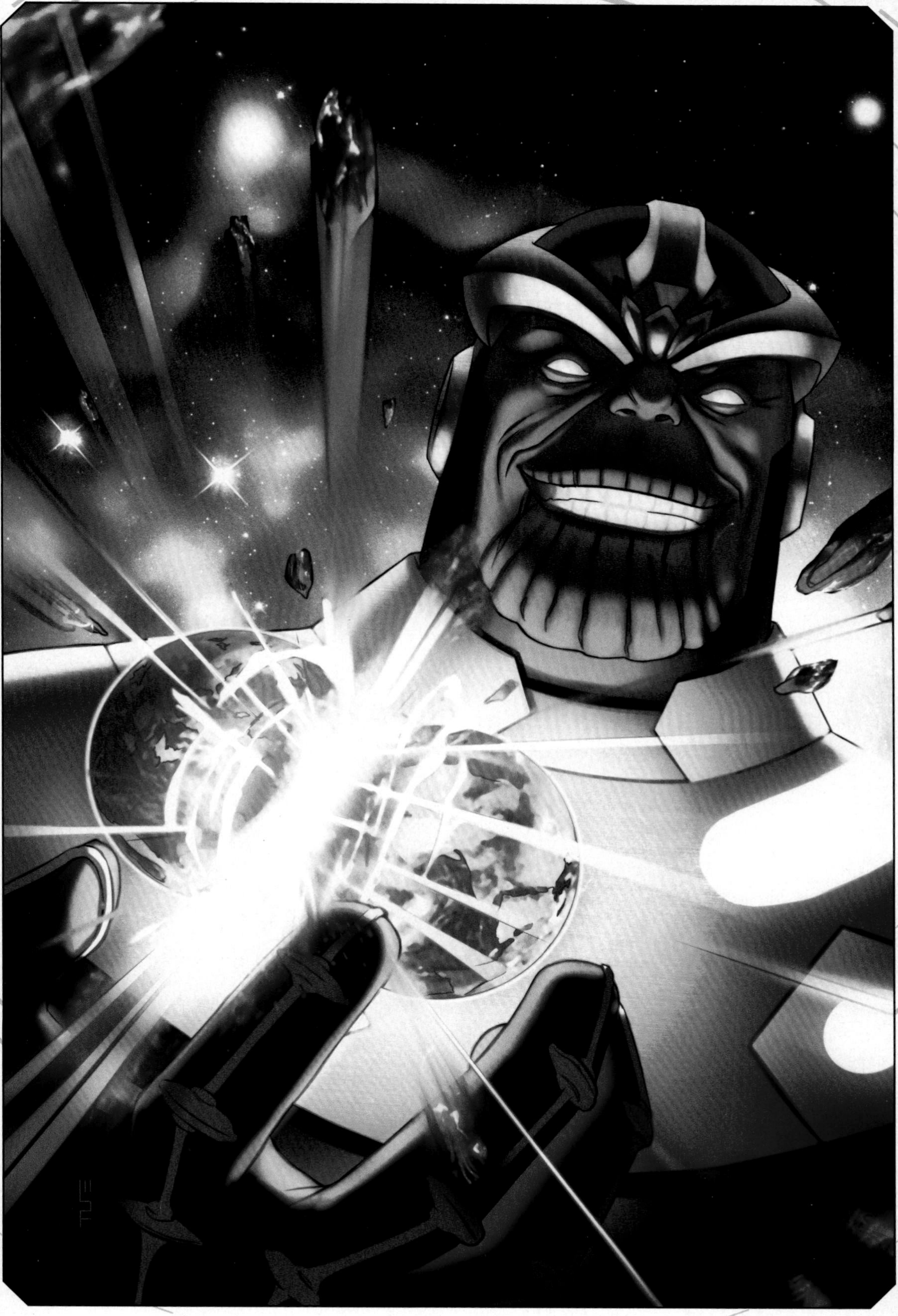

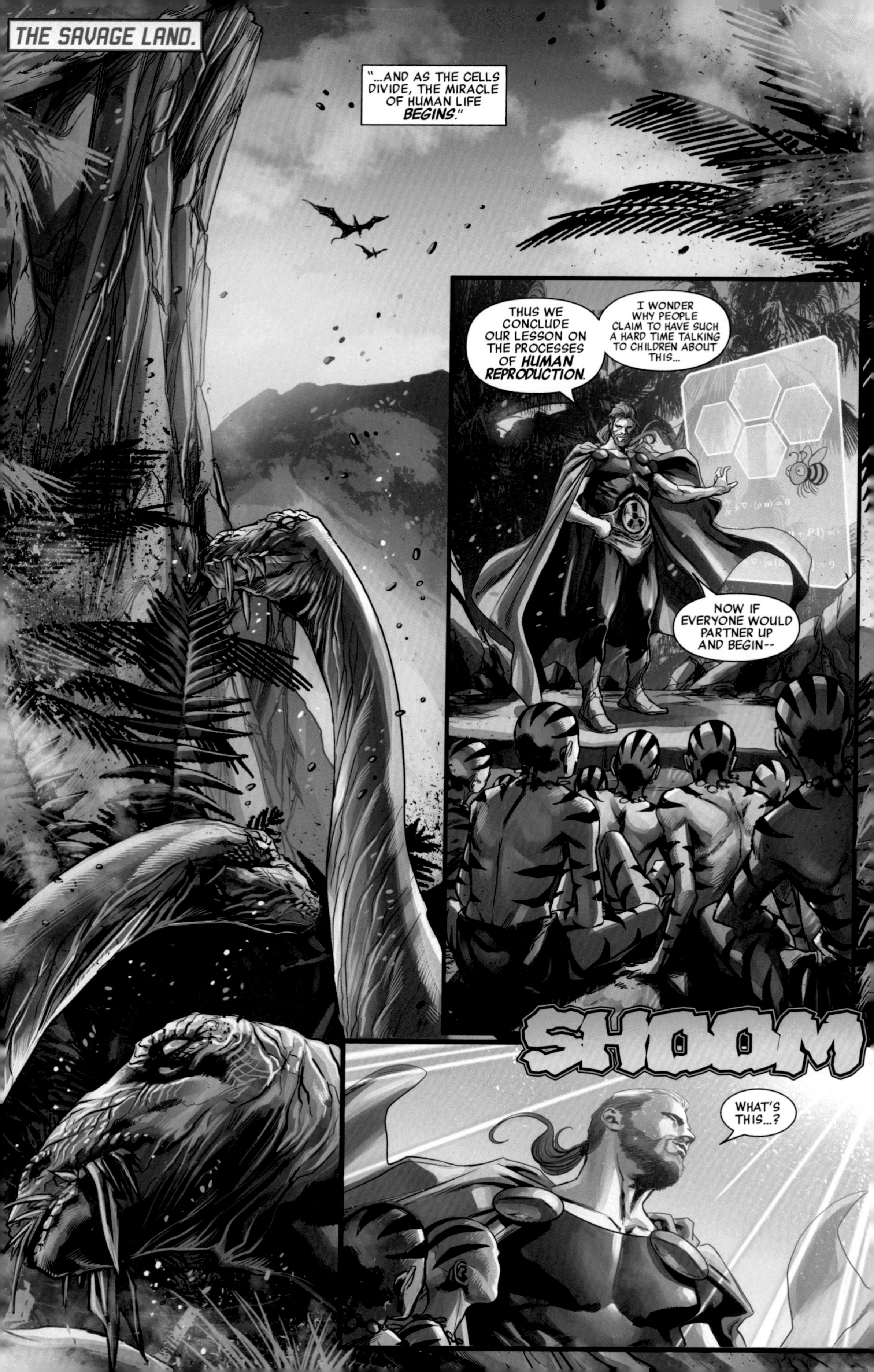
THE SAVAGE LAND.
"...AND AS THE CELLS DIVIDE, THE MIRACLE OF HUMAN LIFE BEGINS."
THUS WE CONCLUDE OUR LESSON ON THE PROCESSES OF HUMAN REPRODUCTION.
I WONDER WHY PEOPLE CLAIM TO HAVE SUCH A HARD TIME TALKING TO CHILDREN ABOUT THIS...
NOW IF EVERYONE WOULD PARTNER UP AND BEGIN--
SHOOM
WHAT'S THIS...?

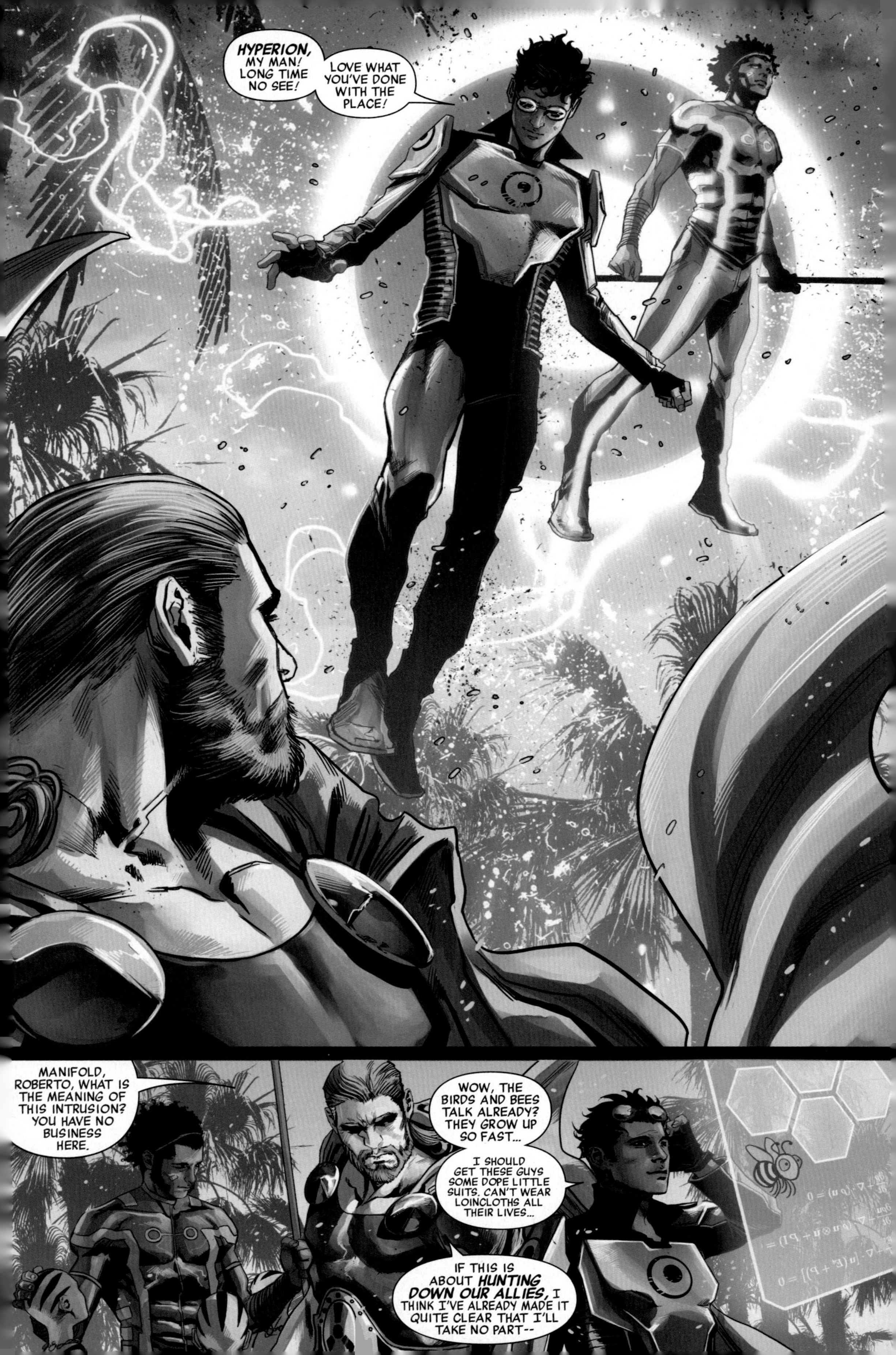
HYPERION, MY MAN! LONG TIME NO SEE!
LOVE WHAT YOU'VE DONE WITH THE PLACE!
MANIFOLD, ROBERTO, WHAT IS THE MEANING OF THIS INTRUSION? YOU HAVE NO BUSINESS HERE.
WOW, THE BIRDS AND BEES TALK ALREADY? THEY GROW UP SO FAST...
I SHOULD GET THESE GUYS SOME DOPE LITTLE SUITS. CAN'T WEAR LOINCLOTHS ALL THEIR LIVES...
IF THIS IS ABOUT HUNTING DOWN OUR ALLIES, I THINK I'VE ALREADY MADE IT QUITE CLEAR THAT I'LL TAKE NO PART--

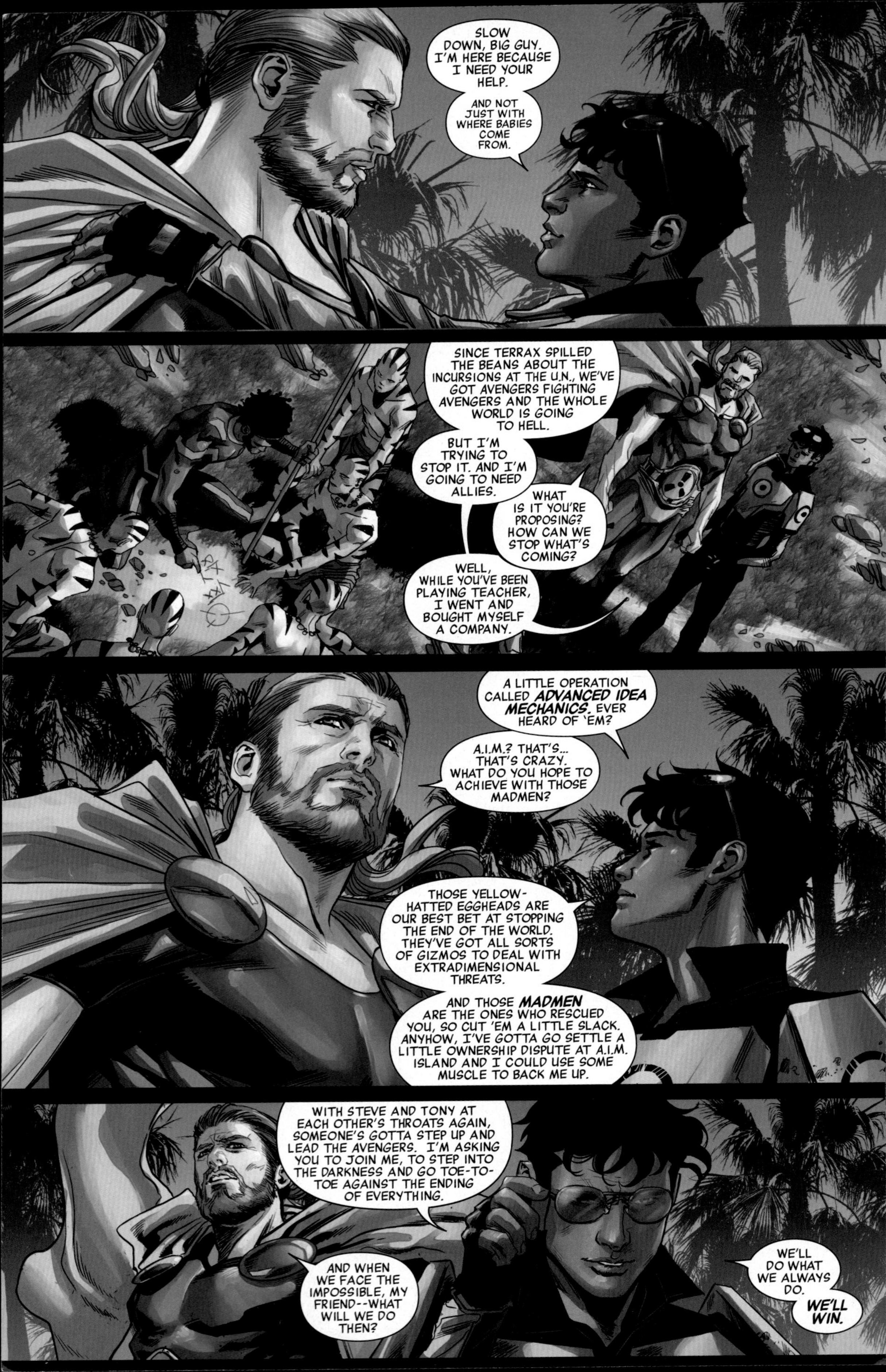
SLOW DOWN, BIG GUY. I'M HERE BECAUSE I NEED YOUR HELP.
AND NOT JUST WITH WHERE BABIES COME FROM.
SINCE TERRAX SPILLED THE BEANS ABOUT THE INCURSIONS AT THE U.N., WE'VE GOT AVENGERS FIGHTING AVENGERS AND THE WHOLE WORLD IS GOING TO HELL.
BUT I'M TRYING TO STOP IT. AND I'M GOING TO NEED ALLIES.
WHAT IS IT YOU'RE PROPOSING? HOW CAN WE STOP WHAT'S COMING?
WELL, WHILE YOU'VE BEEN PLAYING TEACHER, I WENT AND BOUGHT MYSELF A COMPANY.
A LITTLE OPERATION CALLED ADVANCED IDEA MECHANICS. EVER HEARD OF 'EM?
A.I.M.? THAT'S... THAT'S CRAZY. WHAT DO YOU HOPE TO ACHIEVE WITH THOSE MADMEN?
THOSE YELLOW-HATTED EGGHEADS ARE OUR BEST BET AT STOPPING THE END OF THE WORLD. THEY'VE GOT ALL SORTS OF GIZMOS TO DEAL WITH EXTRADIMENSIONAL THREATS.
AND THOSE MADMEN ARE THE ONES WHO RESCUED YOU, SO CUT 'EM A LITTLE SLACK. ANYHOW, I'VE GOTTA GO SETTLE A LITTLE OWNERSHIP DISPUTE AT A.I.M. ISLAND AND I COULD USE SOME MUSCLE TO BACK ME UP.
WITH STEVE AND TONY AT EACH OTHER'S THROATS AGAIN, SOMEONE'S GOTTA STEP UP AND LEAD THE AVENGERS. I'M ASKING YOU TO JOIN ME, TO STEP INTO THE DARKNESS AND GO TOE-TO-TOE AGAINST THE ENDING OF EVERYTHING.
AND WHEN WE FACE THE IMPOSSIBLE, MY FRIEND--WHAT WILL WE DO THEN?
WE'LL DO WHAT WE ALWAYS DO.
WE'LL WIN.

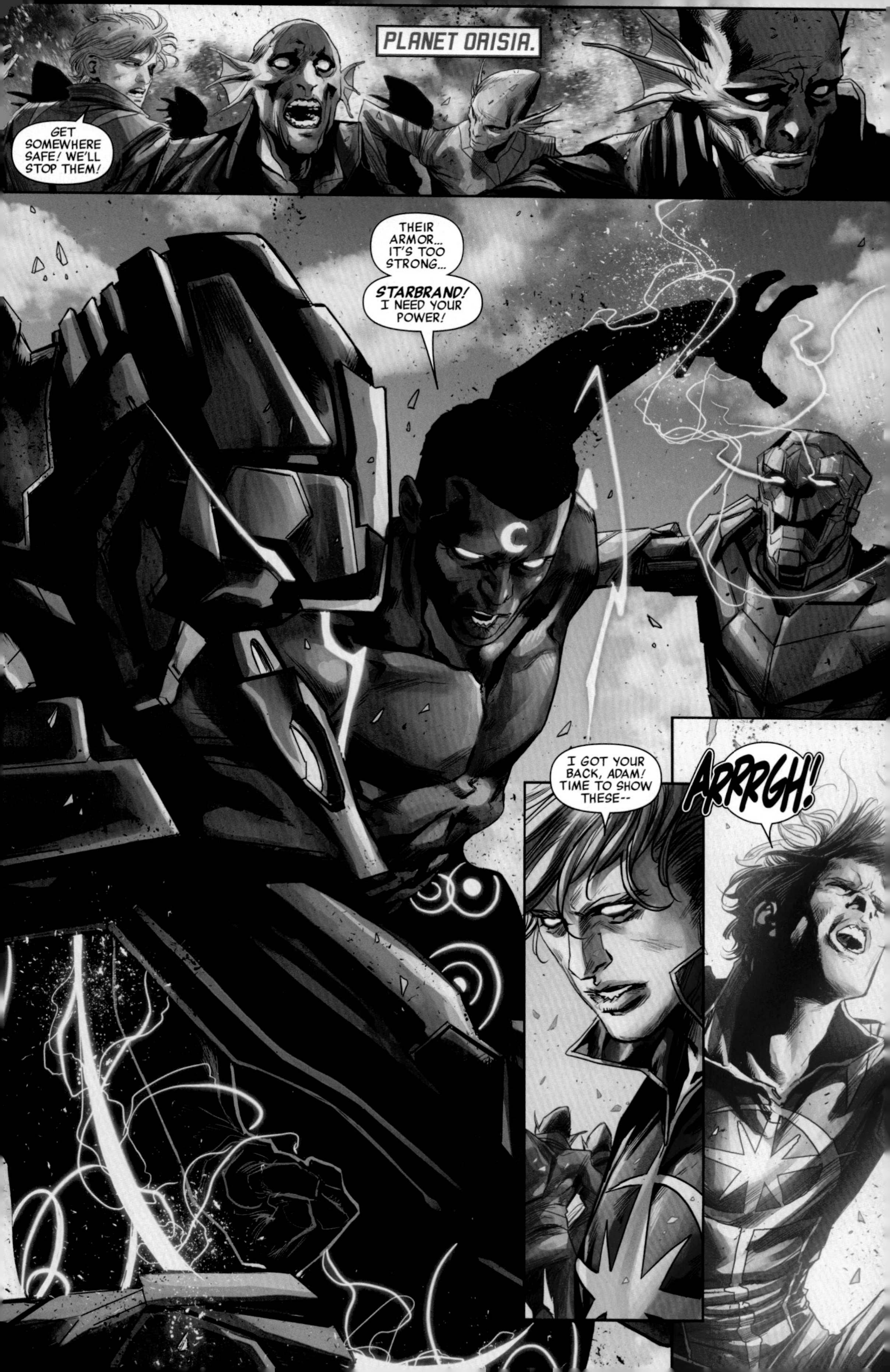
PLANET ORISIA.
GET SOMEWHERE SAFE! WE'LL STOP THEM!
THEIR ARMOR... IT'S TOO STRONG...
STARBRAND! I NEED YOUR POWER!
I GOT YOUR BACK, ADAM! TIME TO SHOW THESE--
ARRRGH!

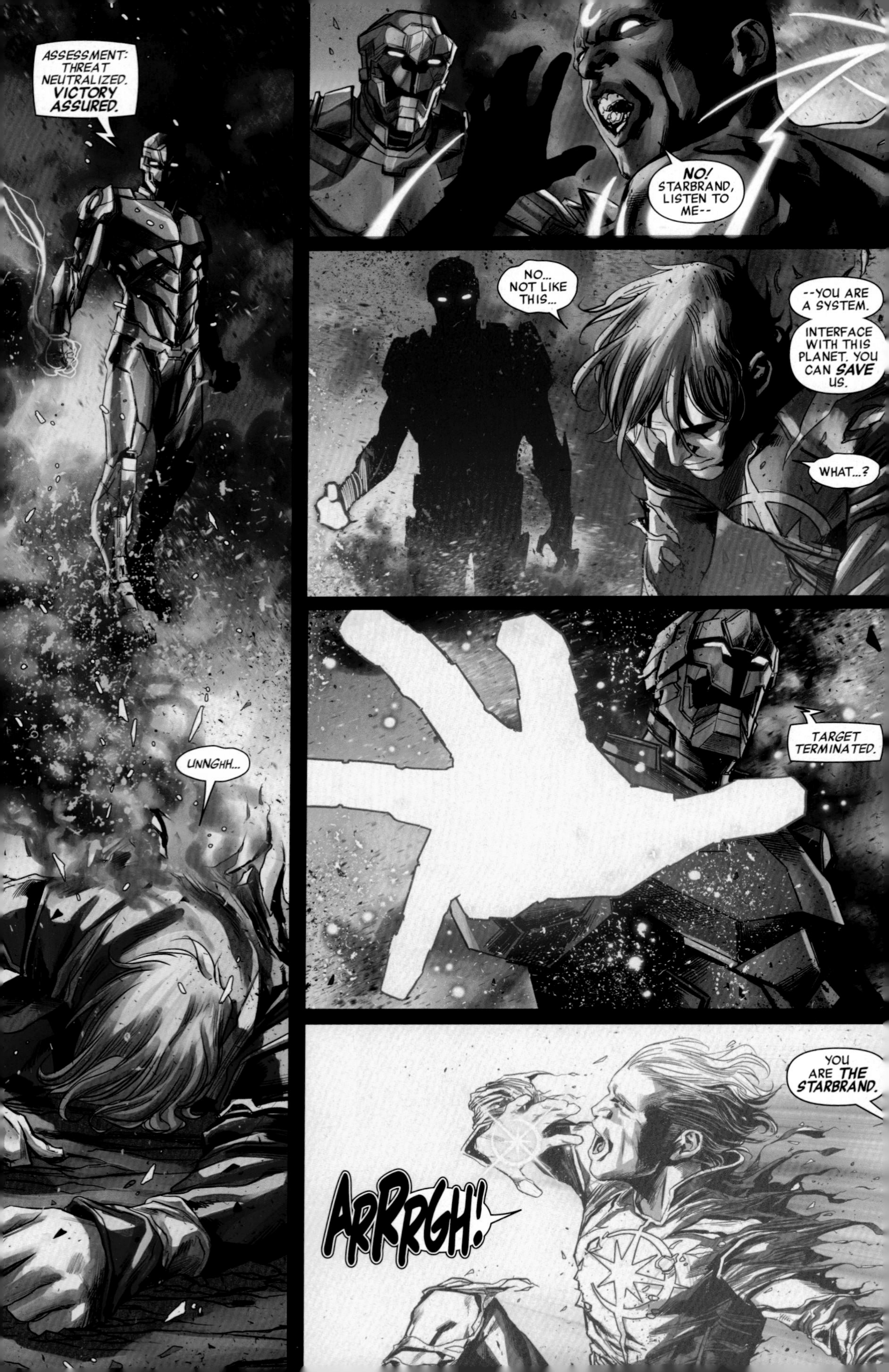

ASSESSMENT: THREAT NEUTRALIZED. **VICTORY ASSURED.**
UNNGHH...
**NO!** STARBRAND, LISTEN TO ME--
NO... NOT LIKE THIS...
--YOU ARE A SYSTEM.
INTERFACE WITH THIS PLANET. YOU CAN **SAVE** US.
WHAT...?
TARGET TERMINATED.
YOU ARE **THE STARBRAND.**
ARRRGH!

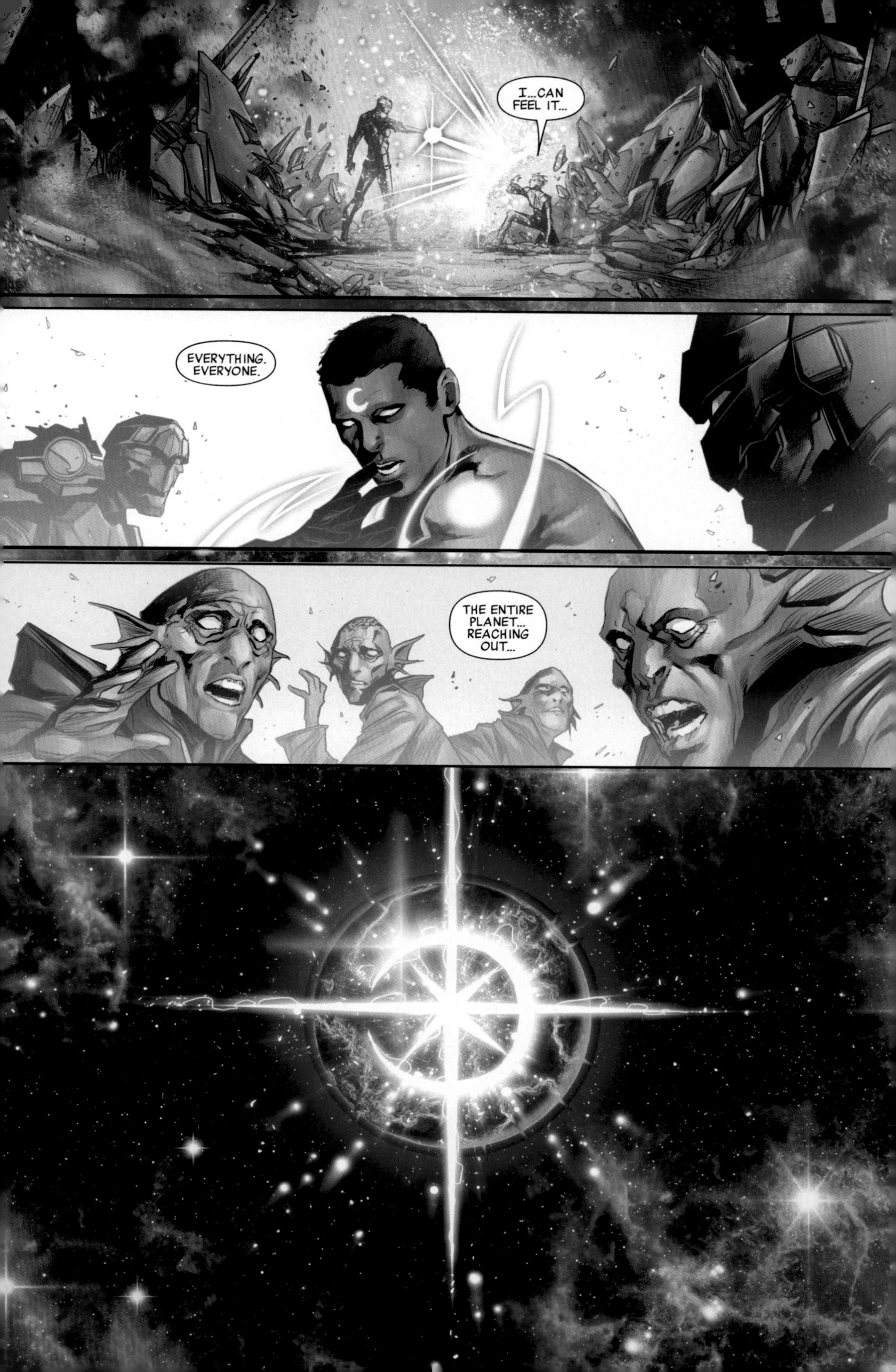
I...CAN FEEL IT...
EVERYTHING. EVERYONE.
THE ENTIRE PLANET... REACHING OUT...

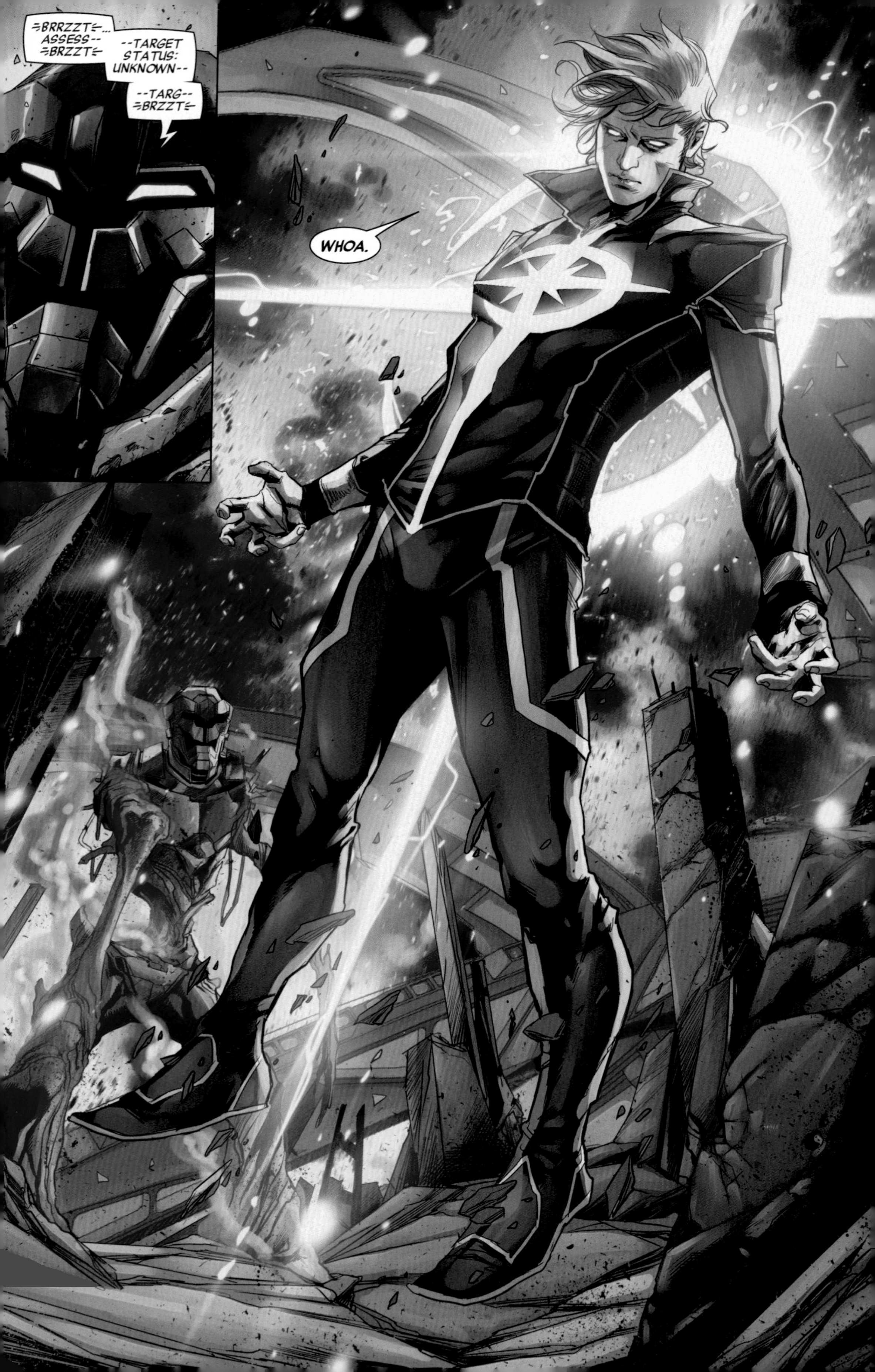

=BRRZZT=...
ASSESS--
=BRZZT=
--TARGET
STATUS:
UNKNOWN--
--TARG--
BRZZT=
WHOA.

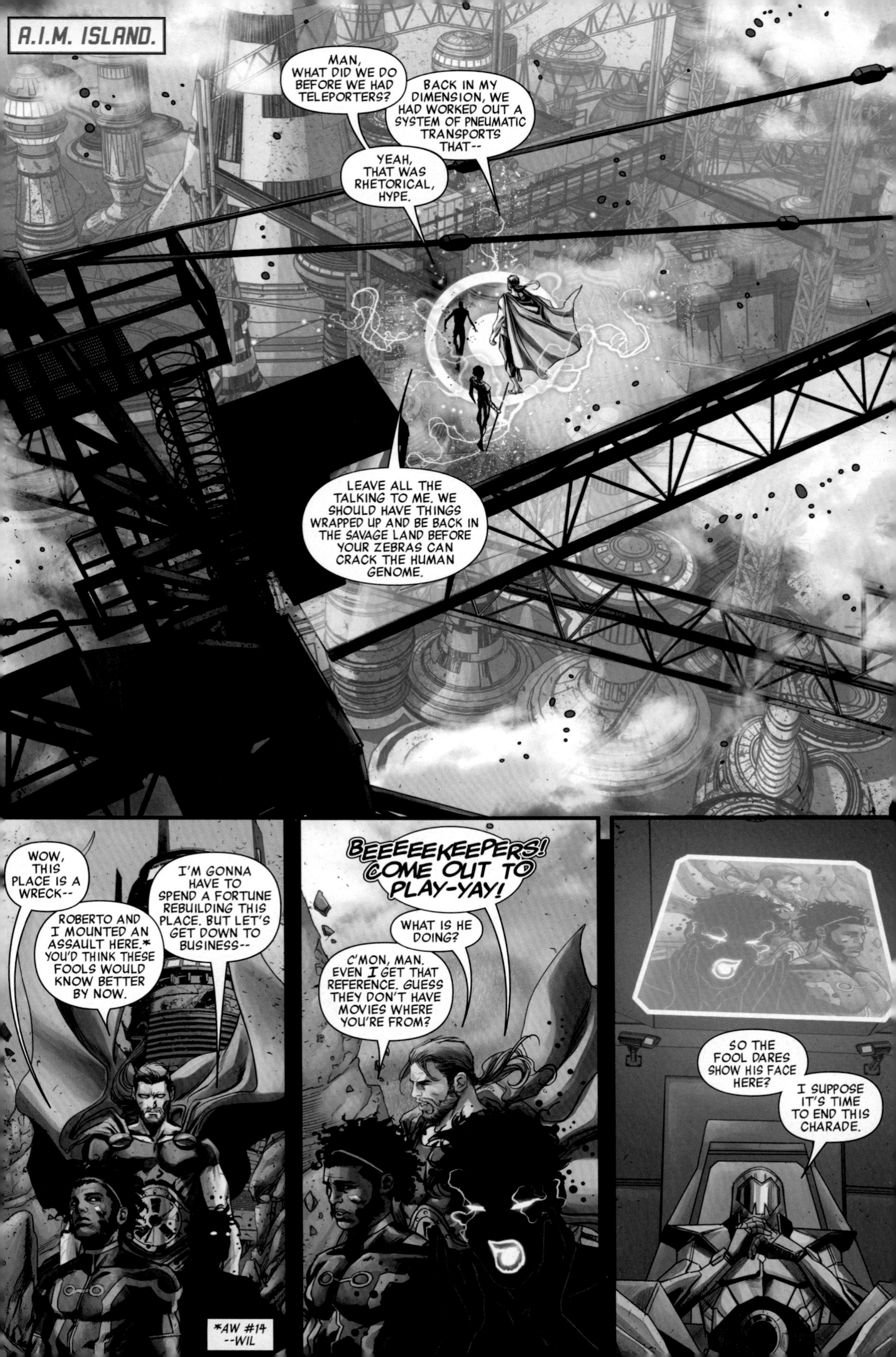
A.I.M. ISLAND.
MAN, WHAT DID WE DO BEFORE WE HAD TELEPORTERS?
BACK IN MY DIMENSION, WE HAD WORKED OUT A SYSTEM OF PNEUMATIC TRANSPORTS THAT--
YEAH, THAT WAS RHETORICAL, HYPE.
LEAVE ALL THE TALKING TO ME. WE SHOULD HAVE THINGS WRAPPED UP AND BE BACK IN THE SAVAGE LAND BEFORE YOUR ZEBRAS CAN CRACK THE HUMAN GENOME.
WOW, THIS PLACE IS A WRECK--
ROBERTO AND I MOUNTED AN ASSAULT HERE.* YOU'D THINK THESE FOOLS WOULD KNOW BETTER BY NOW.
I'M GONNA HAVE TO SPEND A FORTUNE REBUILDING THIS PLACE. BUT LET'S GET DOWN TO BUSINESS--
*AW #14 --WIL
BEEEEEKEEPERS! COME OUT TO PLAY-YAY!
WHAT IS HE DOING?
C'MON, MAN. EVEN I GET THAT REFERENCE. GUESS THEY DON'T HAVE MOVIES WHERE YOU'RE FROM?
SO THE FOOL DARES SHOW HIS FACE HERE?
I SUPPOSE IT'S TIME TO END THIS CHARADE.

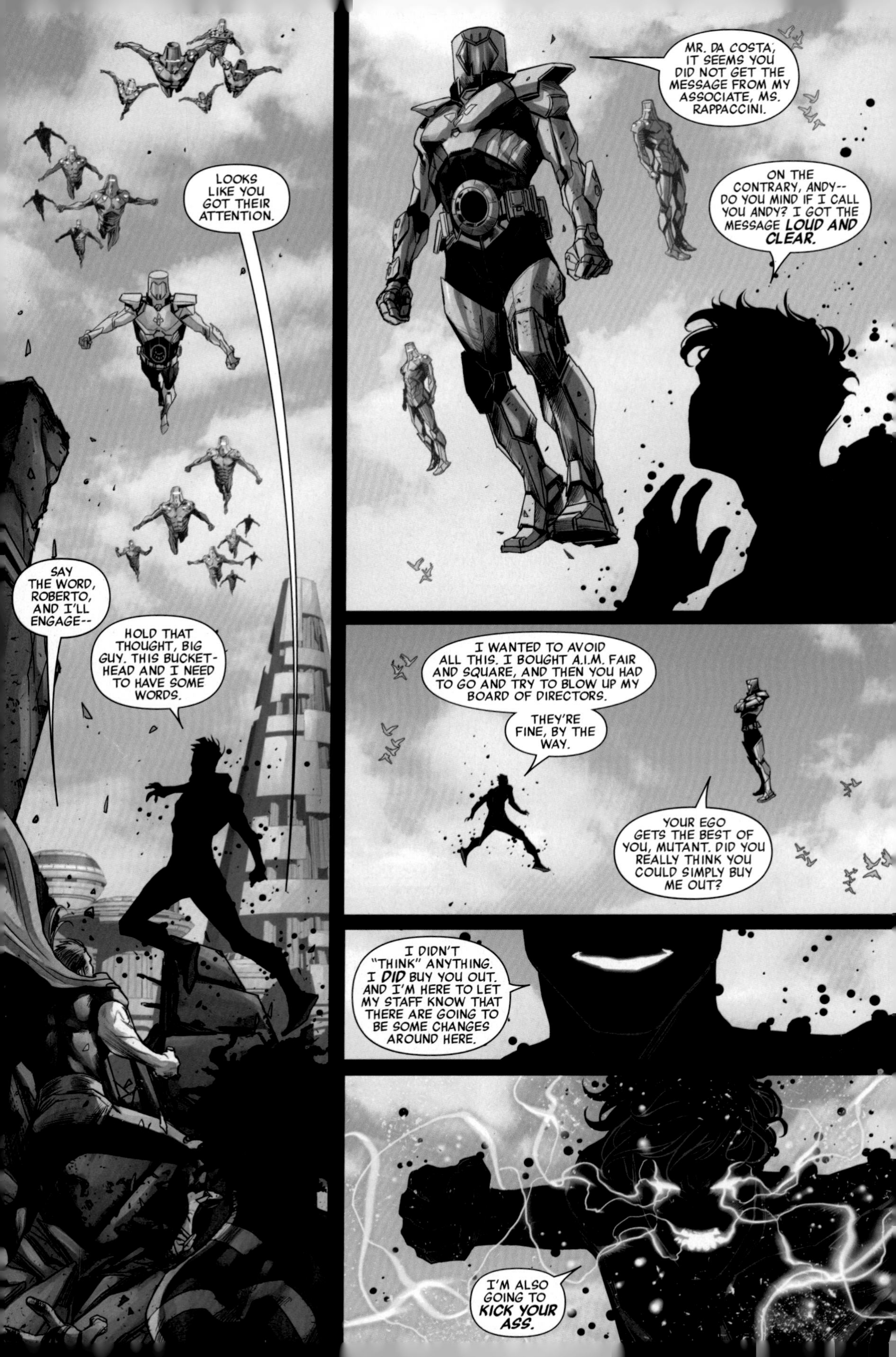
LOOKS LIKE YOU GOT THEIR ATTENTION.
SAY THE WORD, ROBERTO, AND I'LL ENGAGE--
HOLD THAT THOUGHT, BIG GUY. THIS BUCKET-HEAD AND I NEED TO HAVE SOME WORDS.
MR. DA COSTA, IT SEEMS YOU DID NOT GET THE MESSAGE FROM MY ASSOCIATE, MS. RAPPACCINI.
ON THE CONTRARY, ANDY-- DO YOU MIND IF I CALL YOU ANDY? I GOT THE MESSAGE LOUD AND CLEAR.
I WANTED TO AVOID ALL THIS. I BOUGHT A.I.M. FAIR AND SQUARE, AND THEN YOU HAD TO GO AND TRY TO BLOW UP MY BOARD OF DIRECTORS.
THEY'RE FINE, BY THE WAY.
YOUR EGO GETS THE BEST OF YOU, MUTANT. DID YOU REALLY THINK YOU COULD SIMPLY BUY ME OUT?
I DIDN'T "THINK" ANYTHING. I DID BUY YOU OUT. AND I'M HERE TO LET MY STAFF KNOW THAT THERE ARE GOING TO BE SOME CHANGES AROUND HERE.
I'M ALSO GOING TO KICK YOUR ASS.

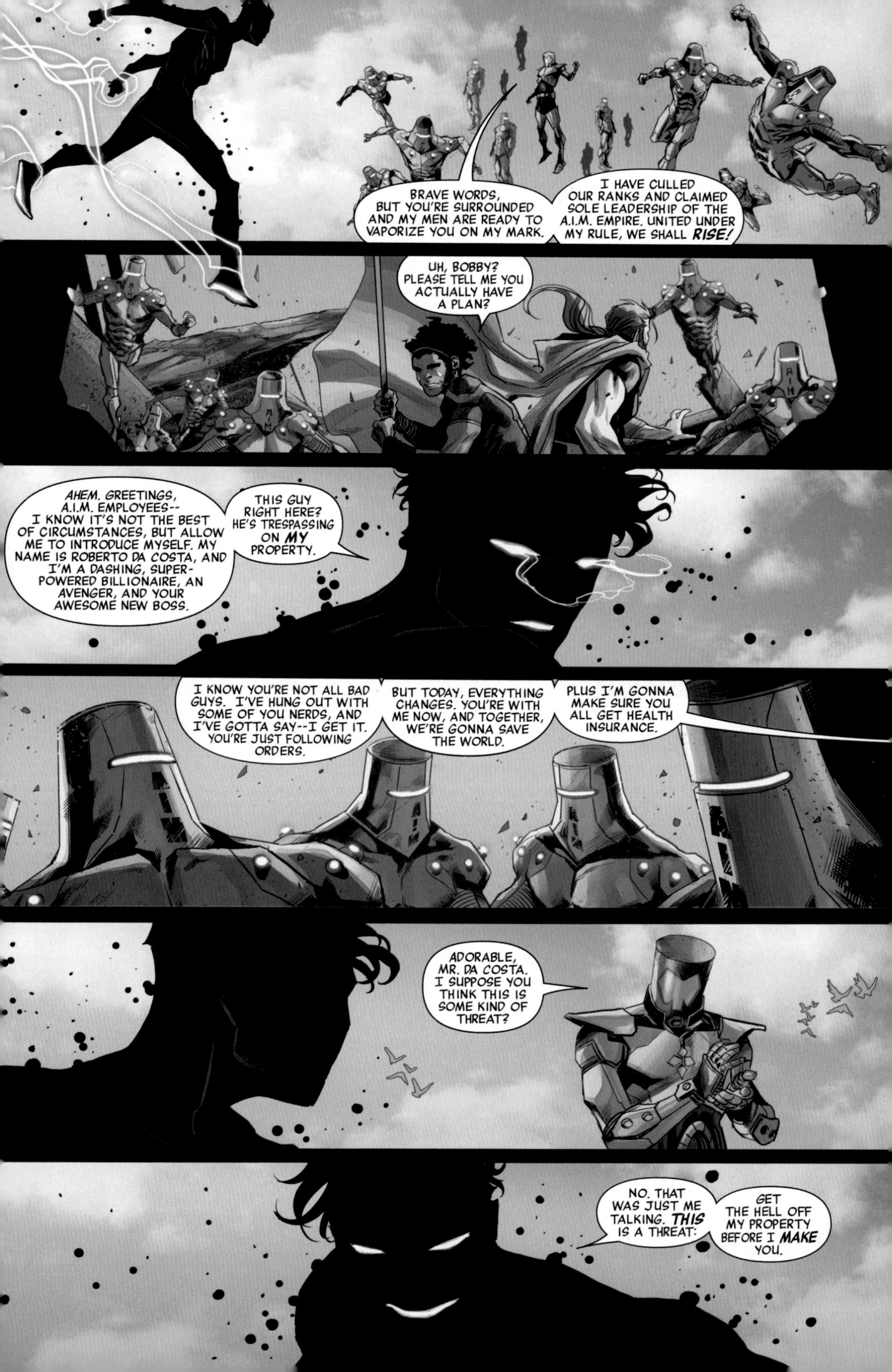
BRAVE WORDS, BUT YOU'RE SURROUNDED AND MY MEN ARE READY TO VAPORIZE YOU ON MY MARK.
I HAVE CULLED OUR RANKS AND CLAIMED SOLE LEADERSHIP OF THE A.I.M. EMPIRE. UNITED UNDER MY RULE, WE SHALL **RISE!**
UH, BOBBY? PLEASE TELL ME YOU ACTUALLY HAVE A PLAN?
AHEM. GREETINGS, A.I.M. EMPLOYEES-- I KNOW IT'S NOT THE BEST OF CIRCUMSTANCES, BUT ALLOW ME TO INTRODUCE MYSELF. MY NAME IS ROBERTO DA COSTA, AND I'M A DASHING, SUPER-POWERED BILLIONAIRE, AN AVENGER, AND YOUR AWESOME NEW BOSS.
THIS GUY RIGHT HERE? HE'S TRESPASSING ON **MY** PROPERTY.
I KNOW YOU'RE NOT ALL BAD GUYS. I'VE HUNG OUT WITH SOME OF YOU NERDS, AND I'VE GOTTA SAY--I GET IT. YOU'RE JUST FOLLOWING ORDERS.
BUT TODAY, EVERYTHING CHANGES. YOU'RE WITH ME NOW, AND TOGETHER, WE'RE GONNA SAVE THE WORLD.
PLUS I'M GONNA MAKE SURE YOU ALL GET HEALTH INSURANCE.
ADORABLE, MR. DA COSTA. I SUPPOSE YOU THINK THIS IS SOME KIND OF THREAT?
NO. THAT WAS JUST ME TALKING. **THIS** IS A THREAT:
GET THE HELL OFF MY PROPERTY BEFORE I **MAKE** YOU.

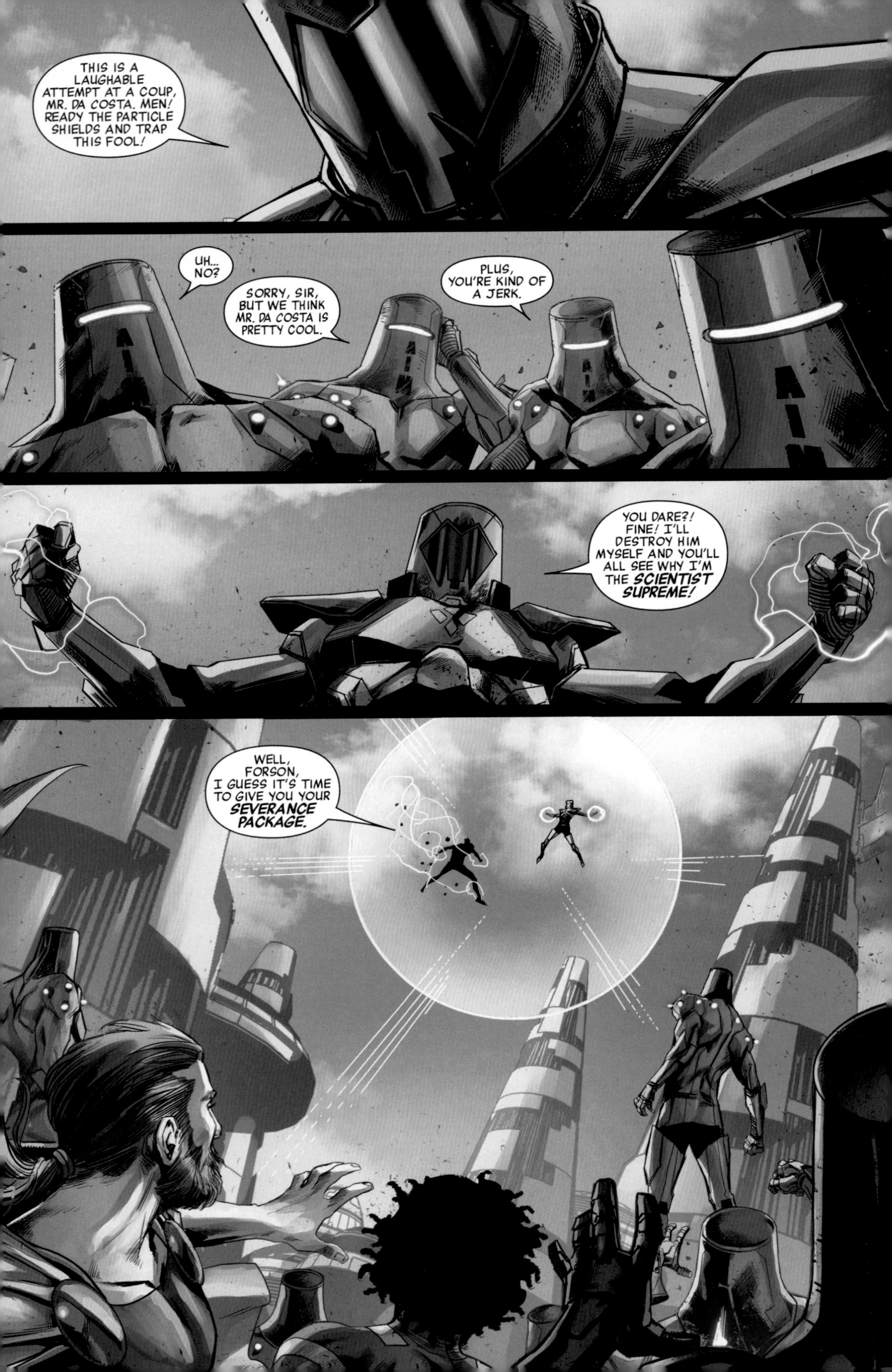
THIS IS A LAUGHABLE ATTEMPT AT A COUP, MR. DA COSTA. MEN! READY THE PARTICLE SHIELDS AND TRAP THIS FOOL!
UH... NO?
SORRY, SIR, BUT WE THINK MR. DA COSTA IS PRETTY COOL.
PLUS, YOU'RE KIND OF A JERK.
YOU DARE?! FINE! I'LL DESTROY HIM MYSELF AND YOU'LL ALL SEE WHY I'M THE SCIENTIST SUPREME!
WELL, FORSON, I GUESS IT'S TIME TO GIVE YOU YOUR SEVERANCE PACKAGE.

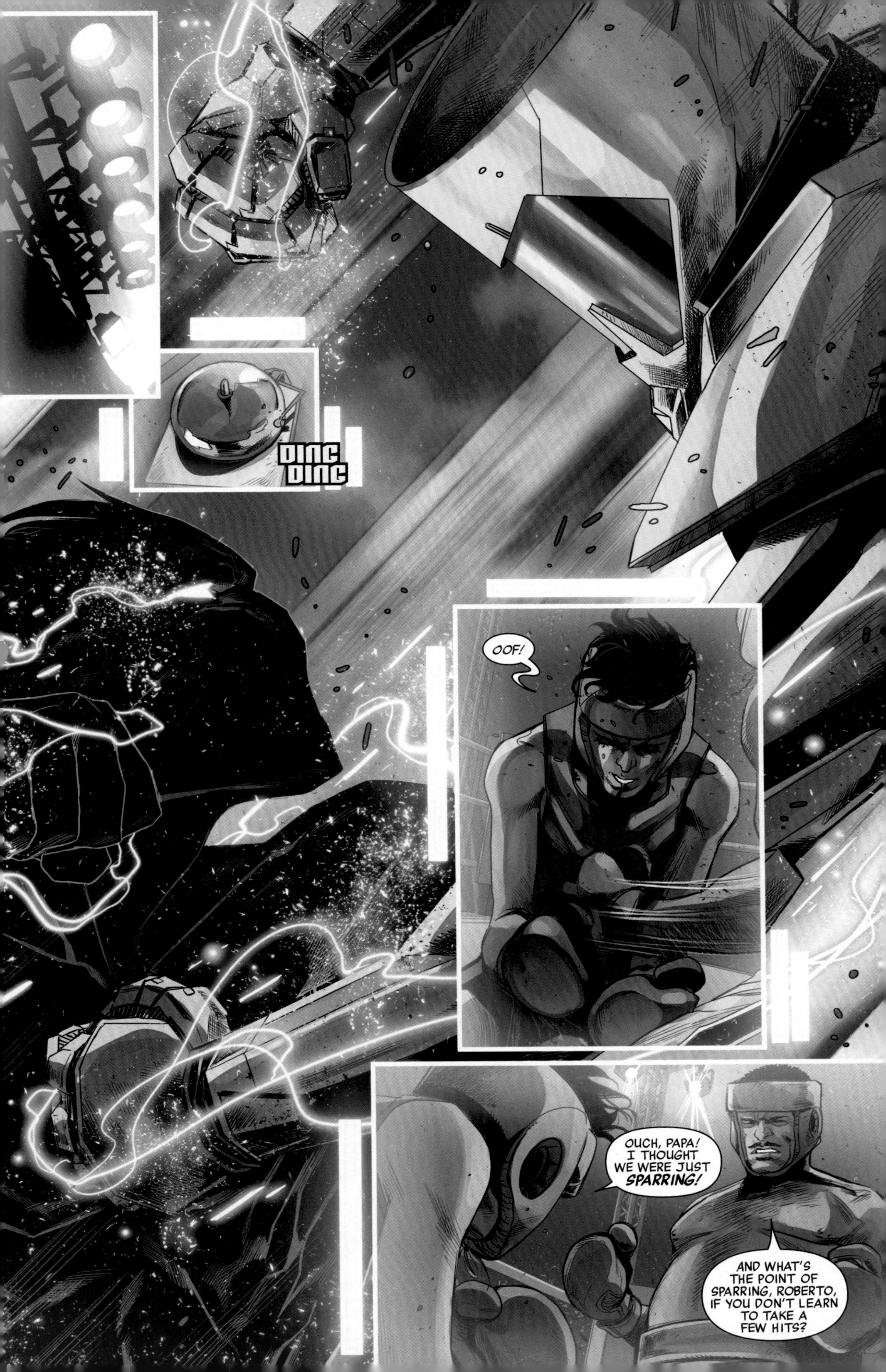
DING DING
OOF!
OUCH, PAPA! I THOUGHT WE WERE JUST SPARRING!
AND WHAT'S THE POINT OF SPARRING, ROBERTO, IF YOU DON'T LEARN TO TAKE A FEW HITS?

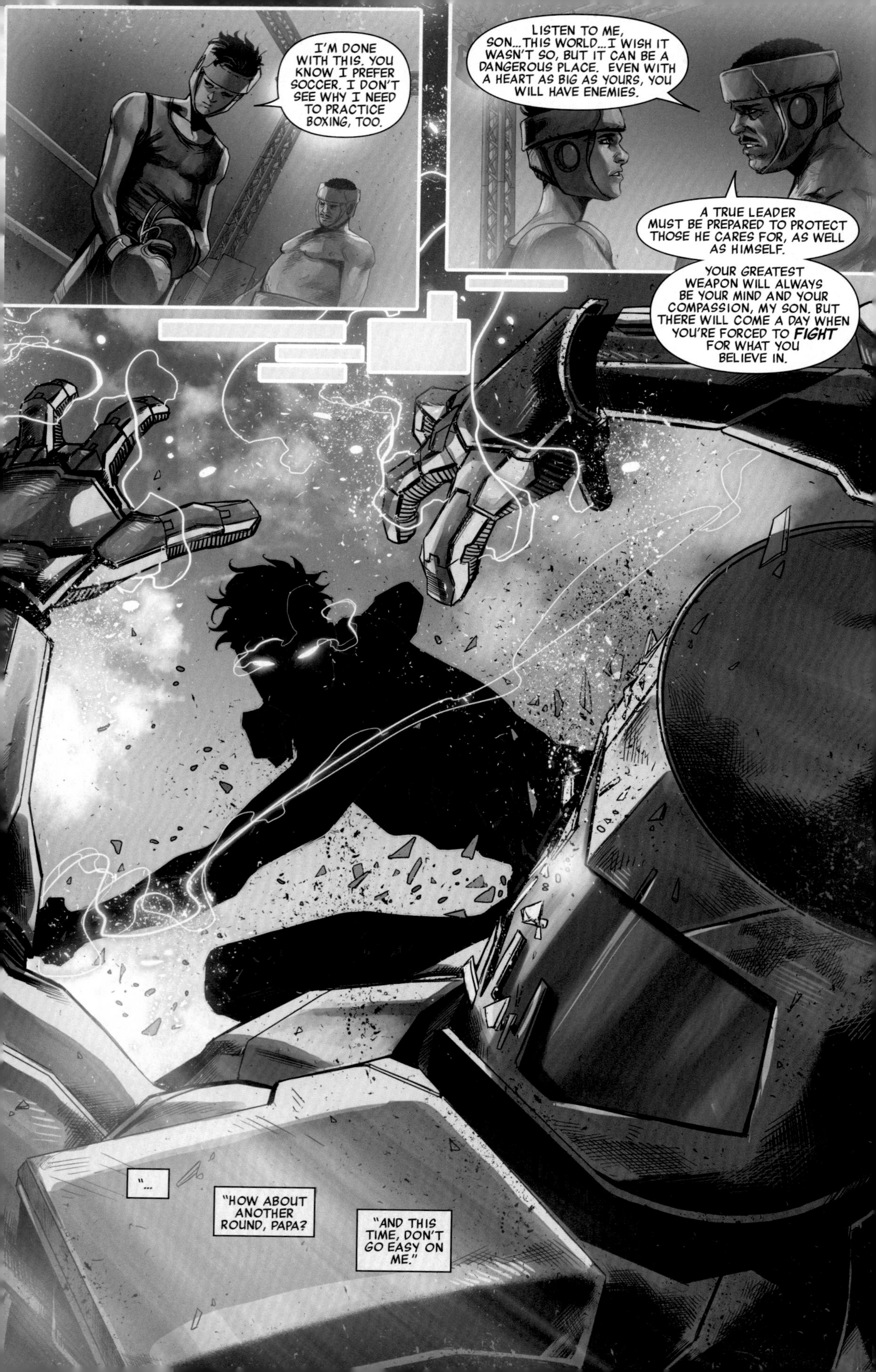
I'M DONE WITH THIS. YOU KNOW I PREFER SOCCER. I DON'T SEE WHY I NEED TO PRACTICE BOXING, TOO.
LISTEN TO ME, SON... THIS WORLD... I WISH IT WASN'T SO, BUT IT CAN BE A DANGEROUS PLACE. EVEN WITH A HEART AS BIG AS YOURS, YOU WILL HAVE ENEMIES.
A TRUE LEADER MUST BE PREPARED TO PROTECT THOSE HE CARES FOR, AS WELL AS HIMSELF.
YOUR GREATEST WEAPON WILL ALWAYS BE YOUR MIND AND YOUR COMPASSION, MY SON. BUT THERE WILL COME A DAY WHEN YOU'RE FORCED TO **FIGHT** FOR WHAT YOU BELIEVE IN.
"...
"HOW ABOUT ANOTHER ROUND, PAPA?
"AND THIS TIME, DON'T GO EASY ON ME."

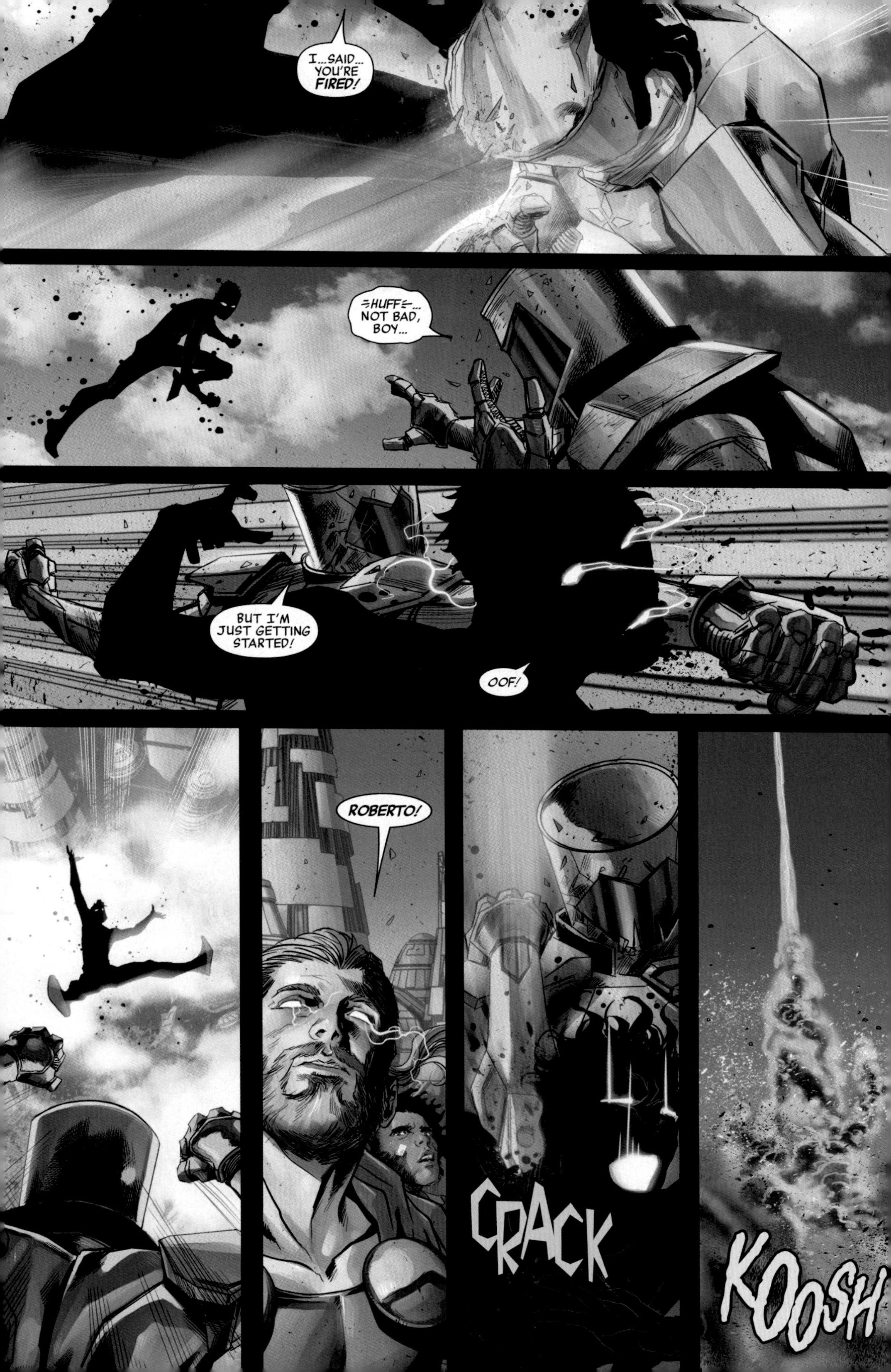

I...SAID... YOU'RE FIRED!
=HUFF=... NOT BAD, BOY...
BUT I'M JUST GETTING STARTED!
OOF!
ROBERTO!
CRACK
KOOSH

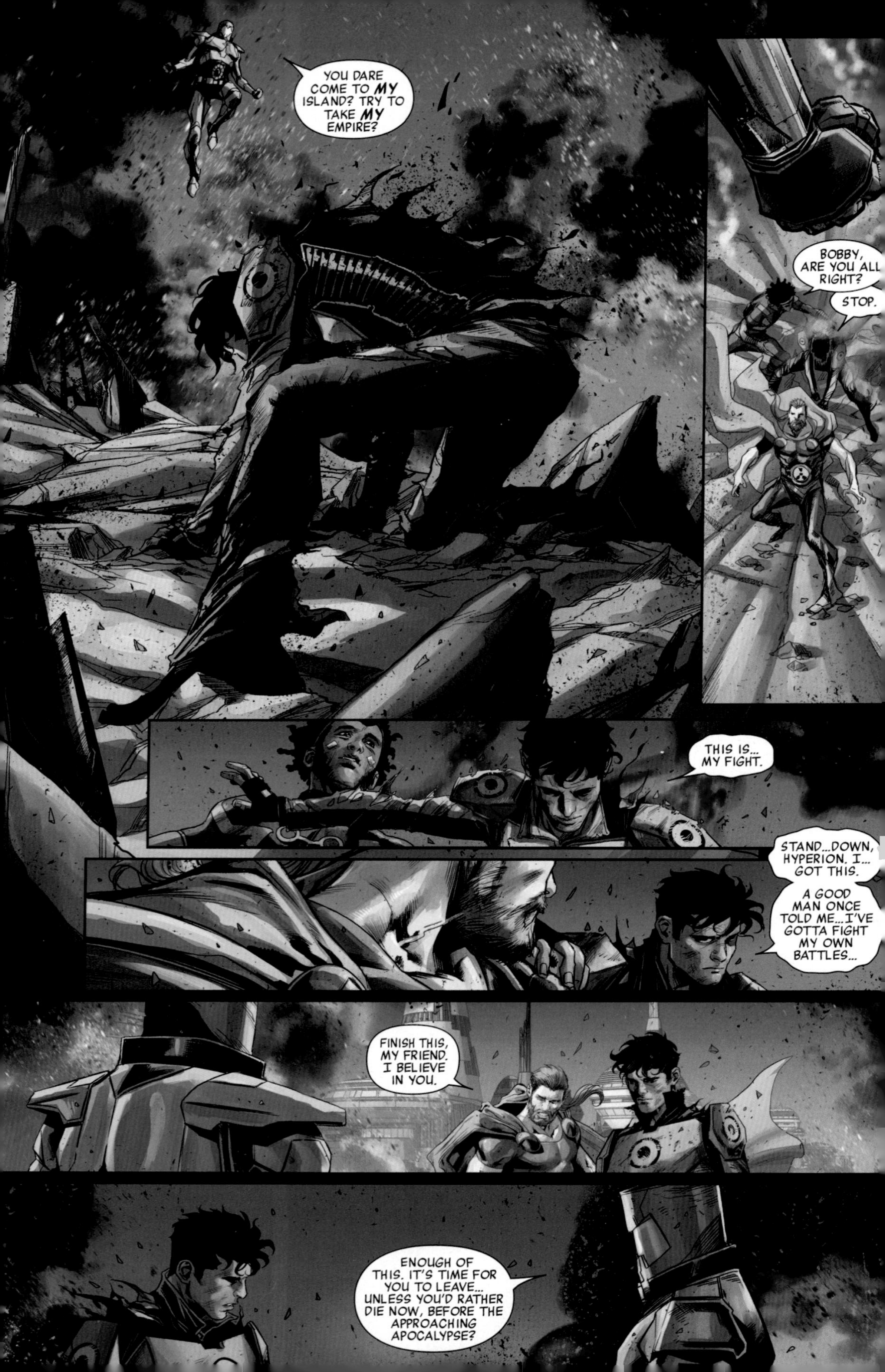
YOU DARE COME TO MY ISLAND? TRY TO TAKE MY EMPIRE?
BOBBY, ARE YOU ALL RIGHT?
STOP.
THIS IS... MY FIGHT.
STAND...DOWN, HYPERION. I... GOT THIS.
A GOOD MAN ONCE TOLD ME...I'VE GOTTA FIGHT MY OWN BATTLES...
FINISH THIS, MY FRIEND. I BELIEVE IN YOU.
ENOUGH OF THIS. IT'S TIME FOR YOU TO LEAVE... UNLESS YOU'D RATHER DIE NOW, BEFORE THE APPROACHING APOCALYPSE?

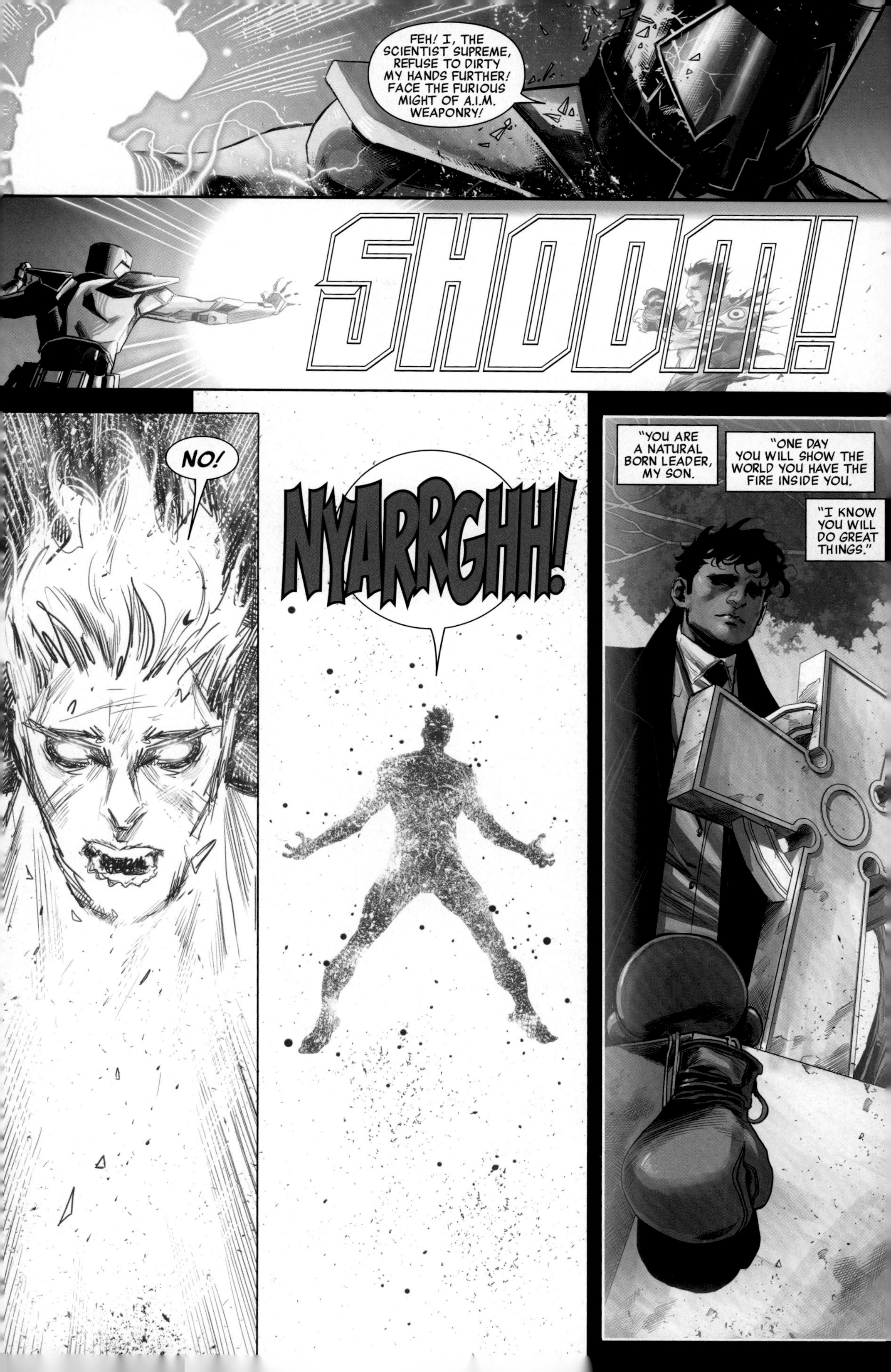
FEH! I, THE SCIENTIST SUPREME, REFUSE TO DIRTY MY HANDS FURTHER! FACE THE FURIOUS MIGHT OF A.I.M. WEAPONRY!
SHOOM!
NO!
NYARRGHH!
"YOU ARE A NATURAL BORN LEADER, MY SON.
"ONE DAY YOU WILL SHOW THE WORLD YOU HAVE THE FIRE INSIDE YOU.
"I KNOW YOU WILL DO GREAT THINGS."

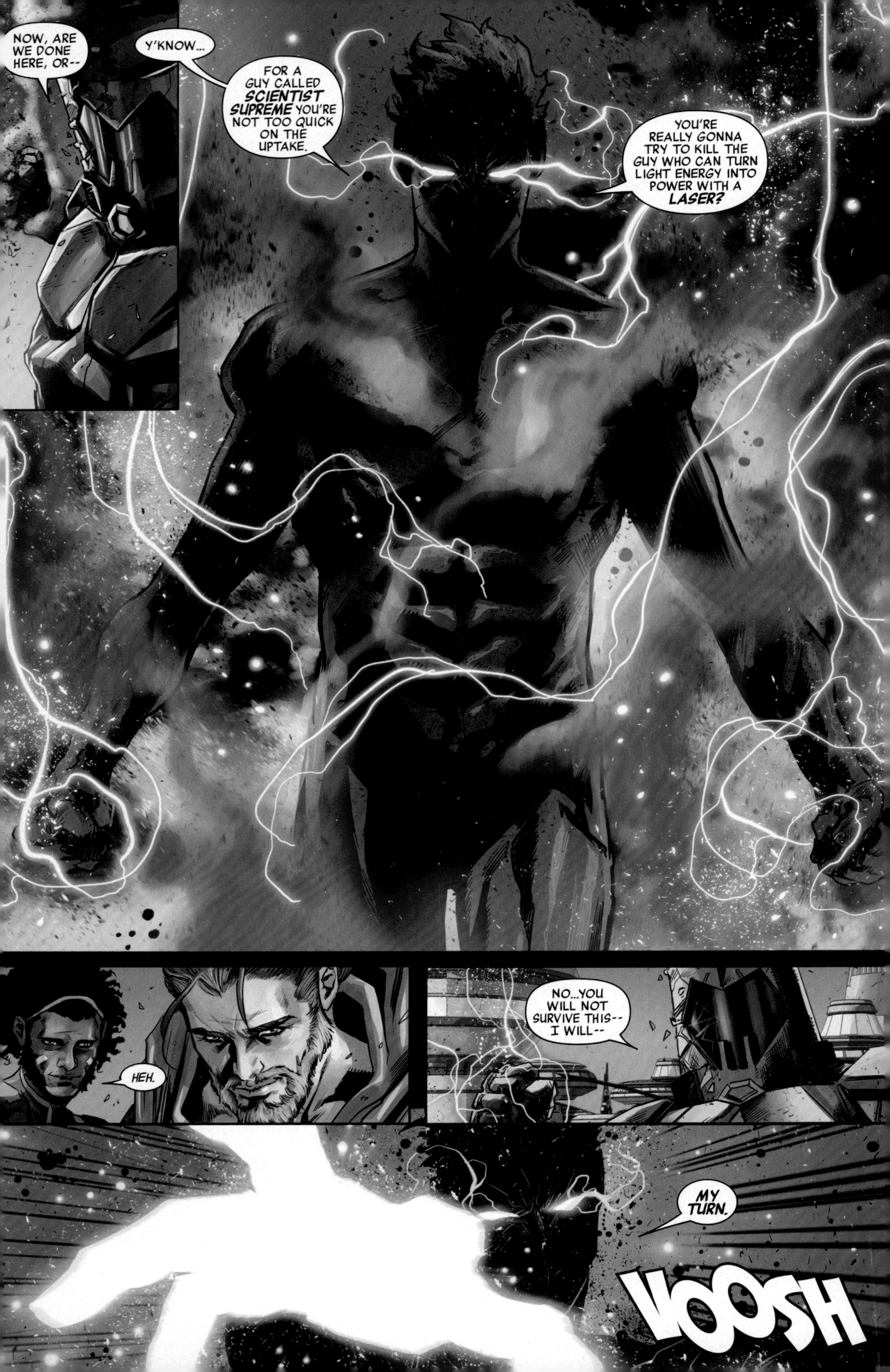
NOW, ARE WE DONE HERE, OR--
Y'KNOW...
FOR A GUY CALLED **SCIENTIST SUPREME** YOU'RE NOT TOO QUICK ON THE UPTAKE.
YOU'RE REALLY GONNA TRY TO KILL THE GUY WHO CAN TURN LIGHT ENERGY INTO POWER WITH A **LASER?**
HEH.
NO...YOU WILL NOT SURVIVE THIS-- I WILL--
MY TURN.
VOOSH

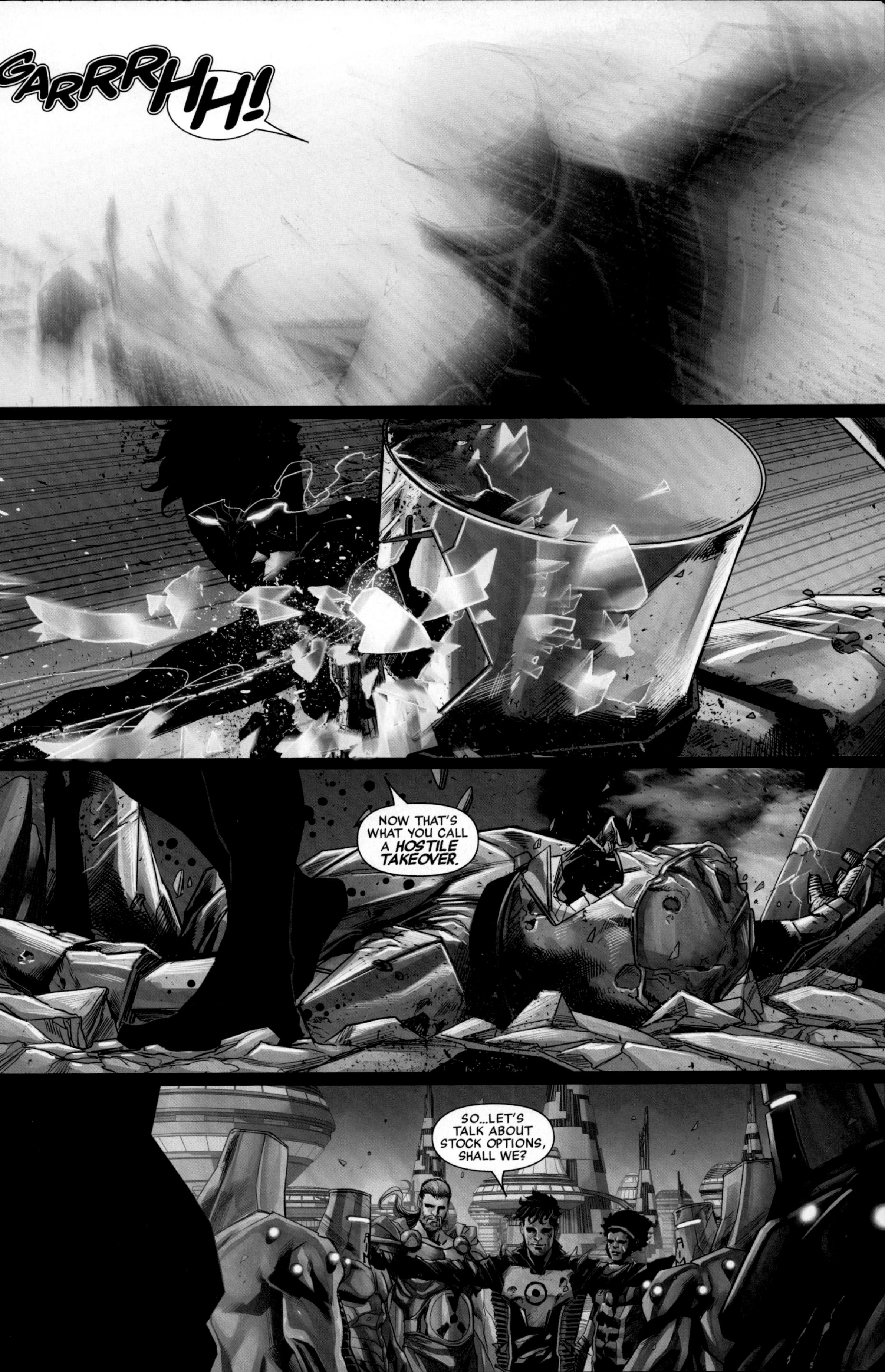

GARRRHH!
NOW THAT'S WHAT YOU CALL A HOSTILE TAKEOVER.
SO...LET'S TALK ABOUT STOCK OPTIONS, SHALL WE?

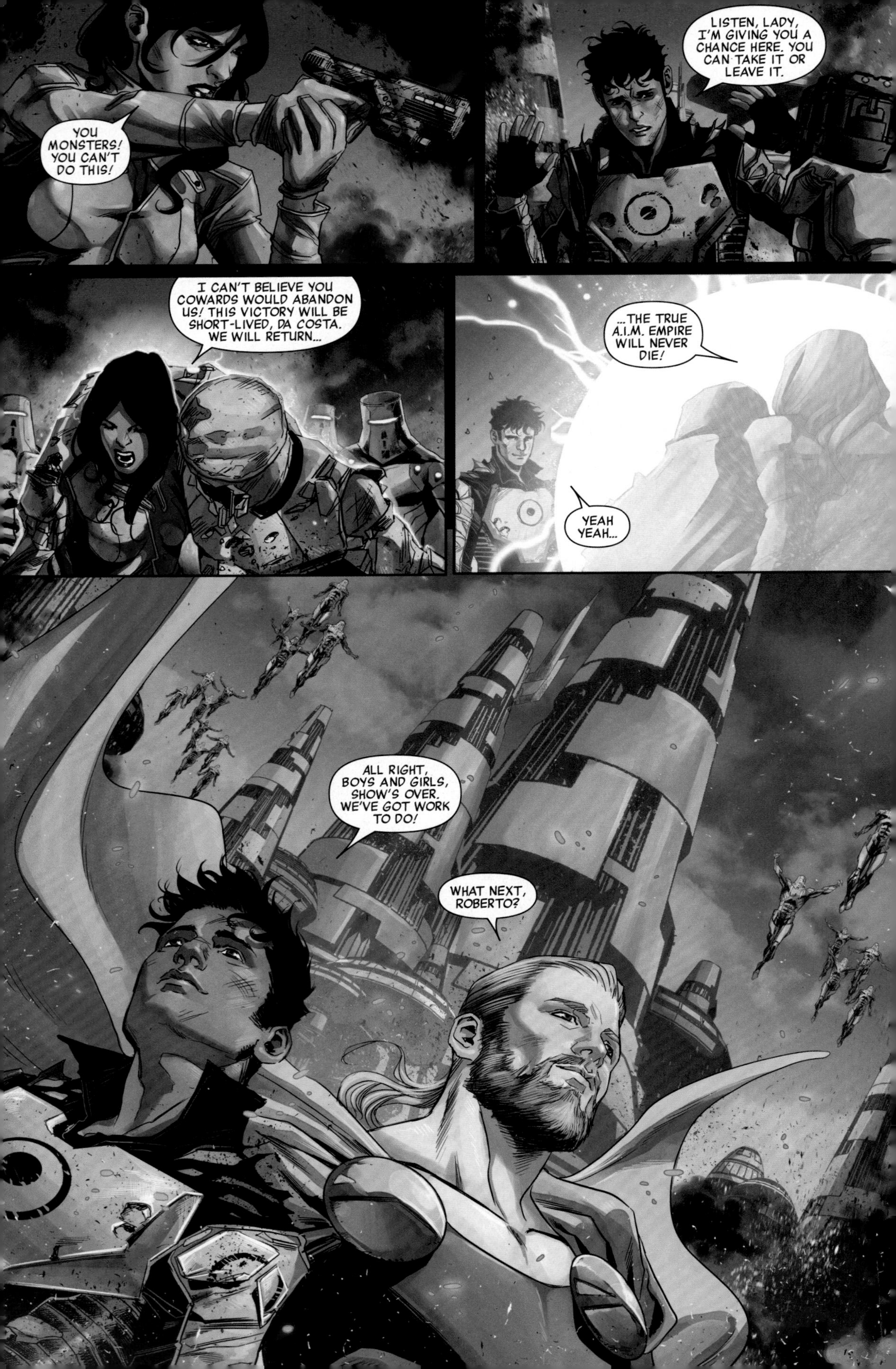

YOU MONSTERS! YOU CAN'T DO THIS!
LISTEN, LADY, I'M GIVING YOU A CHANCE HERE. YOU CAN TAKE IT OR LEAVE IT.
I CAN'T BELIEVE YOU COWARDS WOULD ABANDON US! THIS VICTORY WILL BE SHORT-LIVED, DA COSTA. WE WILL RETURN...
...THE TRUE A.I.M. EMPIRE WILL NEVER DIE!
YEAH YEAH...
ALL RIGHT, BOYS AND GIRLS, SHOW'S OVER. WE'VE GOT WORK TO DO!
WHAT NEXT, ROBERTO?

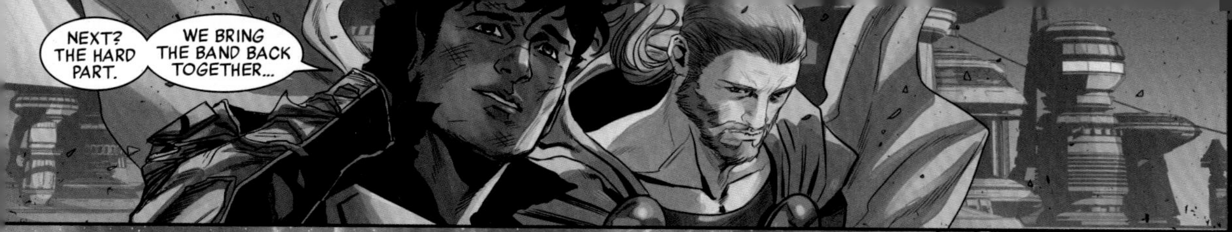
NEXT? THE HARD PART.
WE BRING THE BAND BACK TOGETHER...

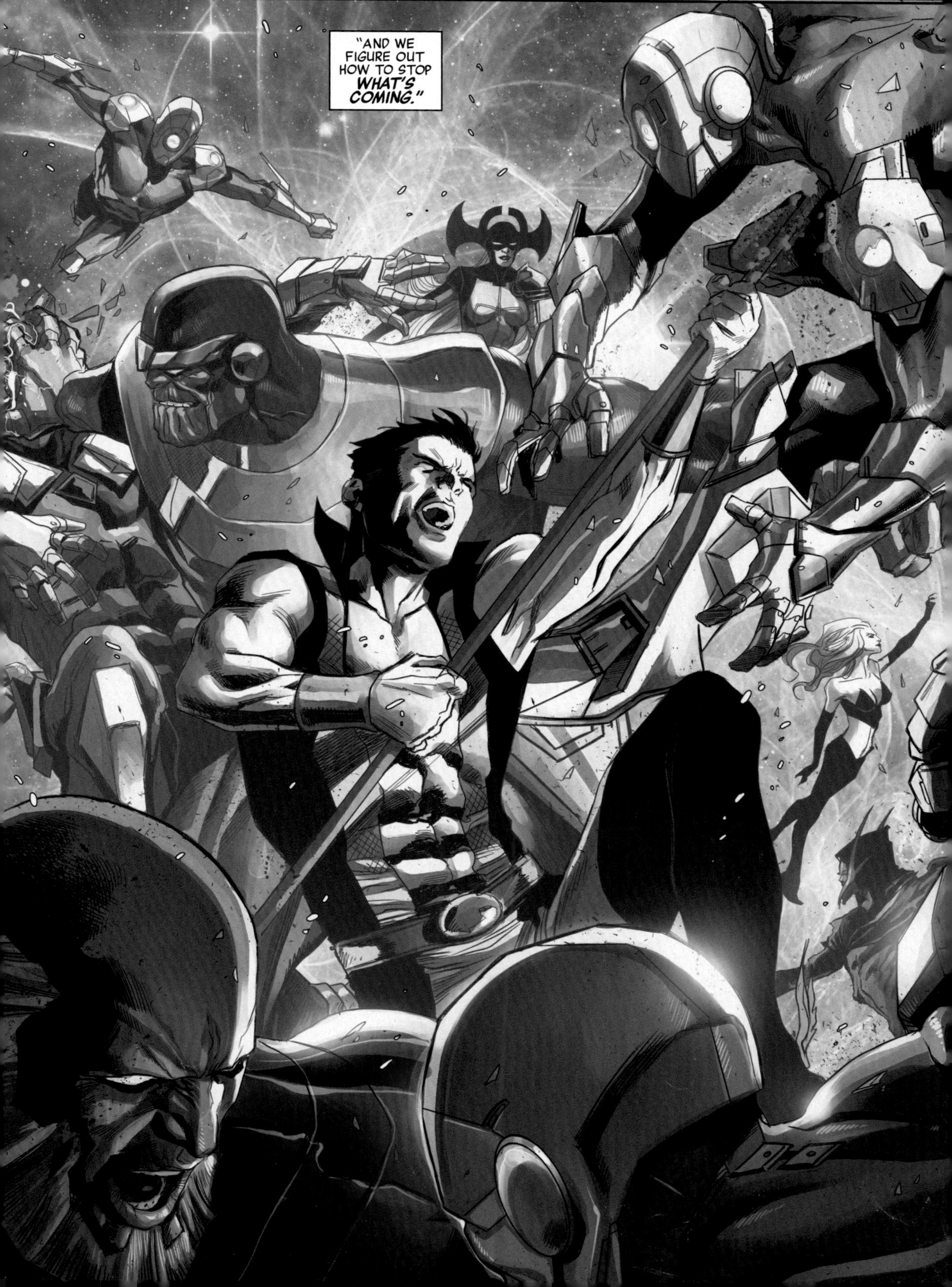
"AND WE FIGURE OUT HOW TO STOP WHAT'S COMING."

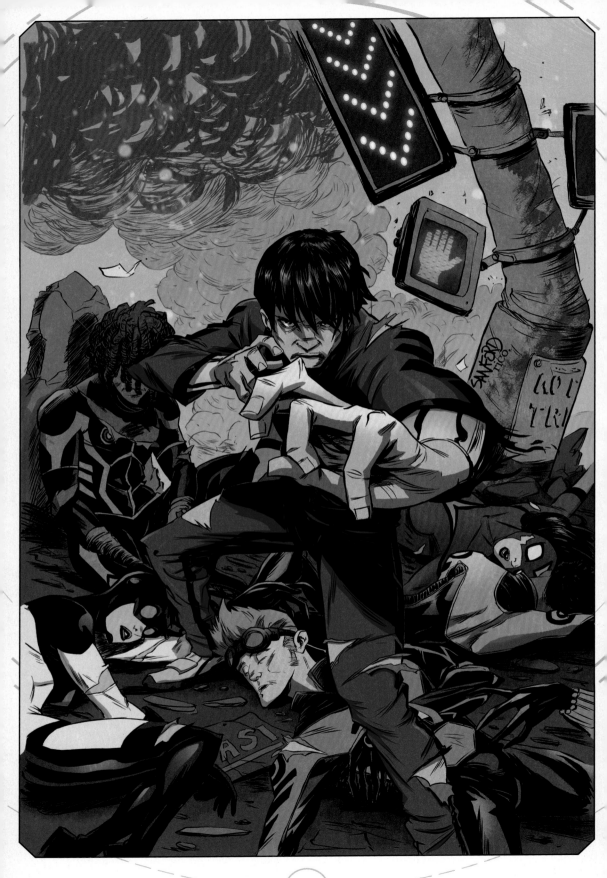

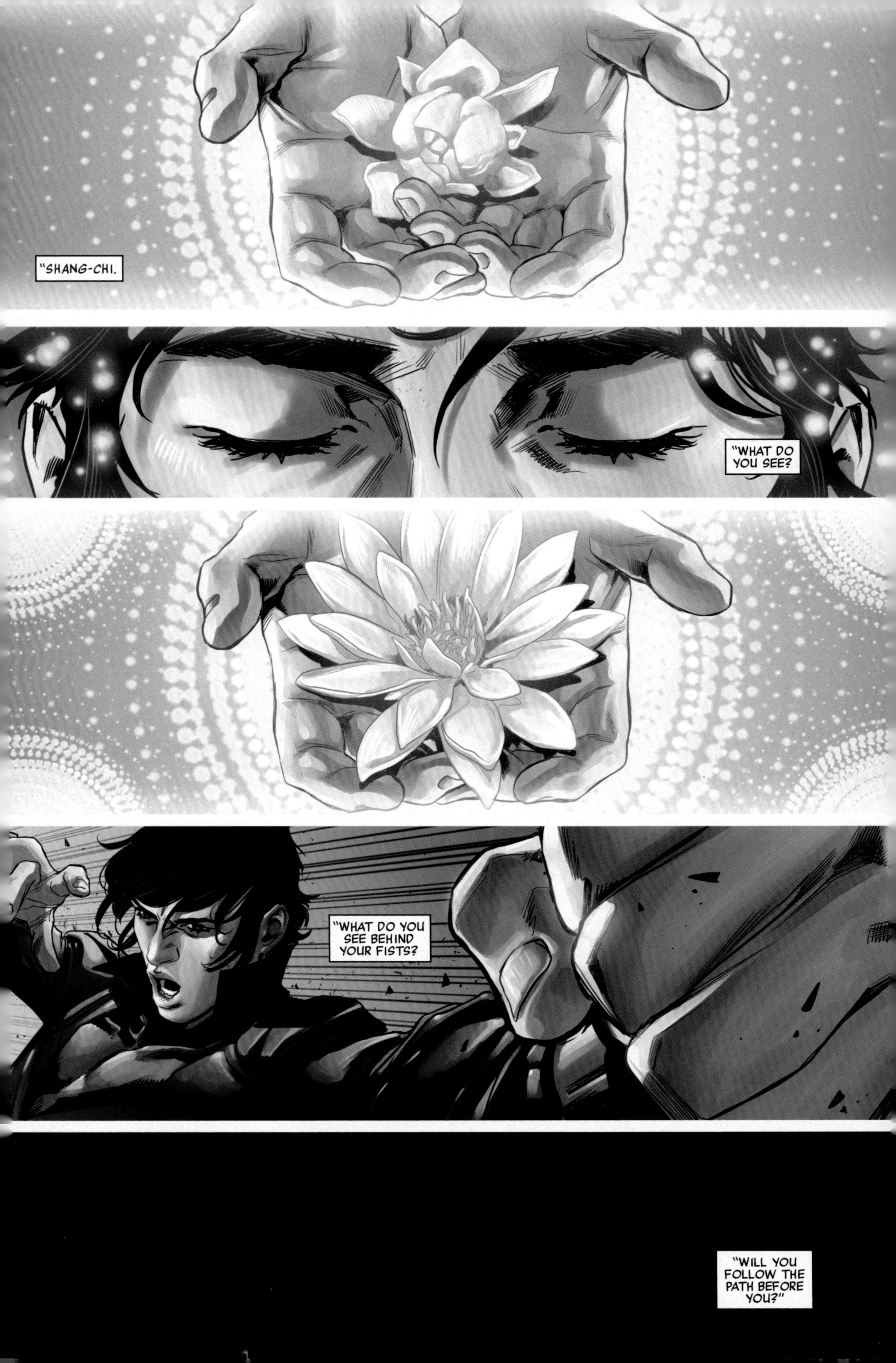
"SHANG-CHI.
"WHAT DO YOU SEE?
"WHAT DO YOU SEE BEHIND YOUR FISTS?
"WILL YOU FOLLOW THE PATH BEFORE YOU?"

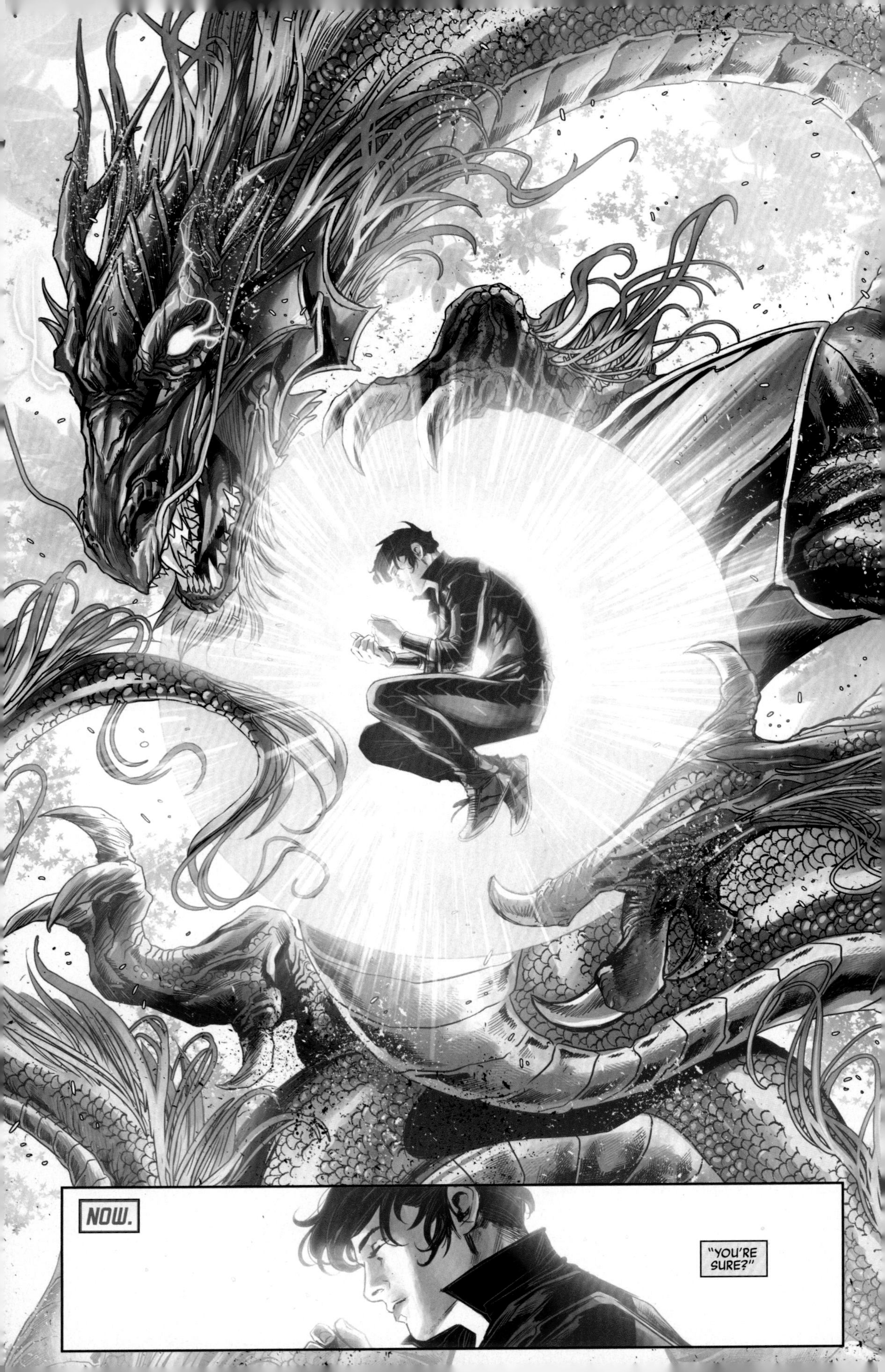
NOW.
"YOU'RE SURE?"

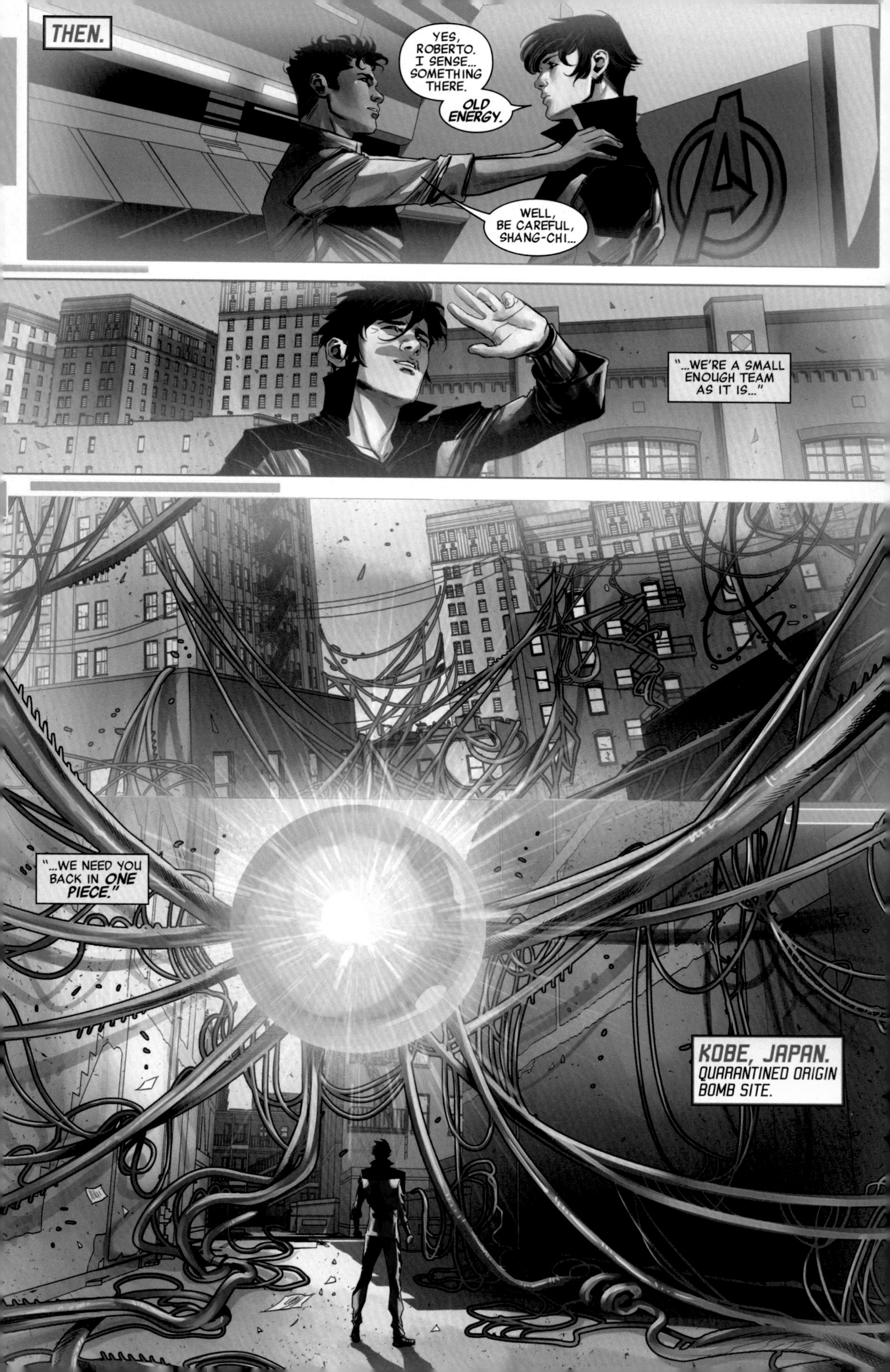
THEN.
YES, ROBERTO. I SENSE... SOMETHING THERE.
OLD ENERGY.
WELL, BE CAREFUL, SHANG-CHI...
"...WE'RE A SMALL ENOUGH TEAM AS IT IS..."
"...WE NEED YOU BACK IN ONE PIECE."
KOBE, JAPAN. QUARANTINED ORIGIN BOMB SITE.

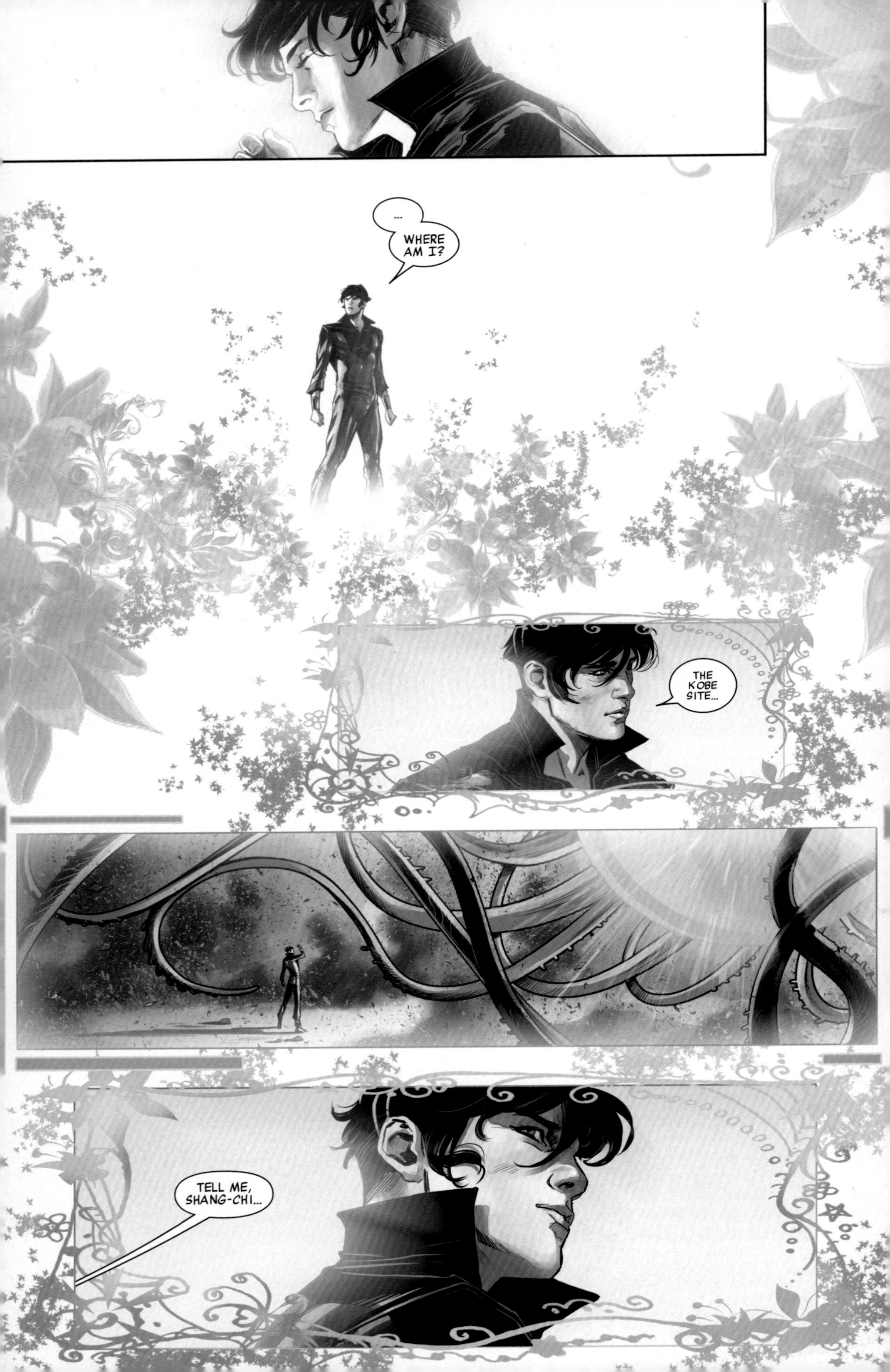

...
WHERE AM I?
THE KOBE SITE...
TELL ME, SHANG-CHI...

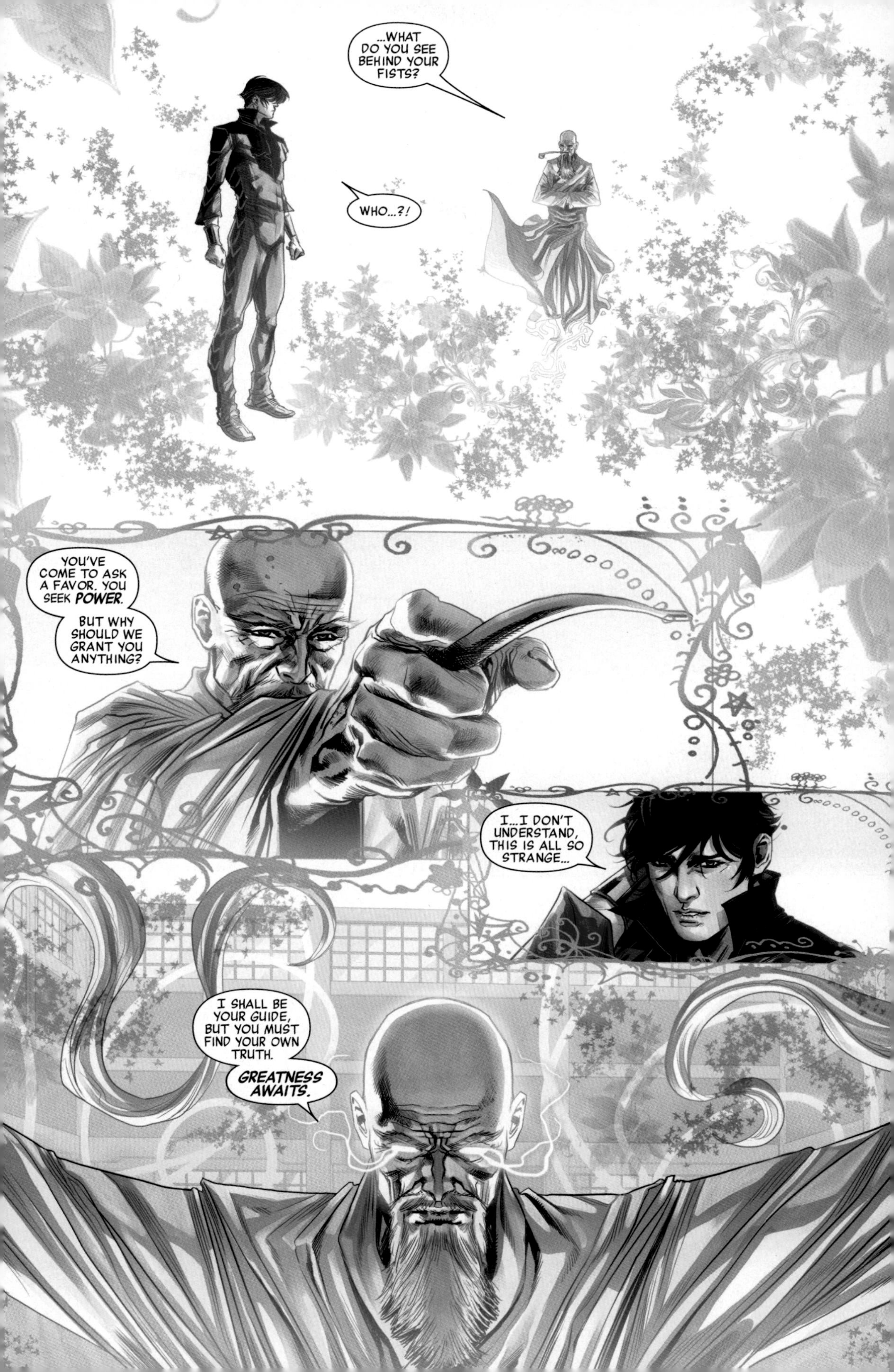
...WHAT DO YOU SEE BEHIND YOUR FISTS?
WHO...?!
YOU'VE COME TO ASK A FAVOR. YOU SEEK POWER.
BUT WHY SHOULD WE GRANT YOU ANYTHING?
I...I DON'T UNDERSTAND, THIS IS ALL SO STRANGE...
I SHALL BE YOUR GUIDE, BUT YOU MUST FIND YOUR OWN TRUTH.
GREATNESS AWAITS.

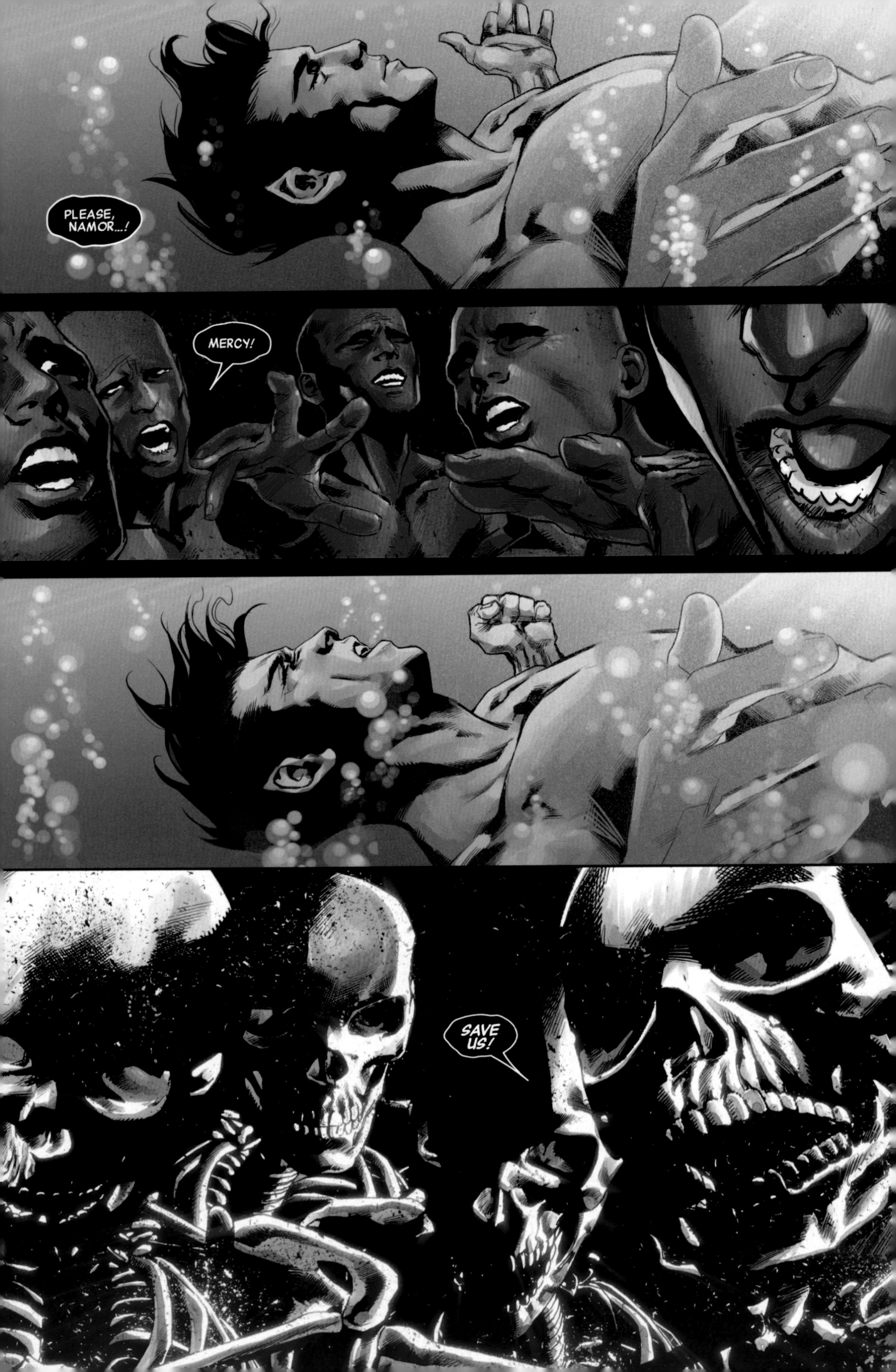
PLEASE, NAMOR...!
MERCY!
SAVE US!

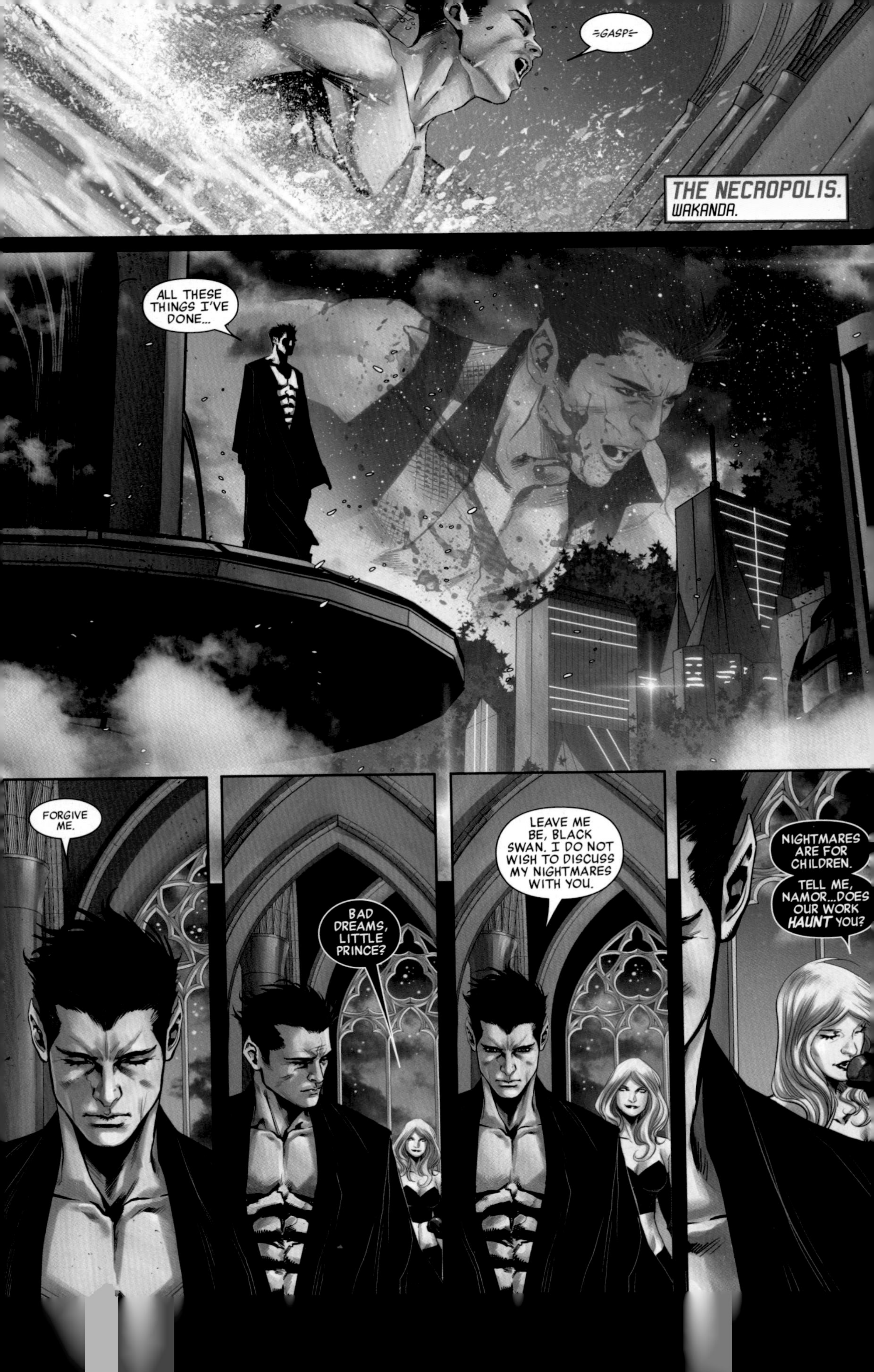

=GASP=
THE NECROPOLIS.
WAKANDA.
ALL THESE THINGS I'VE DONE...
FORGIVE ME.
BAD DREAMS, LITTLE PRINCE?
LEAVE ME BE, BLACK SWAN. I DO NOT WISH TO DISCUSS MY NIGHTMARES WITH YOU.
NIGHTMARES ARE FOR CHILDREN.
TELL ME, NAMOR...DOES OUR WORK HAUNT YOU?

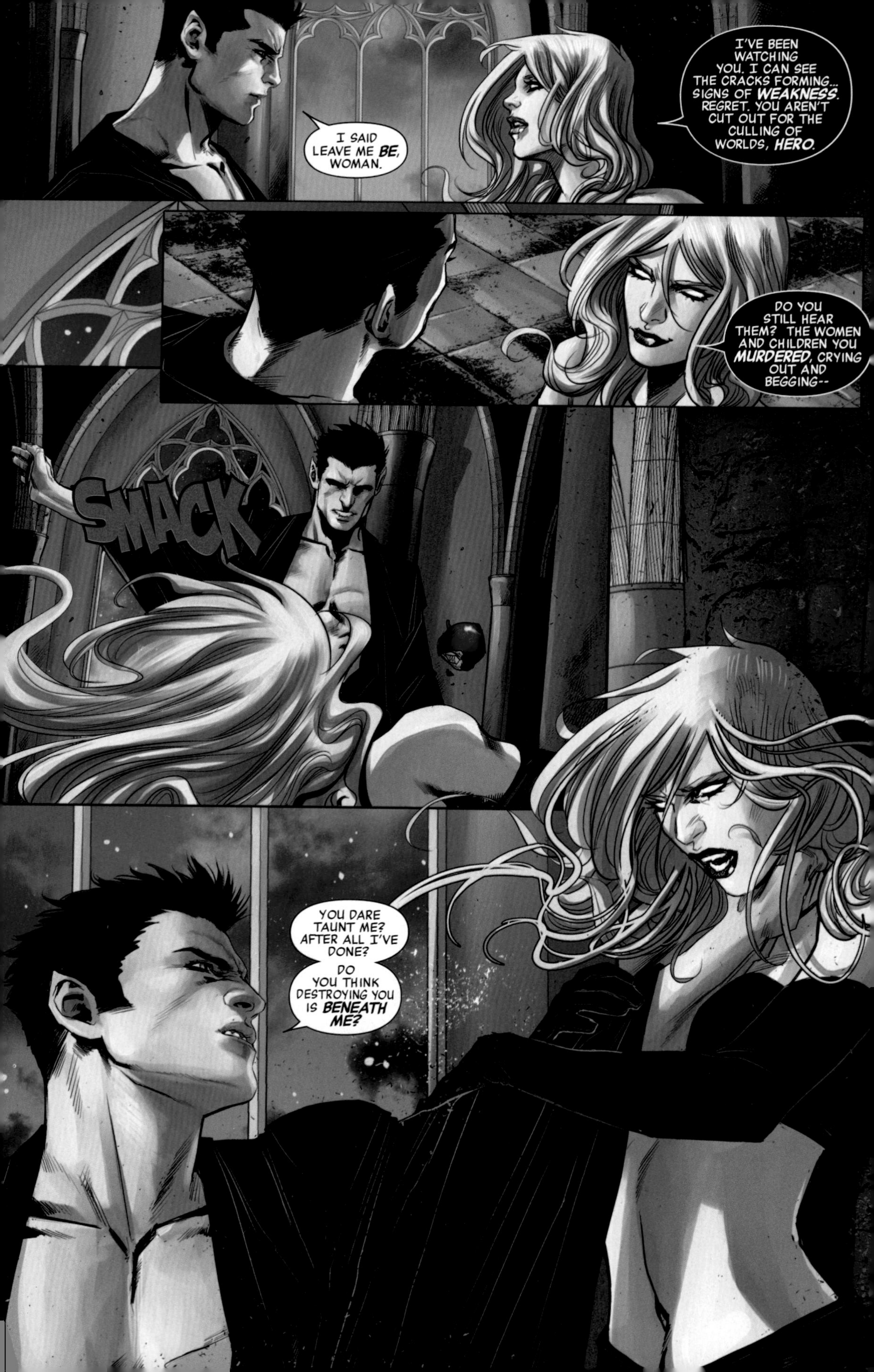
I SAID LEAVE ME BE, WOMAN.
I'VE BEEN WATCHING YOU. I CAN SEE THE CRACKS FORMING... SIGNS OF WEAKNESS. REGRET. YOU AREN'T CUT OUT FOR THE CULLING OF WORLDS, HERO.
DO YOU STILL HEAR THEM? THE WOMEN AND CHILDREN YOU MURDERED, CRYING OUT AND BEGGING--
SMACK
YOU DARE TAUNT ME? AFTER ALL I'VE DONE?
DO YOU THINK DESTROYING YOU IS BENEATH ME?

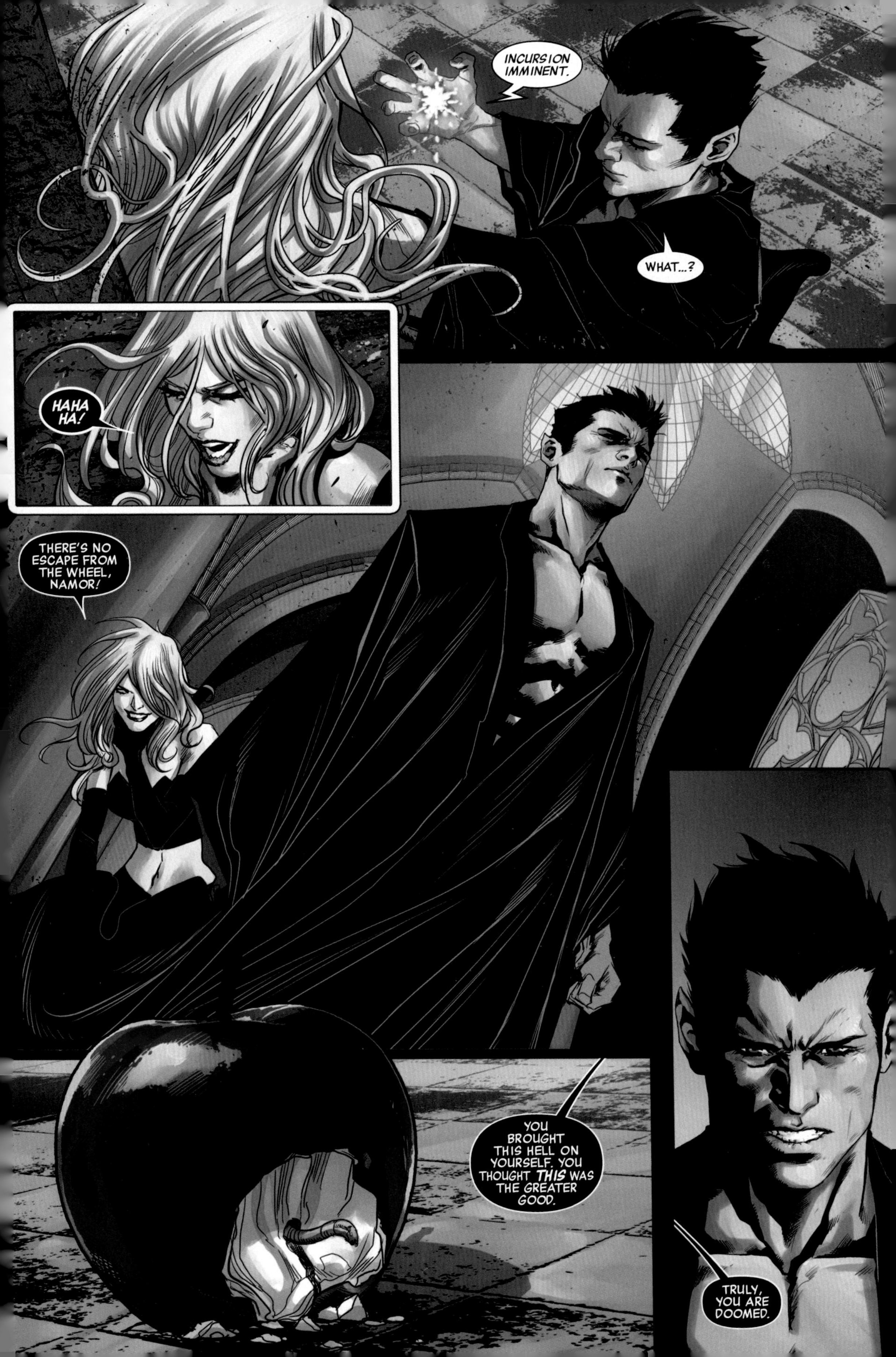
INCURSION IMMINENT.
WHAT...?
HAHA HA!
THERE'S NO ESCAPE FROM THE WHEEL, NAMOR!
YOU BROUGHT THIS HELL ON YOURSELF. YOU THOUGHT THIS WAS THE GREATER GOOD.
TRULY, YOU ARE DOOMED.

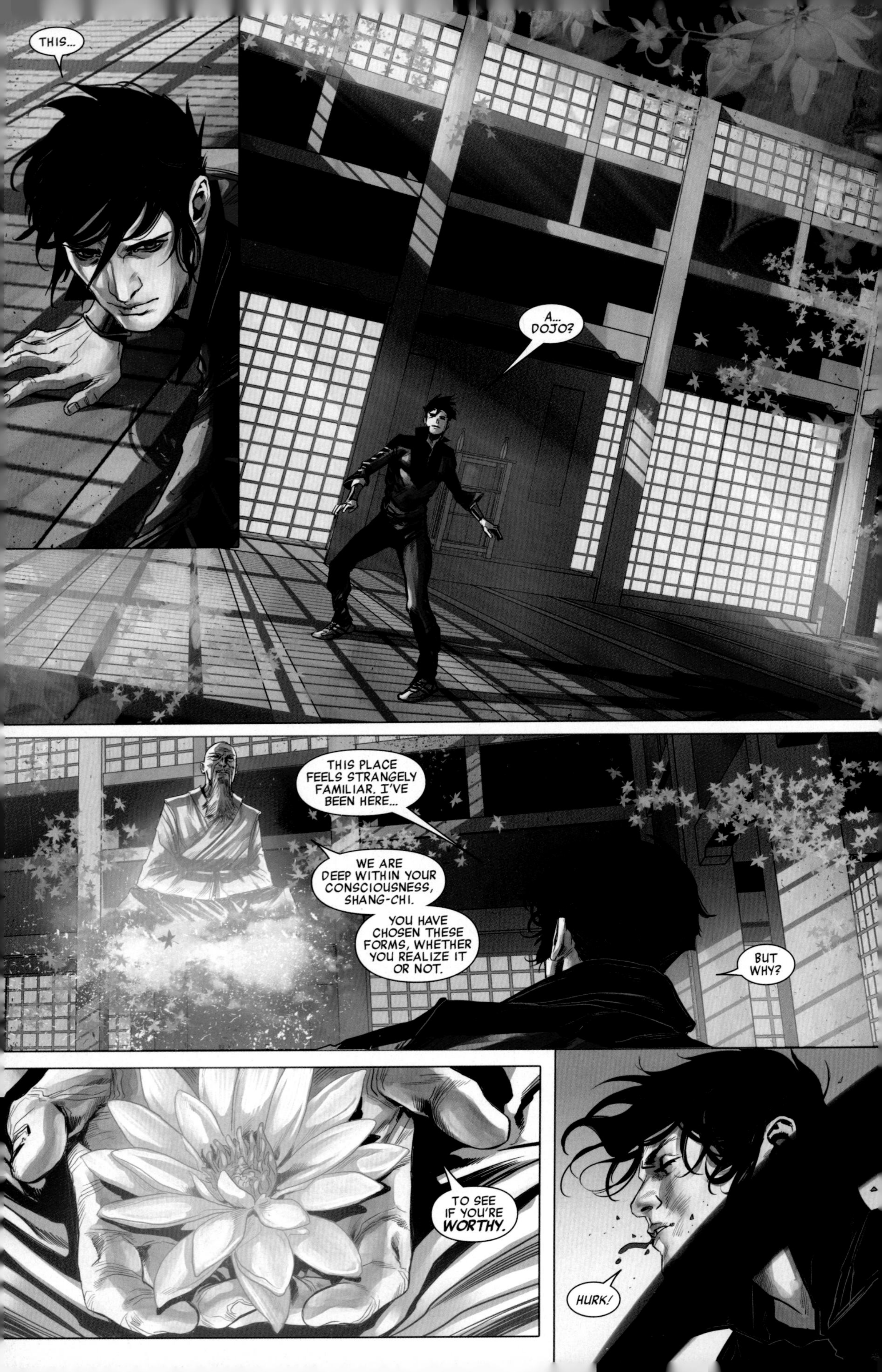
THIS...
A... DOJO?
THIS PLACE FEELS STRANGELY FAMILIAR. I'VE BEEN HERE...
WE ARE DEEP WITHIN YOUR CONSCIOUSNESS, SHANG-CHI.
YOU HAVE CHOSEN THESE FORMS, WHETHER YOU REALIZE IT OR NOT.
BUT WHY?
TO SEE IF YOU'RE WORTHY.
HURK!

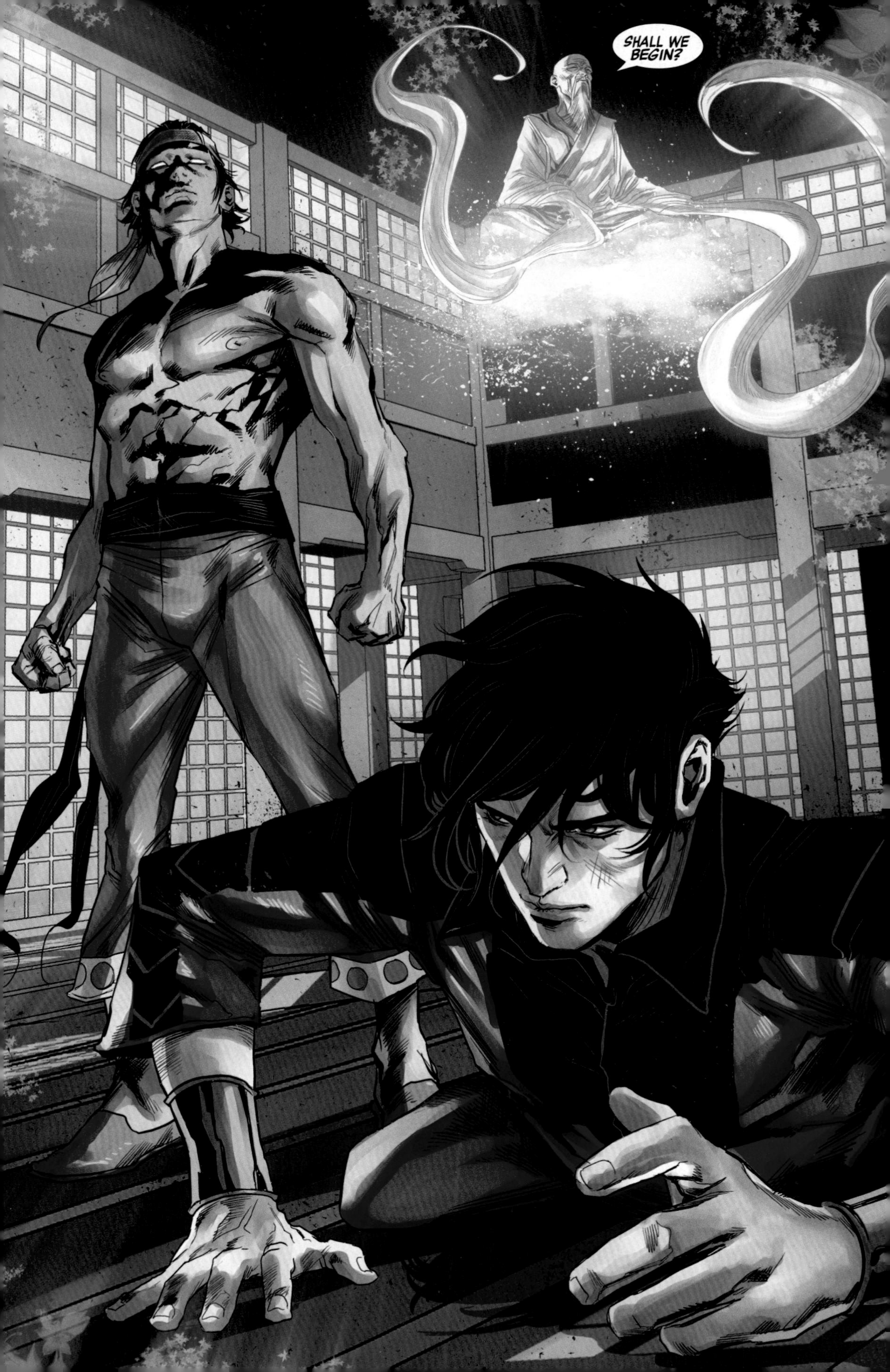
SHALL WE BEGIN?

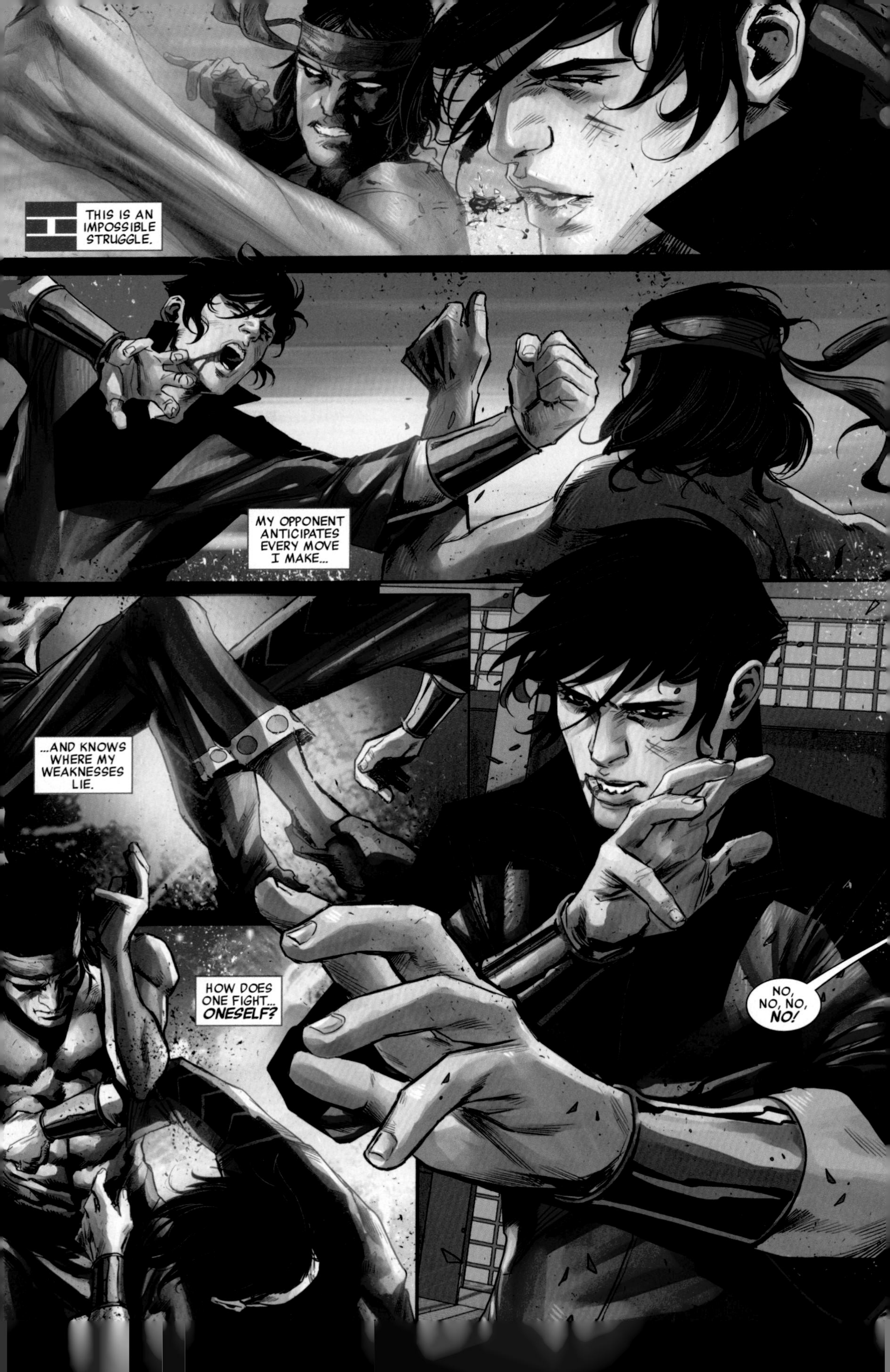
THIS IS AN IMPOSSIBLE STRUGGLE.
MY OPPONENT ANTICIPATES EVERY MOVE I MAKE...
...AND KNOWS WHERE MY WEAKNESSES LIE.
HOW DOES ONE FIGHT... ONESELF?
NO, NO, NO, NO!

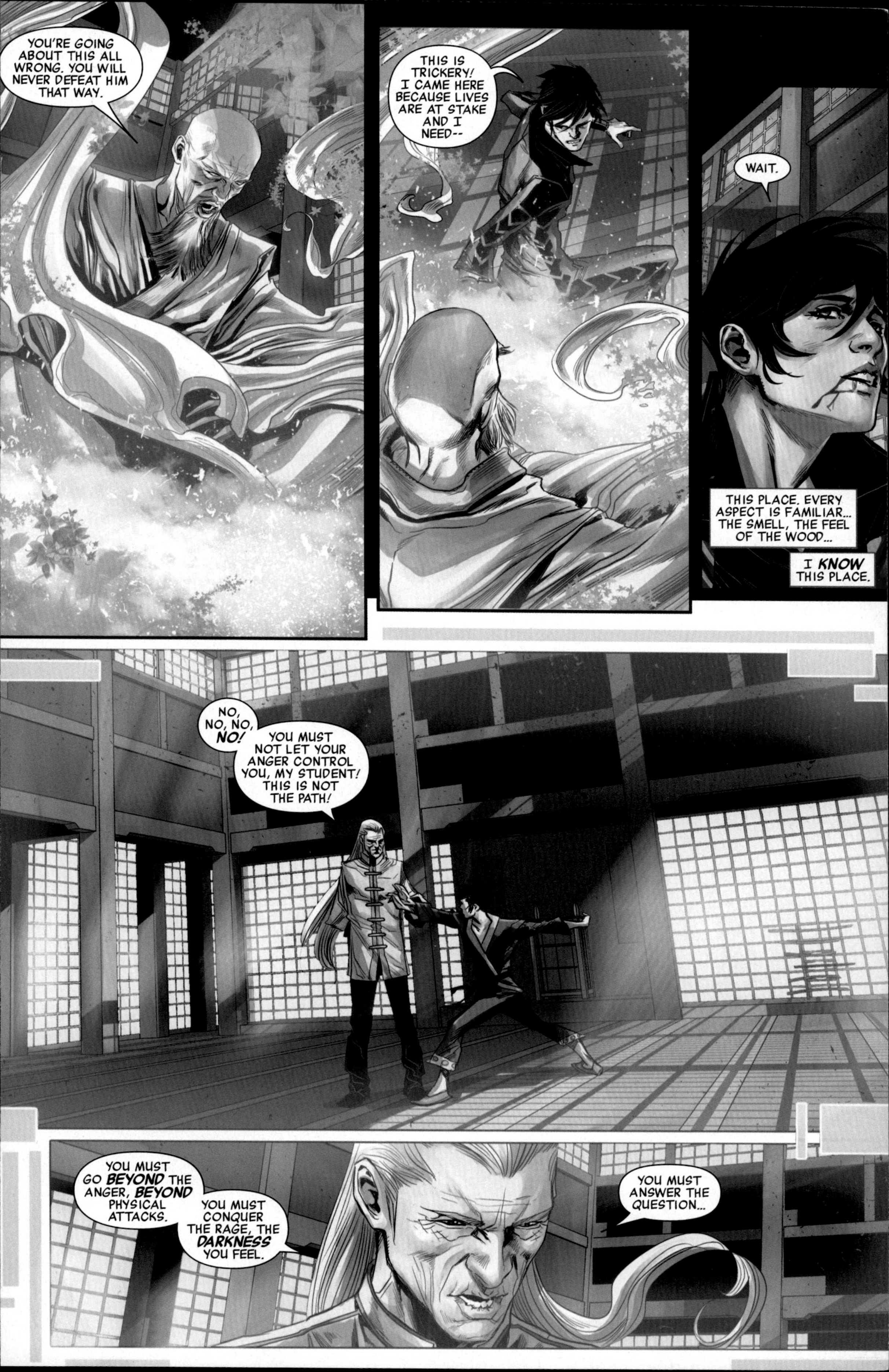
YOU'RE GOING ABOUT THIS ALL WRONG. YOU WILL NEVER DEFEAT HIM THAT WAY.
THIS IS TRICKERY! I CAME HERE BECAUSE LIVES ARE AT STAKE AND I NEED--
WAIT.
THIS PLACE. EVERY ASPECT IS FAMILIAR... THE SMELL, THE FEEL OF THE WOOD...
I KNOW THIS PLACE.
NO, NO, NO, NO!
YOU MUST NOT LET YOUR ANGER CONTROL YOU, MY STUDENT! THIS IS NOT THE PATH!
YOU MUST GO BEYOND THE ANGER, BEYOND PHYSICAL ATTACKS.
YOU MUST CONQUER THE RAGE, THE DARKNESS YOU FEEL.
YOU MUST ANSWER THE QUESTION...

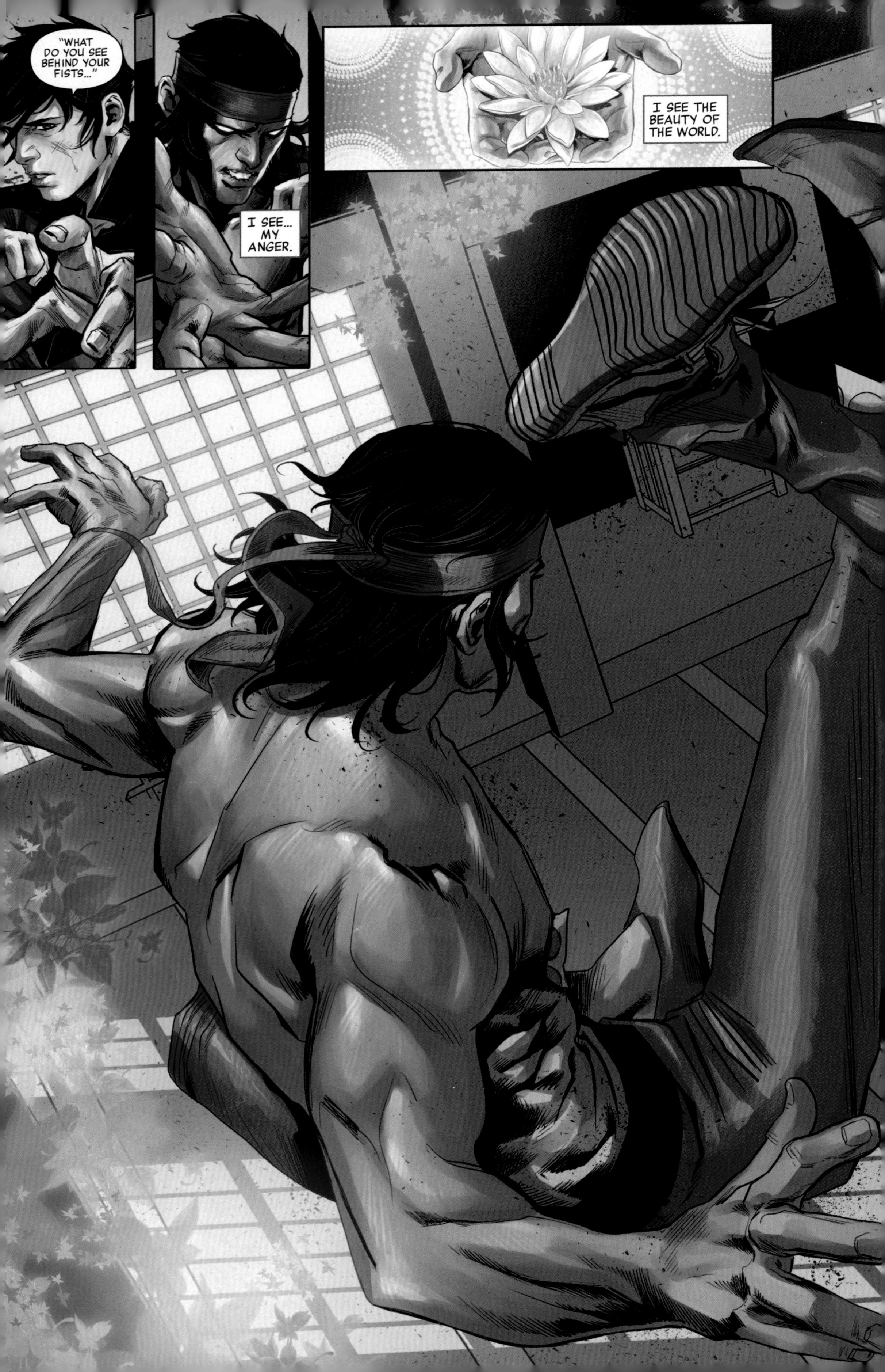
"WHAT DO YOU SEE BEHIND YOUR FISTS..."
I SEE... MY ANGER.
I SEE THE BEAUTY OF THE WORLD.

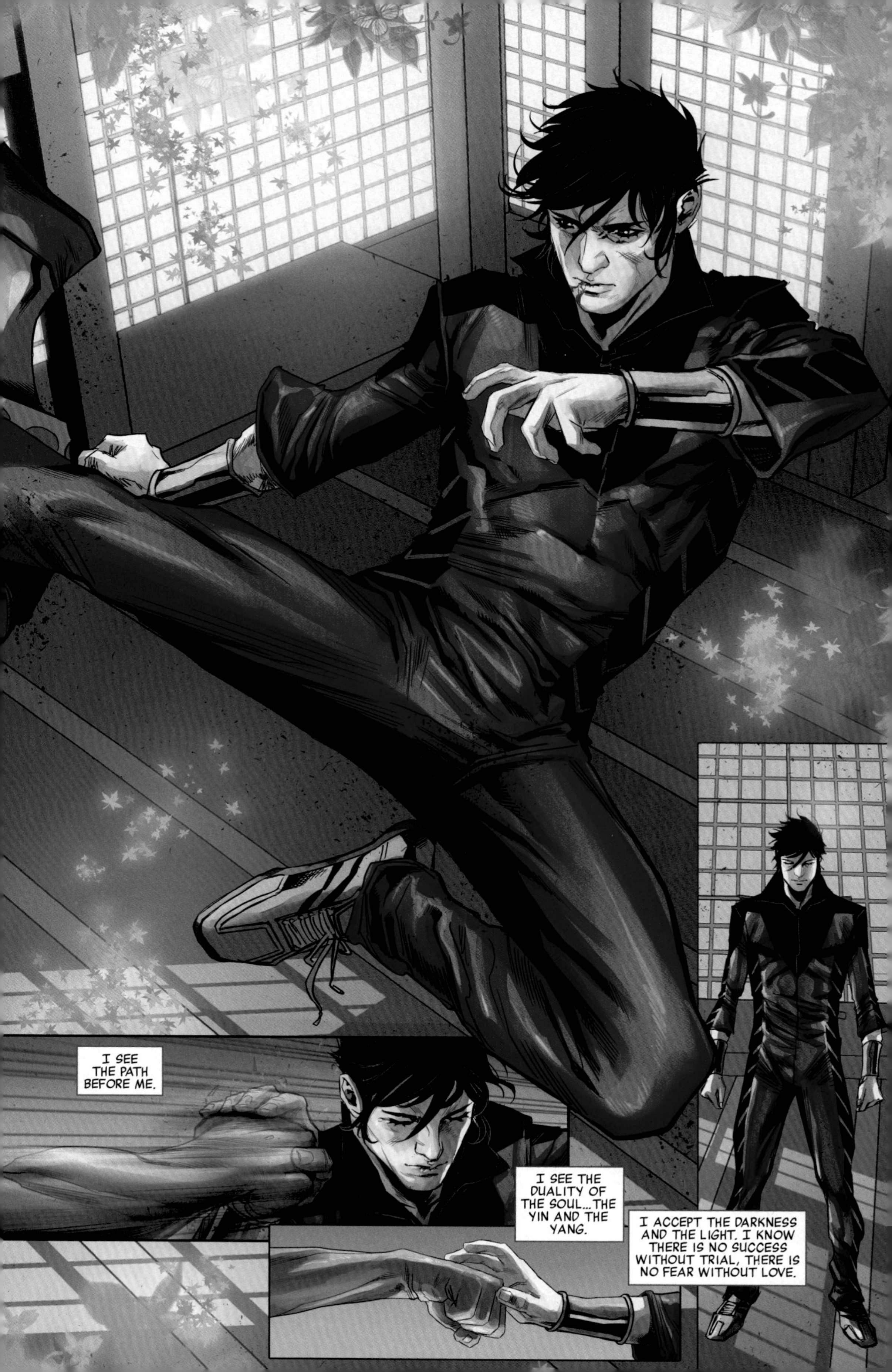
I SEE THE PATH BEFORE ME.
I SEE THE DUALITY OF THE SOUL...THE YIN AND THE YANG.
I ACCEPT THE DARKNESS AND THE LIGHT. I KNOW THERE IS NO SUCCESS WITHOUT TRIAL, THERE IS NO FEAR WITHOUT LOVE.

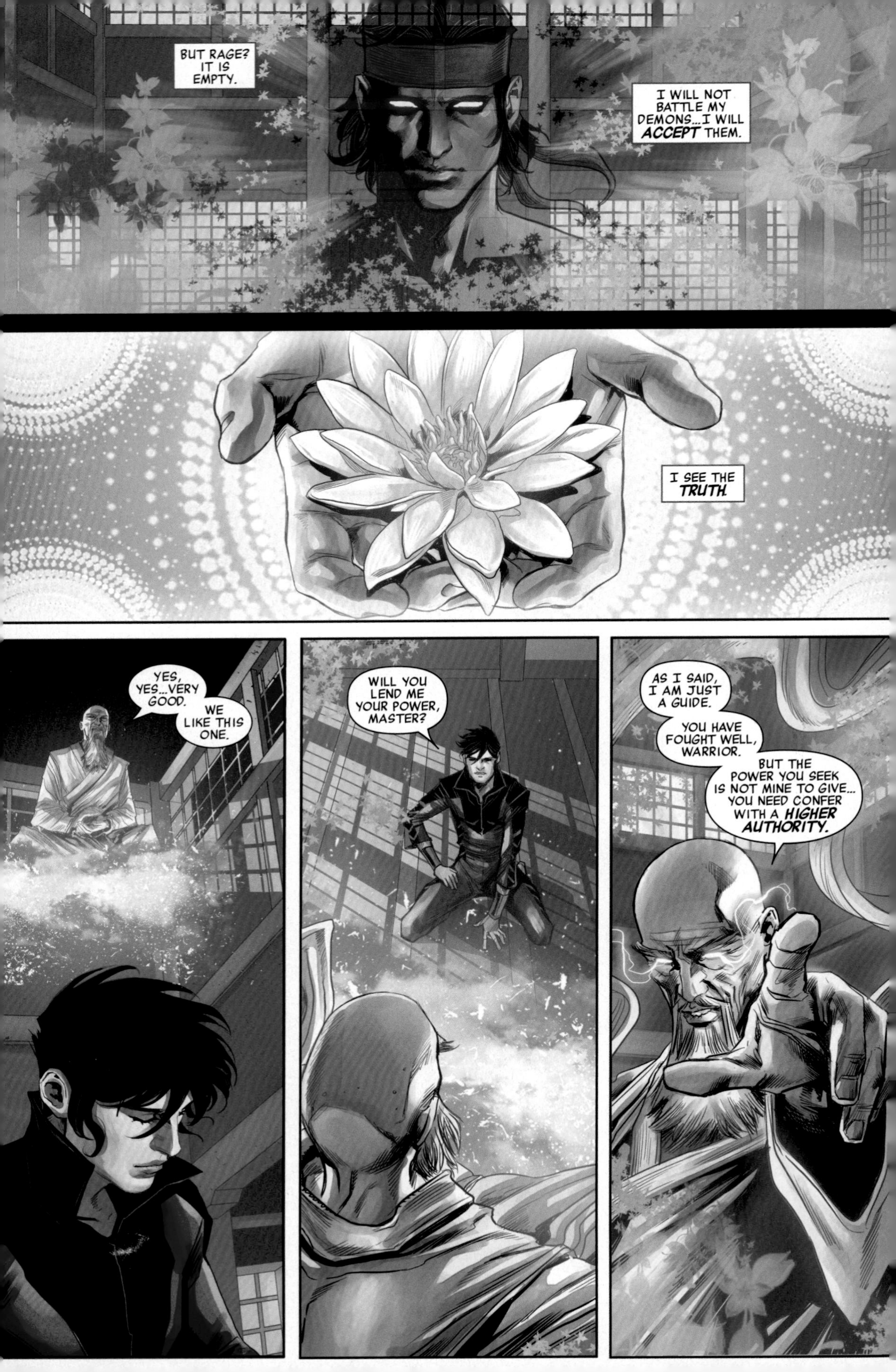
BUT RAGE? IT IS EMPTY.
I WILL NOT BATTLE MY DEMONS...I WILL ACCEPT THEM.
I SEE THE TRUTH.
YES, YES...VERY GOOD.
WE LIKE THIS ONE.
WILL YOU LEND ME YOUR POWER, MASTER?
AS I SAID, I AM JUST A GUIDE.
YOU HAVE FOUGHT WELL, WARRIOR.
BUT THE POWER YOU SEEK IS NOT MINE TO GIVE... YOU NEED CONFER WITH A HIGHER AUTHORITY.

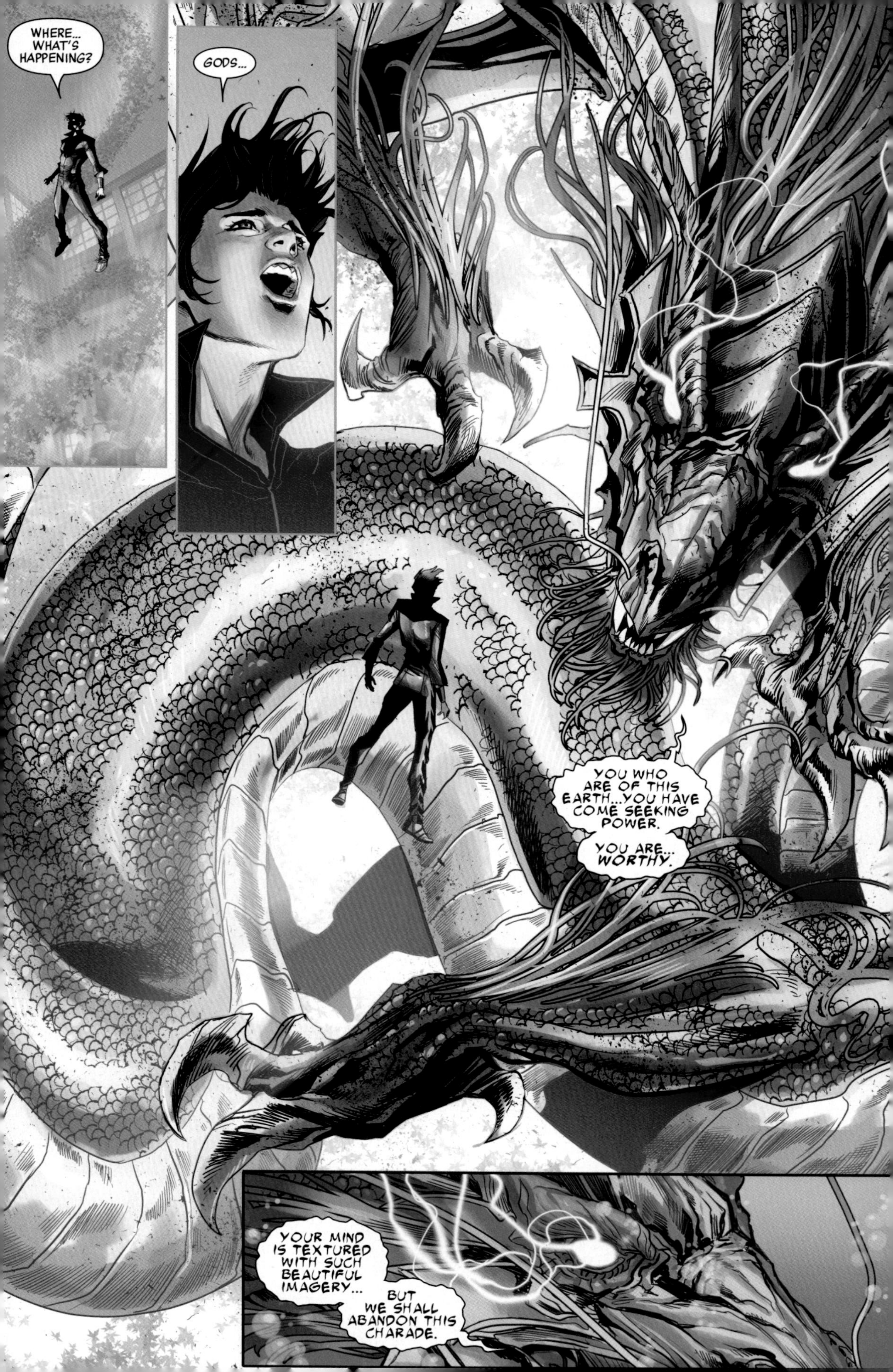
WHERE... WHAT'S HAPPENING?
GODS...
YOU WHO ARE OF THIS EARTH...YOU HAVE COME SEEKING POWER.
YOU ARE... WORTHY.
YOUR MIND IS TEXTURED WITH SUCH BEAUTIFUL IMAGERY...
BUT WE SHALL ABANDON THIS CHARADE.

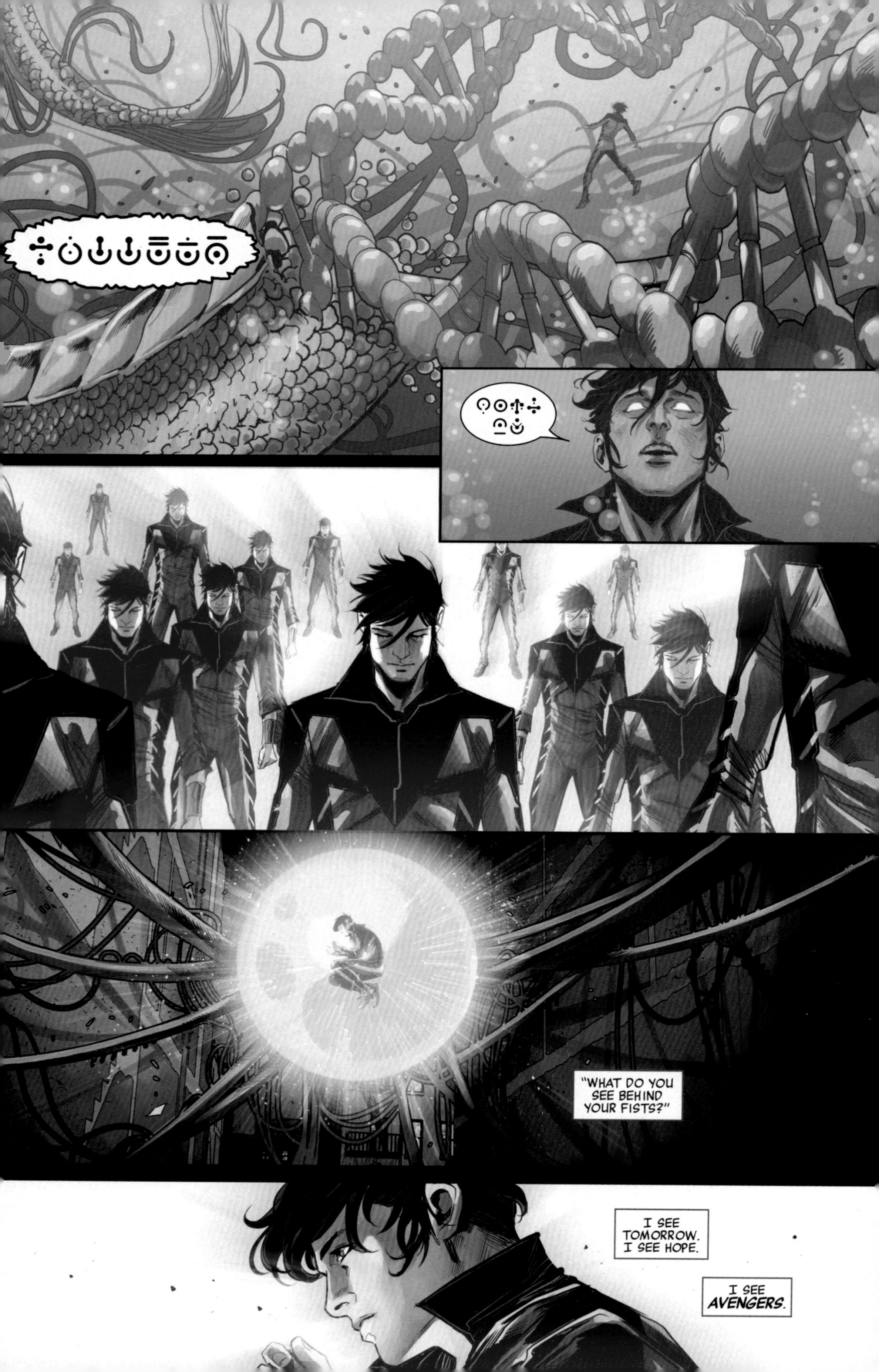
"WHAT DO YOU SEE BEHIND YOUR FISTS?"
I SEE TOMORROW. I SEE HOPE.
I SEE AVENGERS.

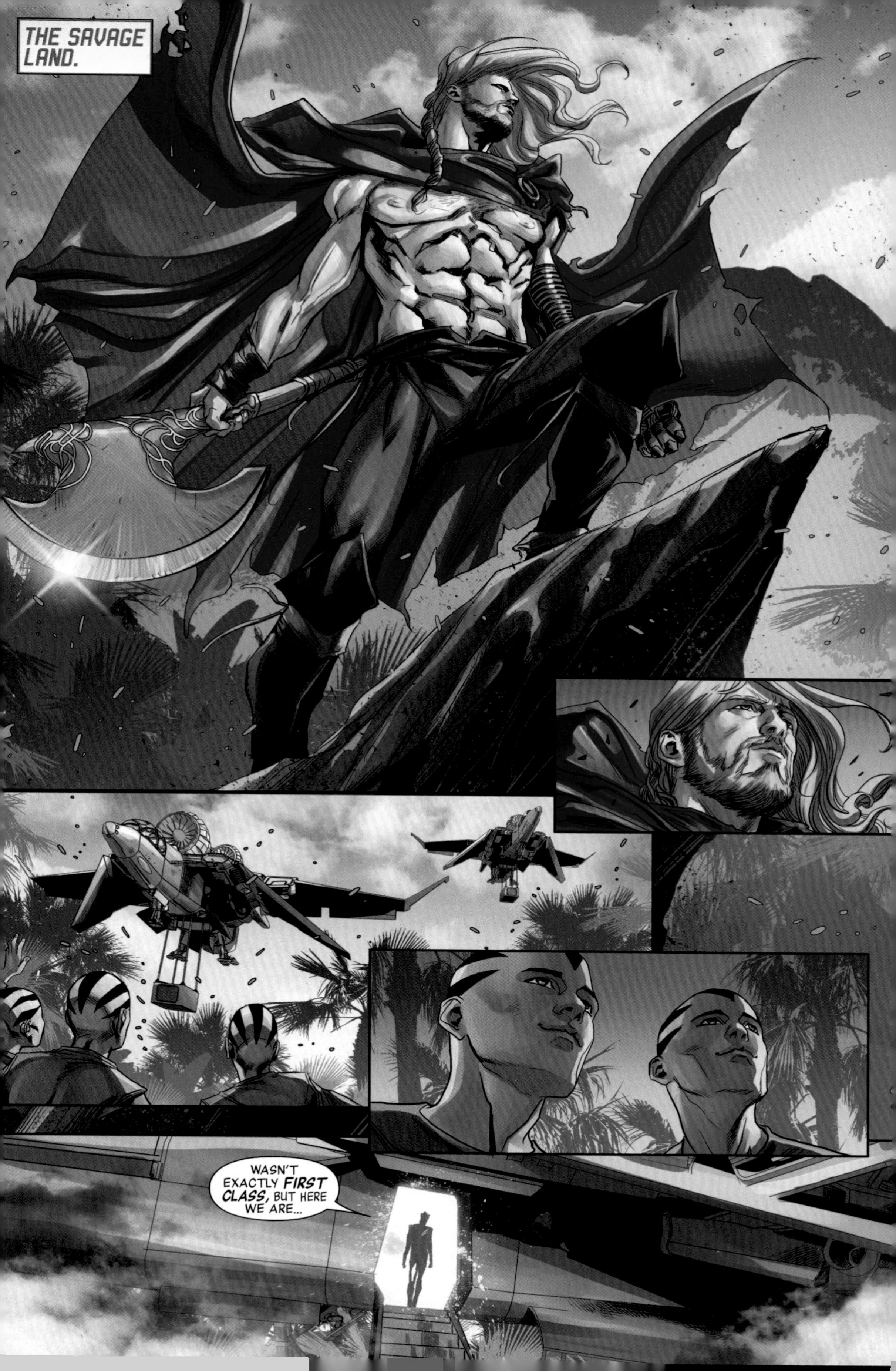
THE SAVAGE LAND.
WASN'T EXACTLY FIRST CLASS, BUT HERE WE ARE...

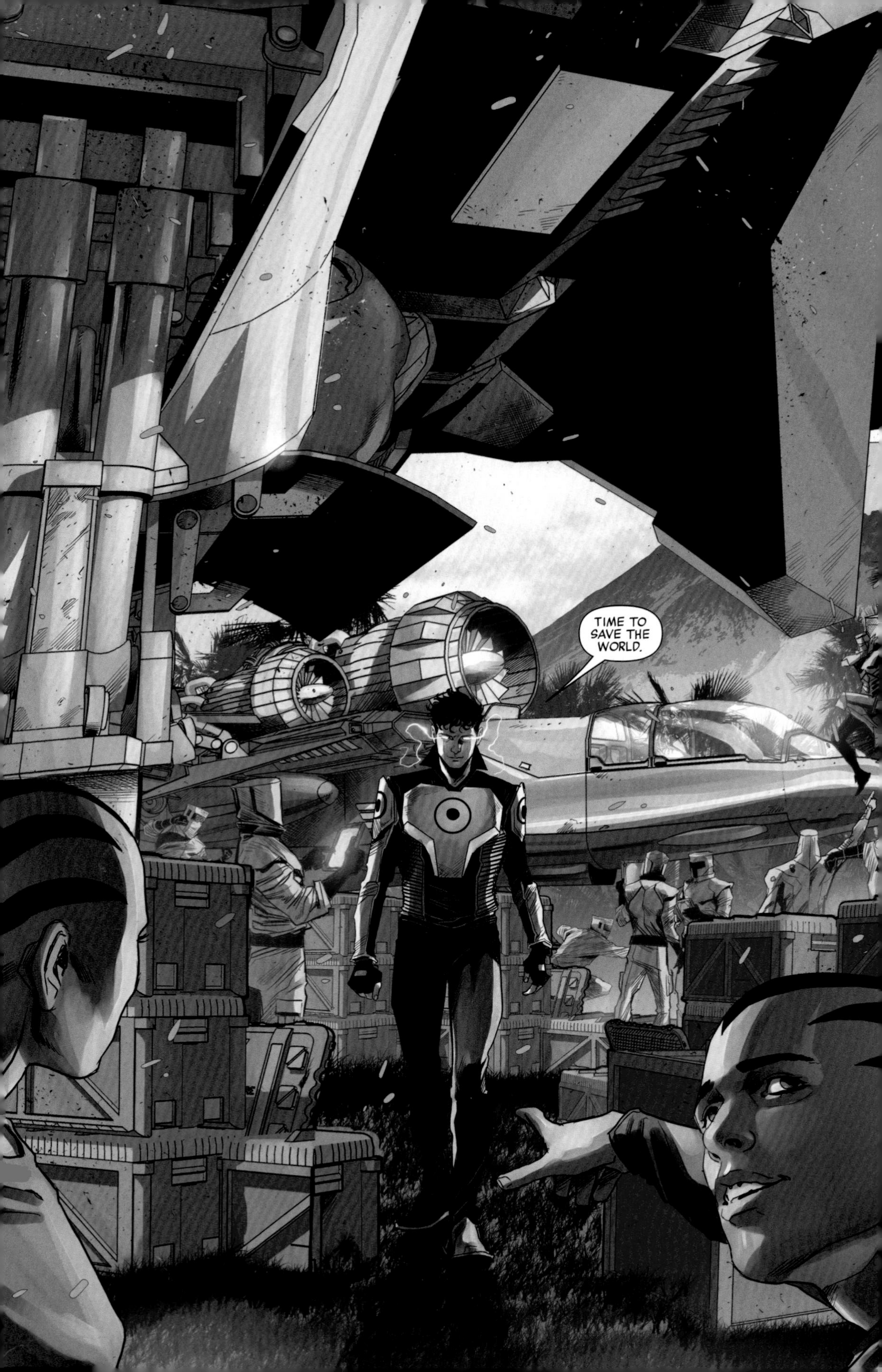
TIME TO SAVE THE WORLD.

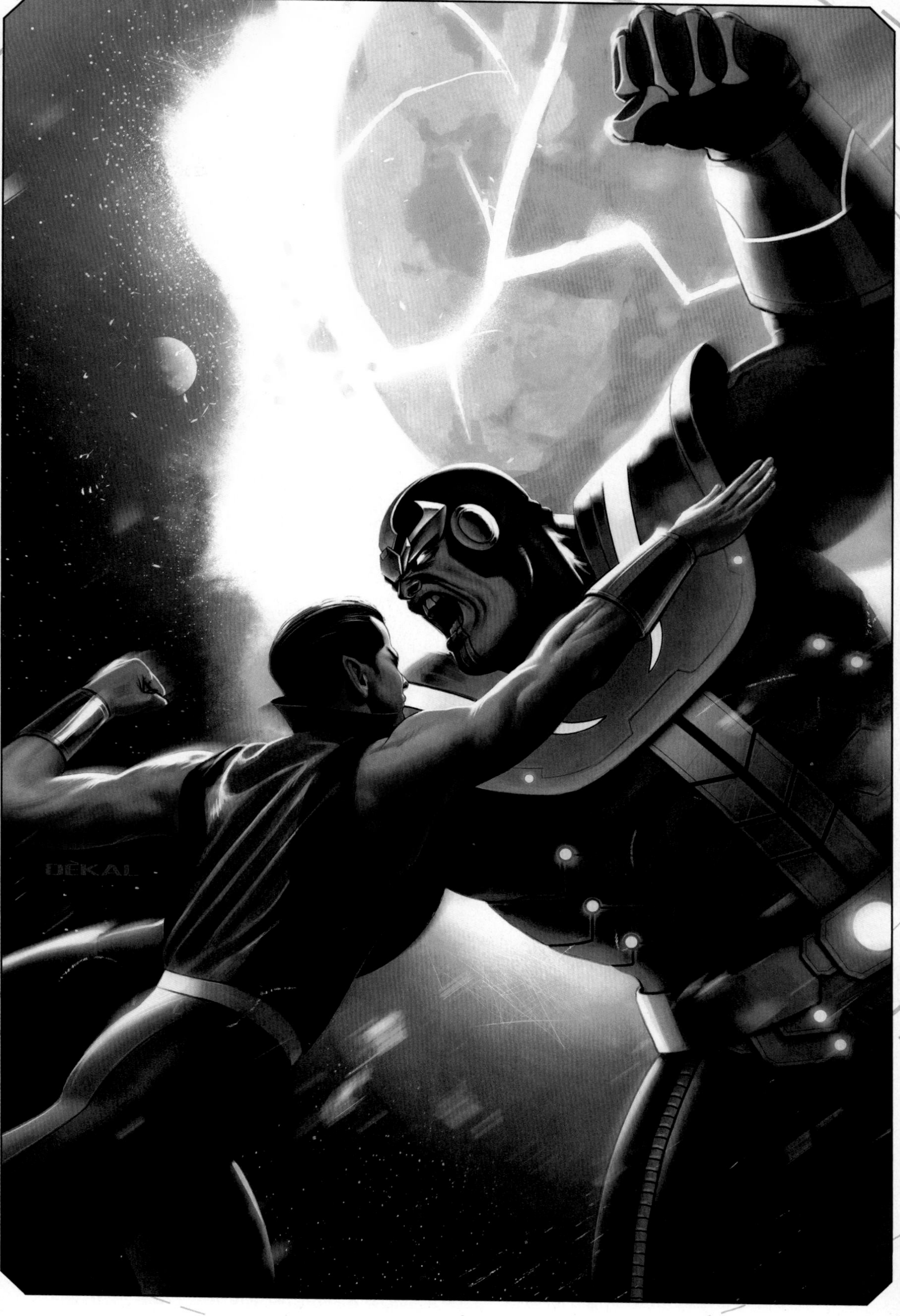
DEKAL

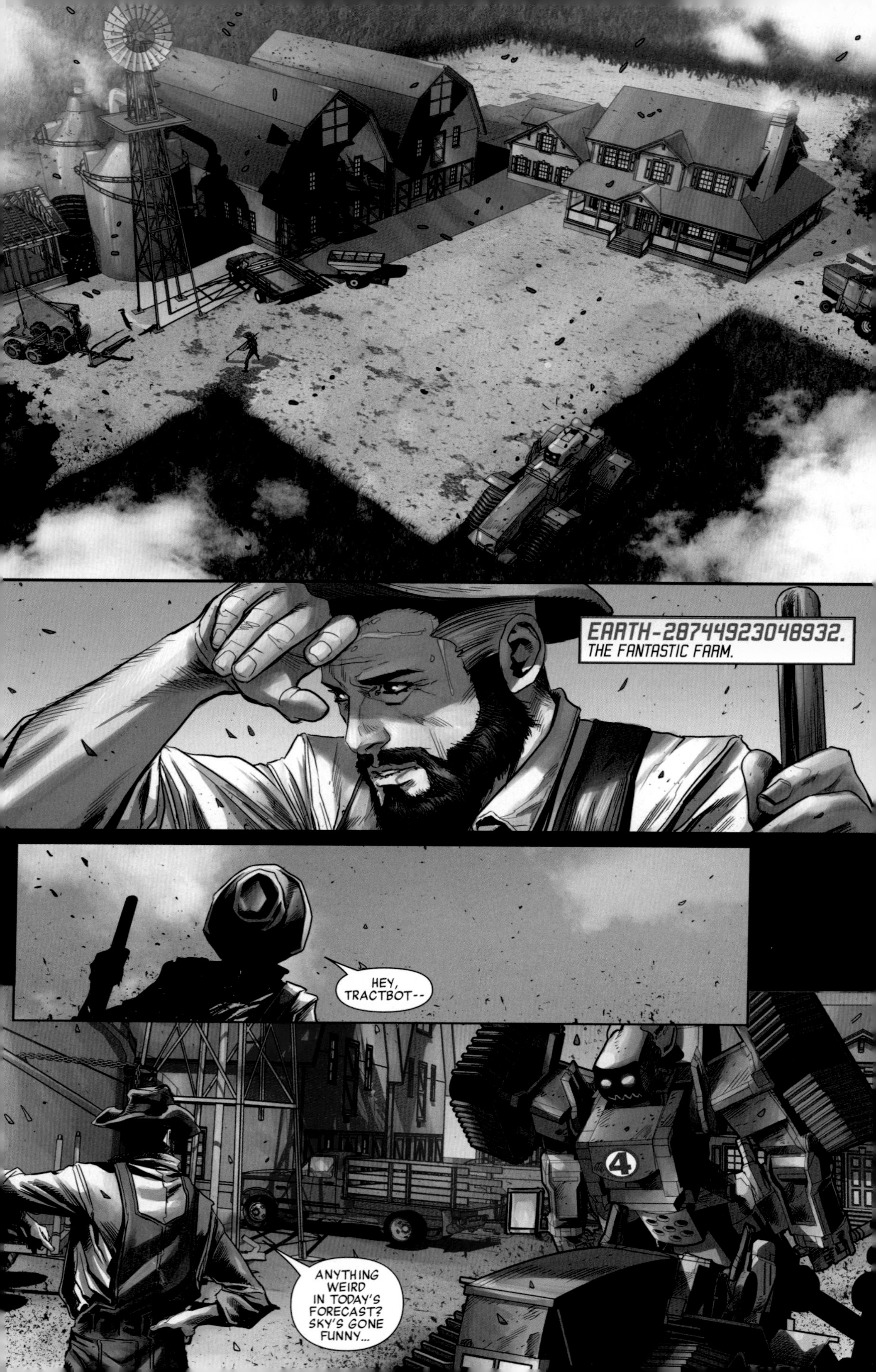
EARTH-28744923048932.
THE FANTASTIC FARM.
HEY, TRACTBOT--
ANYTHING WEIRD IN TODAY'S FORECAST? SKY'S GONE FUNNY...

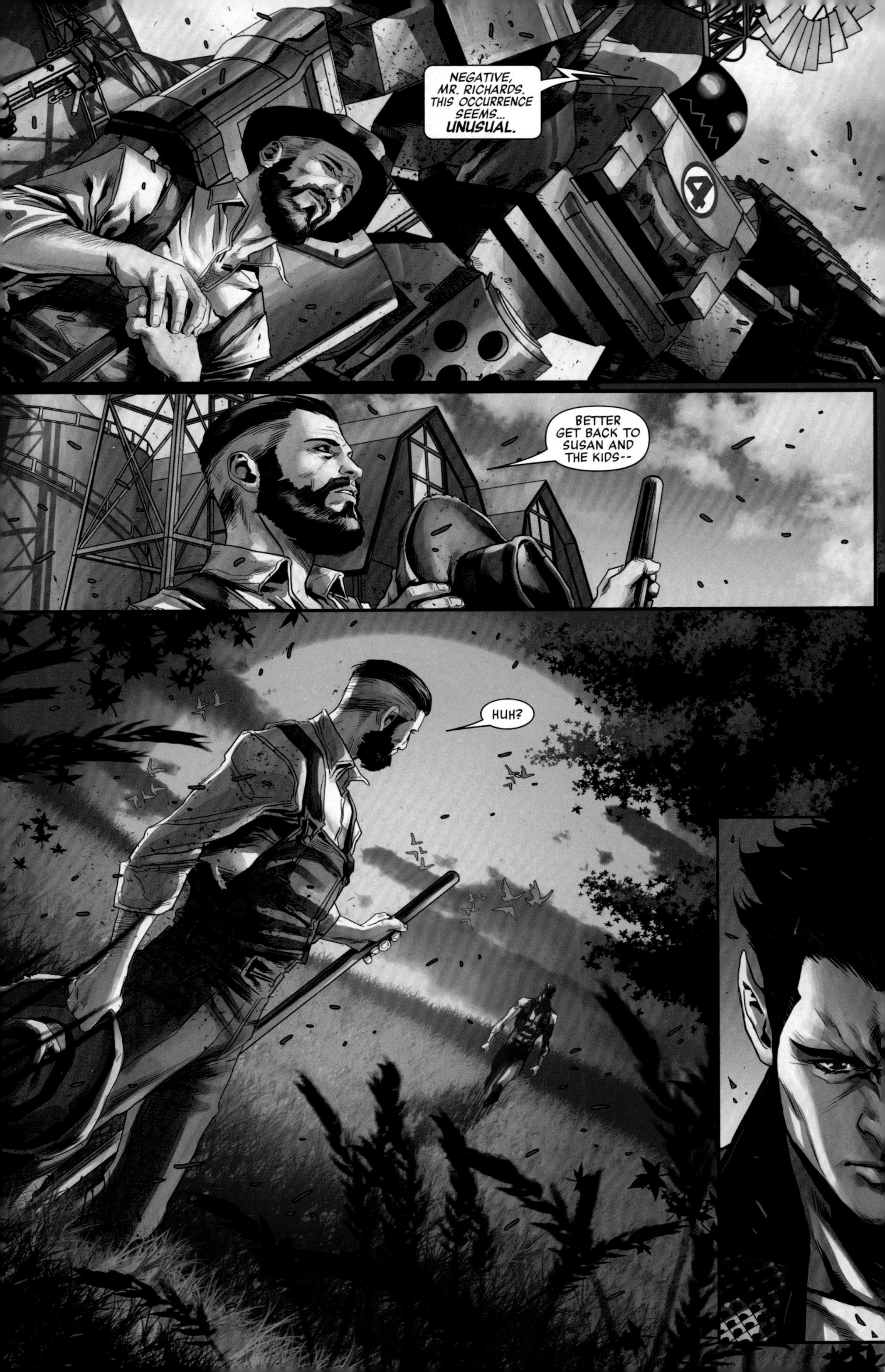
NEGATIVE, MR. RICHARDS. THIS OCCURRENCE SEEMS... UNUSUAL.
BETTER GET BACK TO SUSAN AND THE KIDS--
HUH?

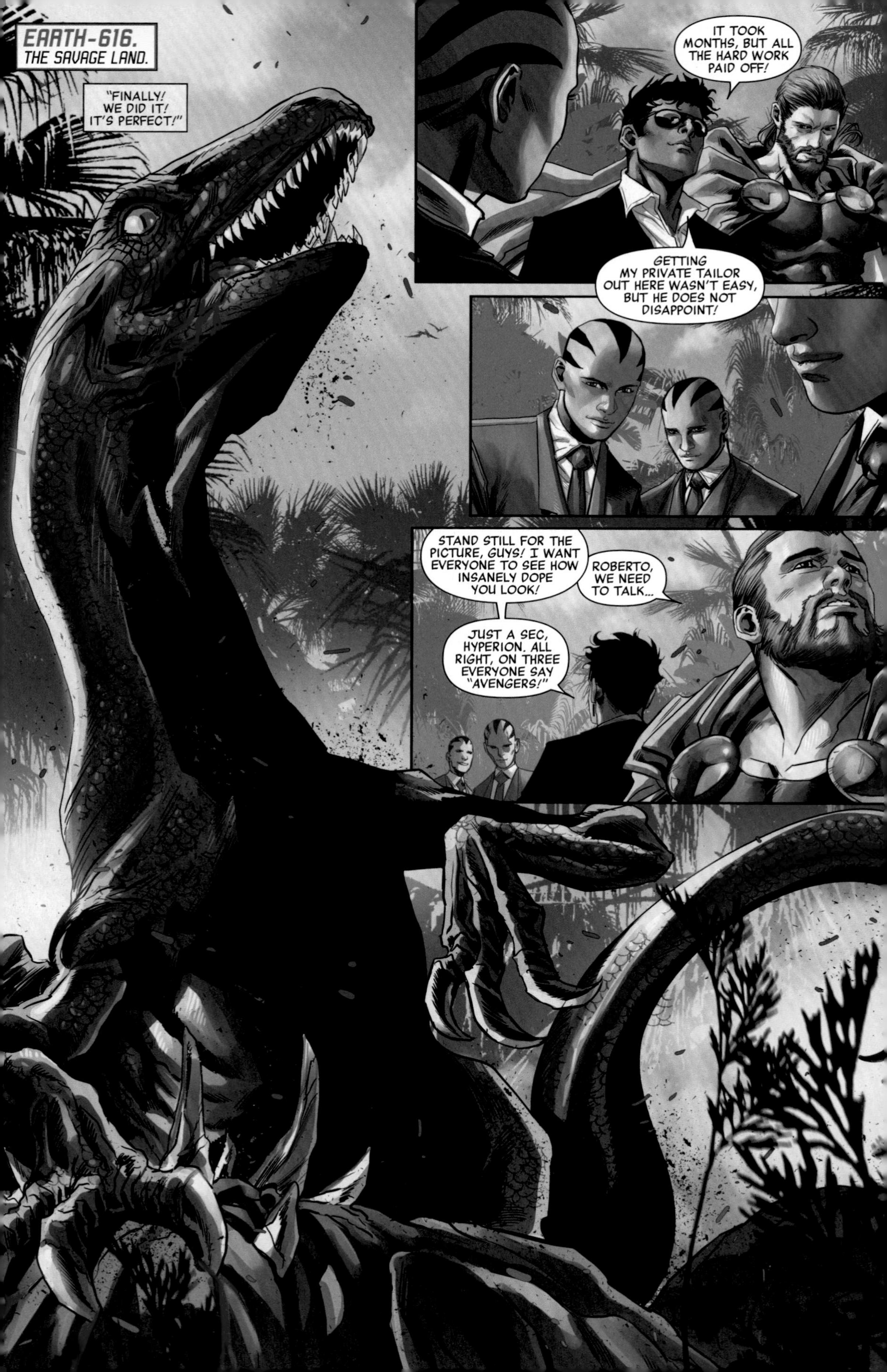
EARTH-616.
THE SAVAGE LAND.
"FINALLY! WE DID IT! IT'S PERFECT!"
IT TOOK MONTHS, BUT ALL THE HARD WORK PAID OFF!
GETTING MY PRIVATE TAILOR OUT HERE WASN'T EASY, BUT HE DOES NOT DISAPPOINT!
STAND STILL FOR THE PICTURE, GUYS! I WANT EVERYONE TO SEE HOW INSANELY DOPE YOU LOOK!
ROBERTO, WE NEED TO TALK...
JUST A SEC, HYPERION. ALL RIGHT, ON THREE EVERYONE SAY "AVENGERS!"

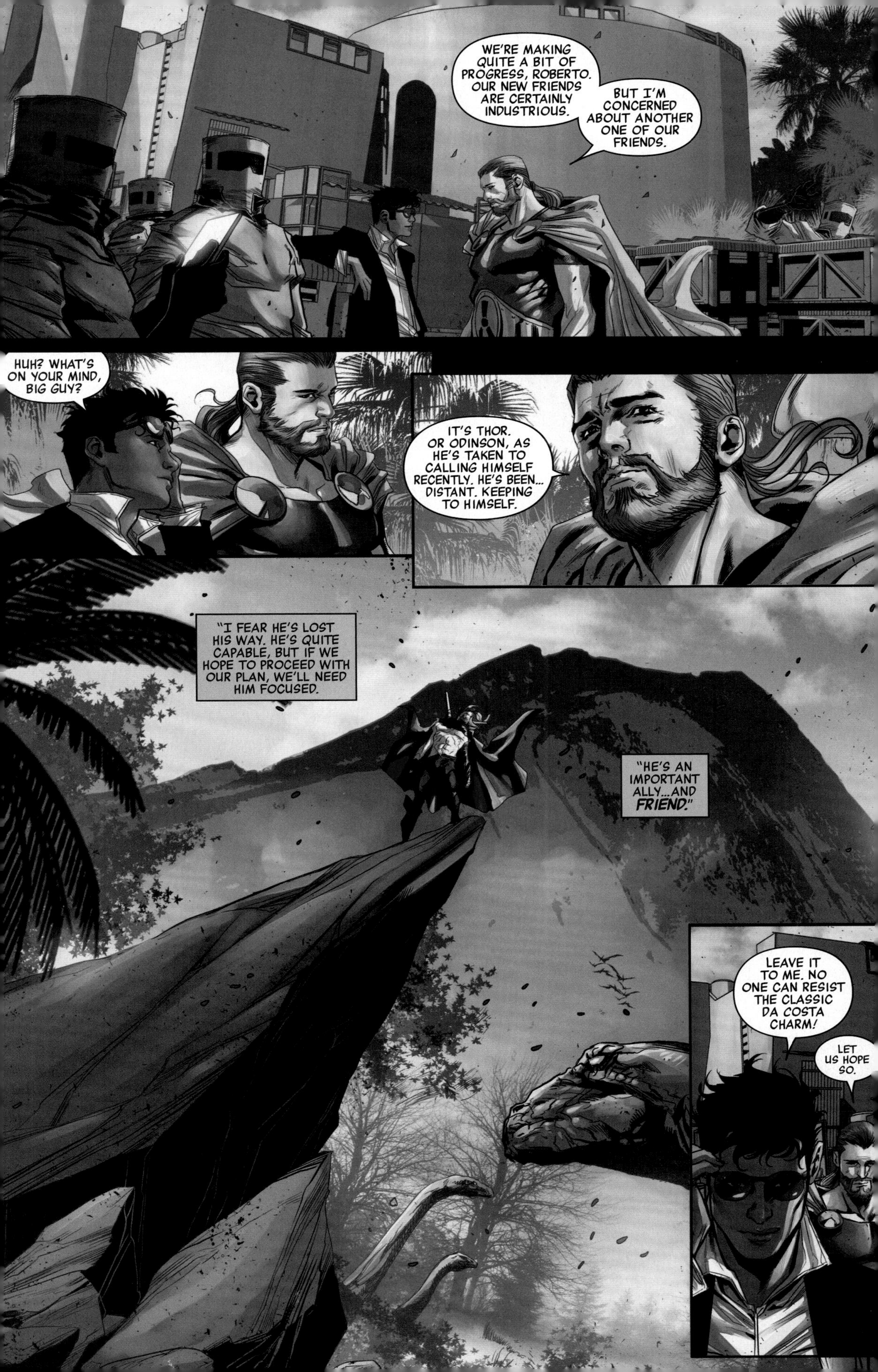
WE'RE MAKING QUITE A BIT OF PROGRESS, ROBERTO. OUR NEW FRIENDS ARE CERTAINLY INDUSTRIOUS.
BUT I'M CONCERNED ABOUT ANOTHER ONE OF OUR FRIENDS.
HUH? WHAT'S ON YOUR MIND, BIG GUY?
IT'S THOR. OR ODINSON, AS HE'S TAKEN TO CALLING HIMSELF RECENTLY. HE'S BEEN... DISTANT. KEEPING TO HIMSELF.
"I FEAR HE'S LOST HIS WAY. HE'S QUITE CAPABLE, BUT IF WE HOPE TO PROCEED WITH OUR PLAN, WE'LL NEED HIM FOCUSED.
"HE'S AN IMPORTANT ALLY...AND *FRIEND*."
LEAVE IT TO ME. NO ONE CAN RESIST THE CLASSIC DA COSTA CHARM!
LET US HOPE SO.

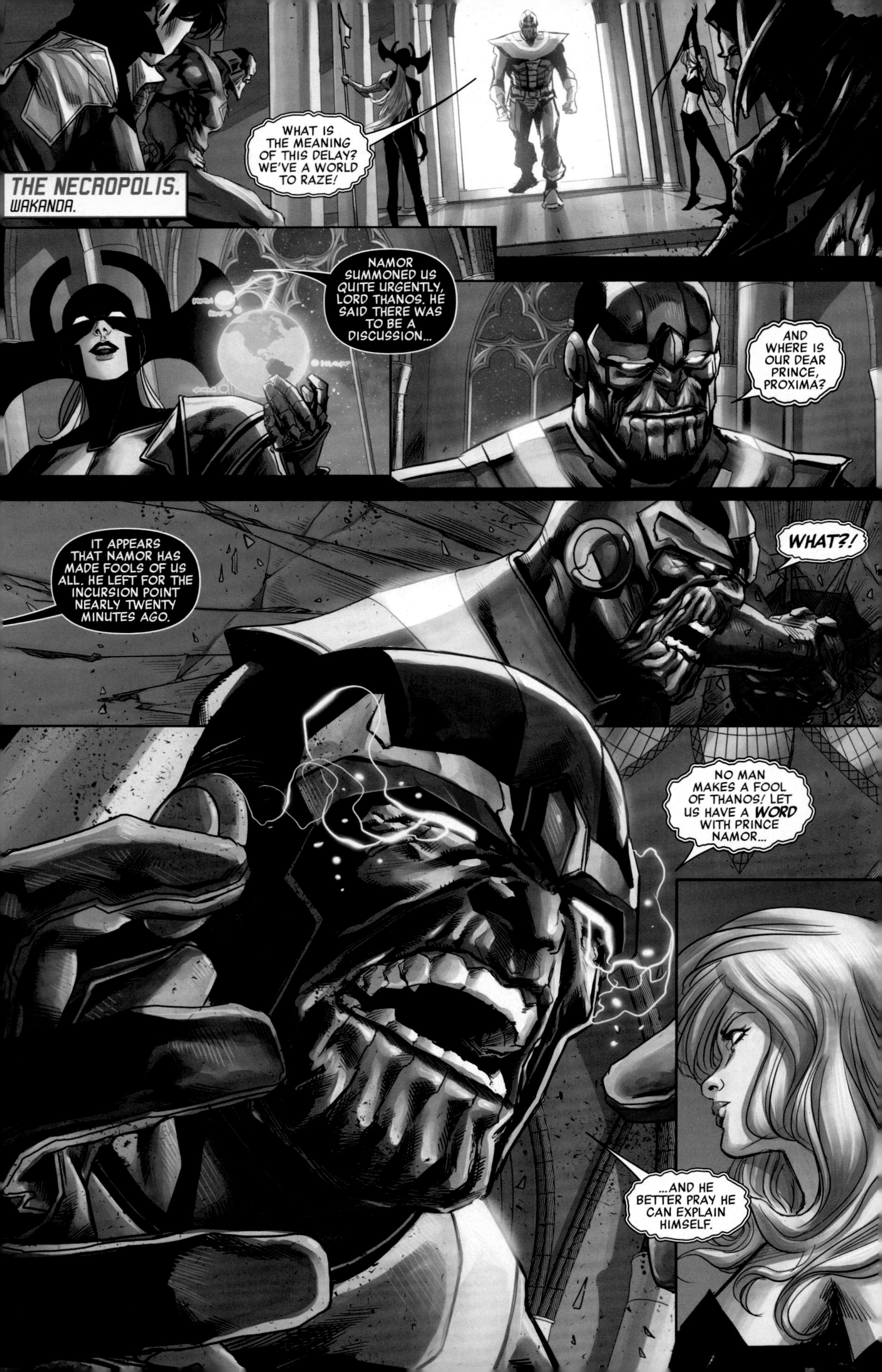
THE NECROPOLIS.
WAKANDA.
WHAT IS THE MEANING OF THIS DELAY? WE'VE A WORLD TO RAZE!
NAMOR SUMMONED US QUITE URGENTLY, LORD THANOS. HE SAID THERE WAS TO BE A DISCUSSION...
AND WHERE IS OUR DEAR PRINCE, PROXIMA?
IT APPEARS THAT NAMOR HAS MADE FOOLS OF US ALL. HE LEFT FOR THE INCURSION POINT NEARLY TWENTY MINUTES AGO.
WHAT?!
NO MAN MAKES A FOOL OF THANOS! LET US HAVE A WORD WITH PRINCE NAMOR...
...AND HE BETTER PRAY HE CAN EXPLAIN HIMSELF.

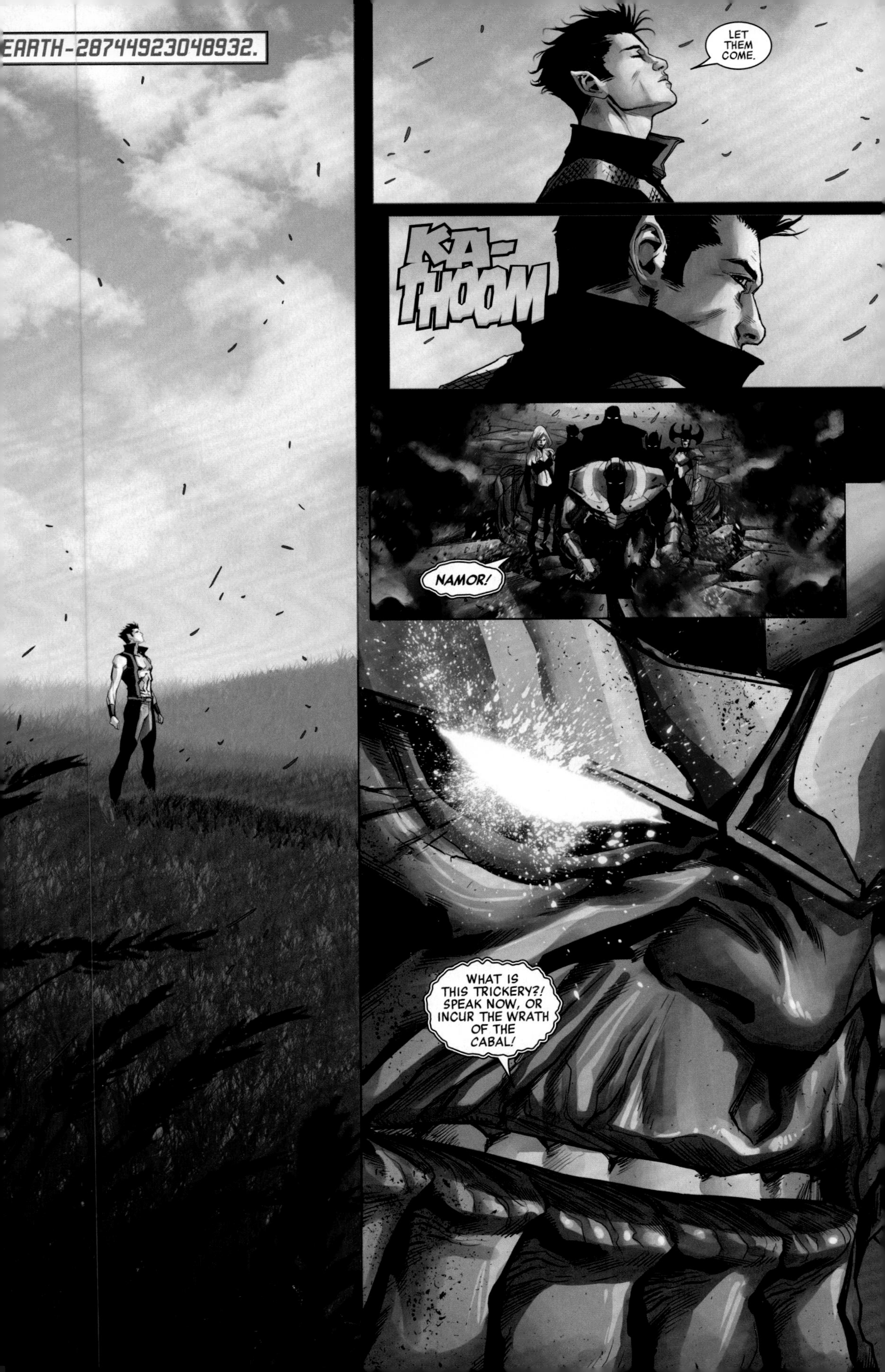
EARTH-28744923048932.
LET THEM COME.
KA-THOOM
NAMOR!
WHAT IS THIS TRICKERY?! SPEAK NOW, OR INCUR THE WRATH OF THE CABAL!

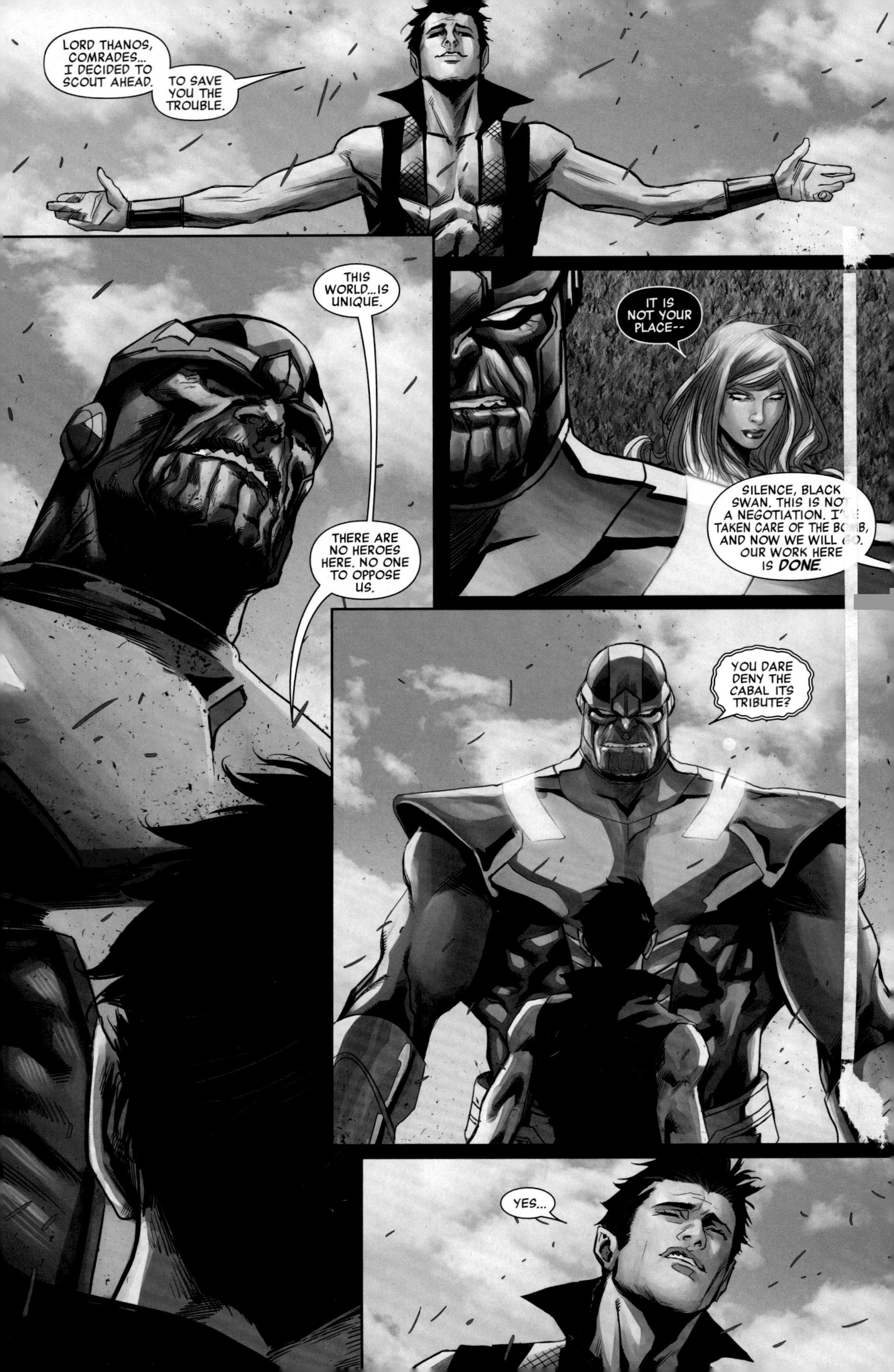
LORD THANOS, COMRADES... I DECIDED TO SCOUT AHEAD.
TO SAVE YOU THE TROUBLE.
THIS WORLD...IS UNIQUE.
THERE ARE NO HEROES HERE. NO ONE TO OPPOSE US.
IT IS NOT YOUR PLACE--
SILENCE, BLACK SWAN. THIS IS NOT A NEGOTIATION. I'VE TAKEN CARE OF THE BOMB, AND NOW WE WILL GO. OUR WORK HERE IS DONE.
YOU DARE DENY THE CABAL ITS TRIBUTE?
YES...

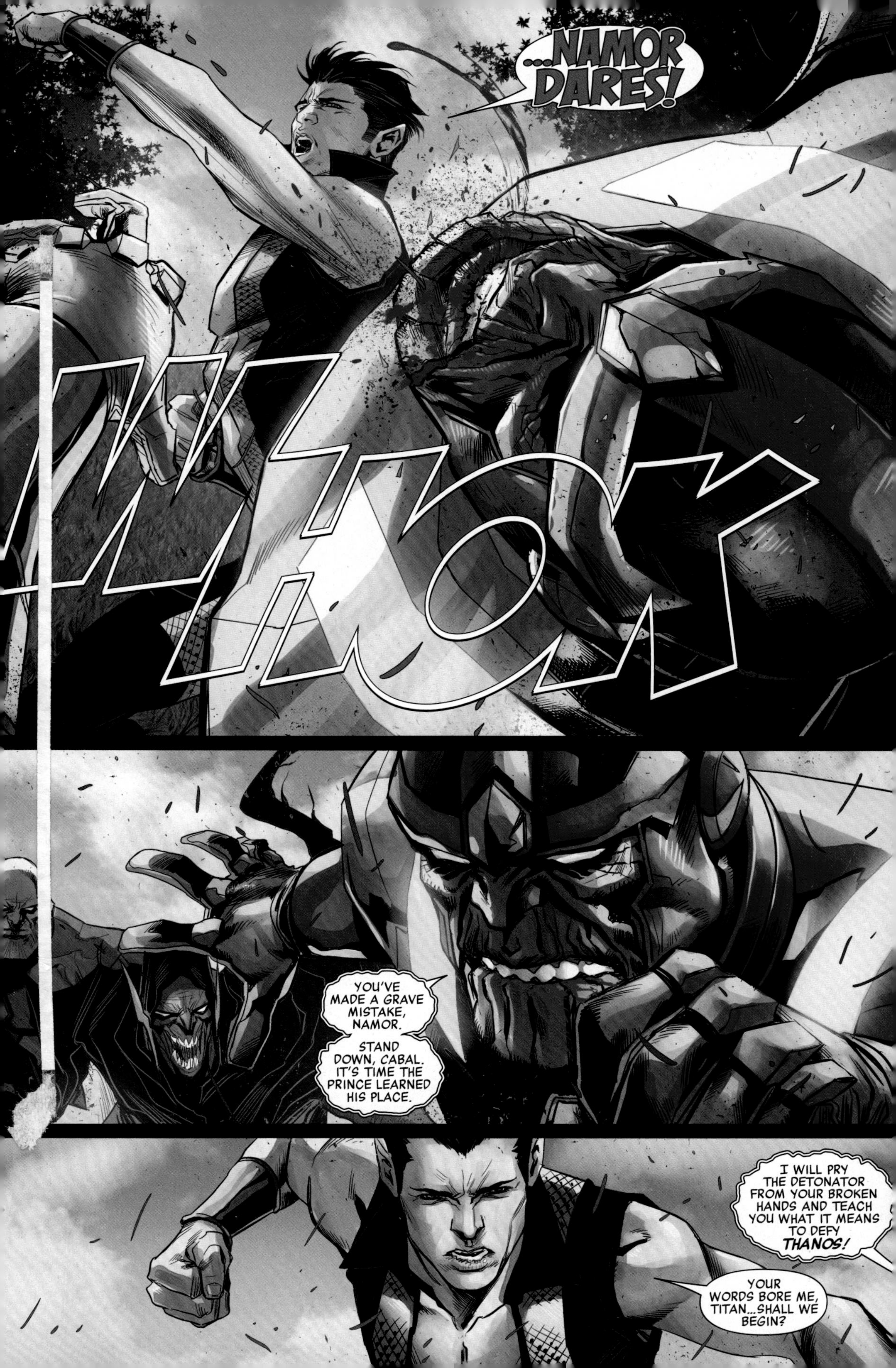
...NAMOR DARES!
WHOOM
YOU'VE MADE A GRAVE MISTAKE, NAMOR.
STAND DOWN, CABAL. IT'S TIME THE PRINCE LEARNED HIS PLACE.
I WILL PRY THE DETONATOR FROM YOUR BROKEN HANDS AND TEACH YOU WHAT IT MEANS TO DEFY *THANOS!*
YOUR WORDS BORE ME, TITAN...SHALL WE BEGIN?

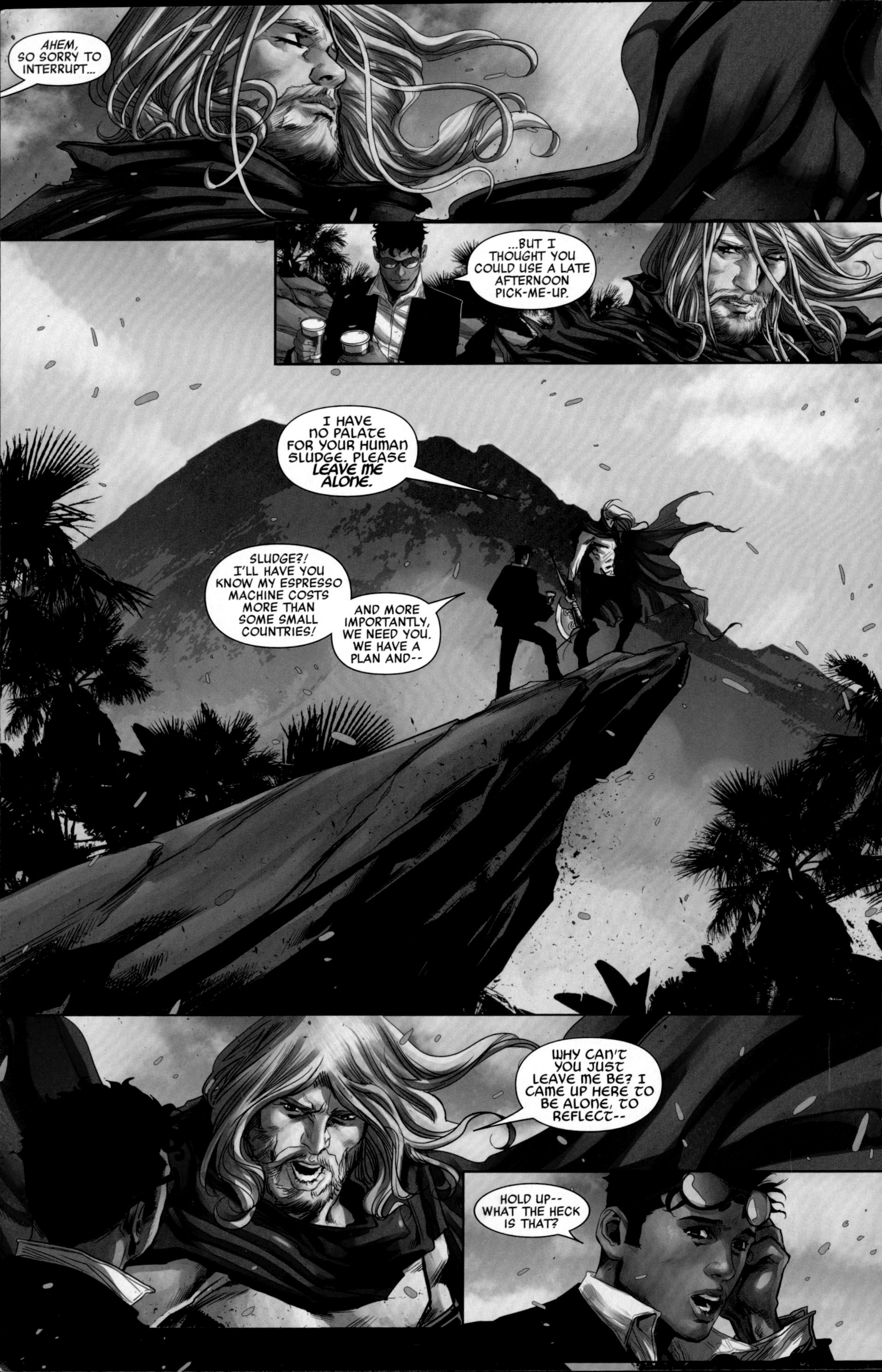
AHEM, SO SORRY TO INTERRUPT...
...BUT I THOUGHT YOU COULD USE A LATE AFTERNOON PICK-ME-UP.
I HAVE NO PALATE FOR YOUR HUMAN SLUDGE. PLEASE LEAVE ME ALONE.
SLUDGE?! I'LL HAVE YOU KNOW MY ESPRESSO MACHINE COSTS MORE THAN SOME SMALL COUNTRIES!
AND MORE IMPORTANTLY, WE NEED YOU. WE HAVE A PLAN AND--
WHY CAN'T YOU JUST LEAVE ME BE? I CAME UP HERE TO BE ALONE, TO REFLECT--
HOLD UP-- WHAT THE HECK IS THAT?

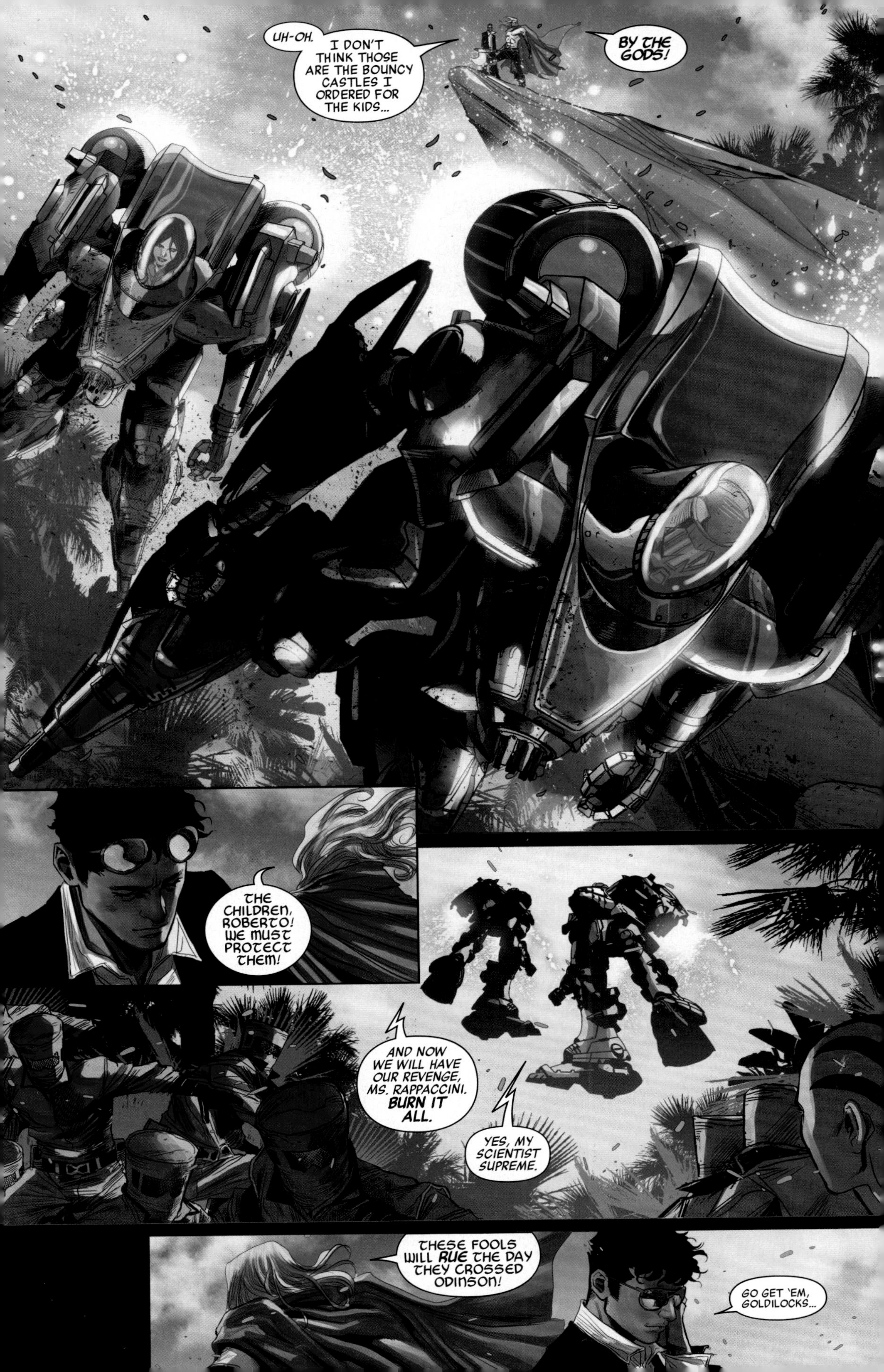
UH-OH.
I DON'T THINK THOSE ARE THE BOUNCY CASTLES I ORDERED FOR THE KIDS...
BY THE GODS!
THE CHILDREN, ROBERTO! WE MUST PROTECT THEM!
AND NOW WE WILL HAVE OUR REVENGE, MS. RAPPACCINI. BURN IT ALL.
YES, MY SCIENTIST SUPREME.
THESE FOOLS WILL RUE THE DAY THEY CROSSED ODINSON!
GO GET 'EM, GOLDILOCKS...

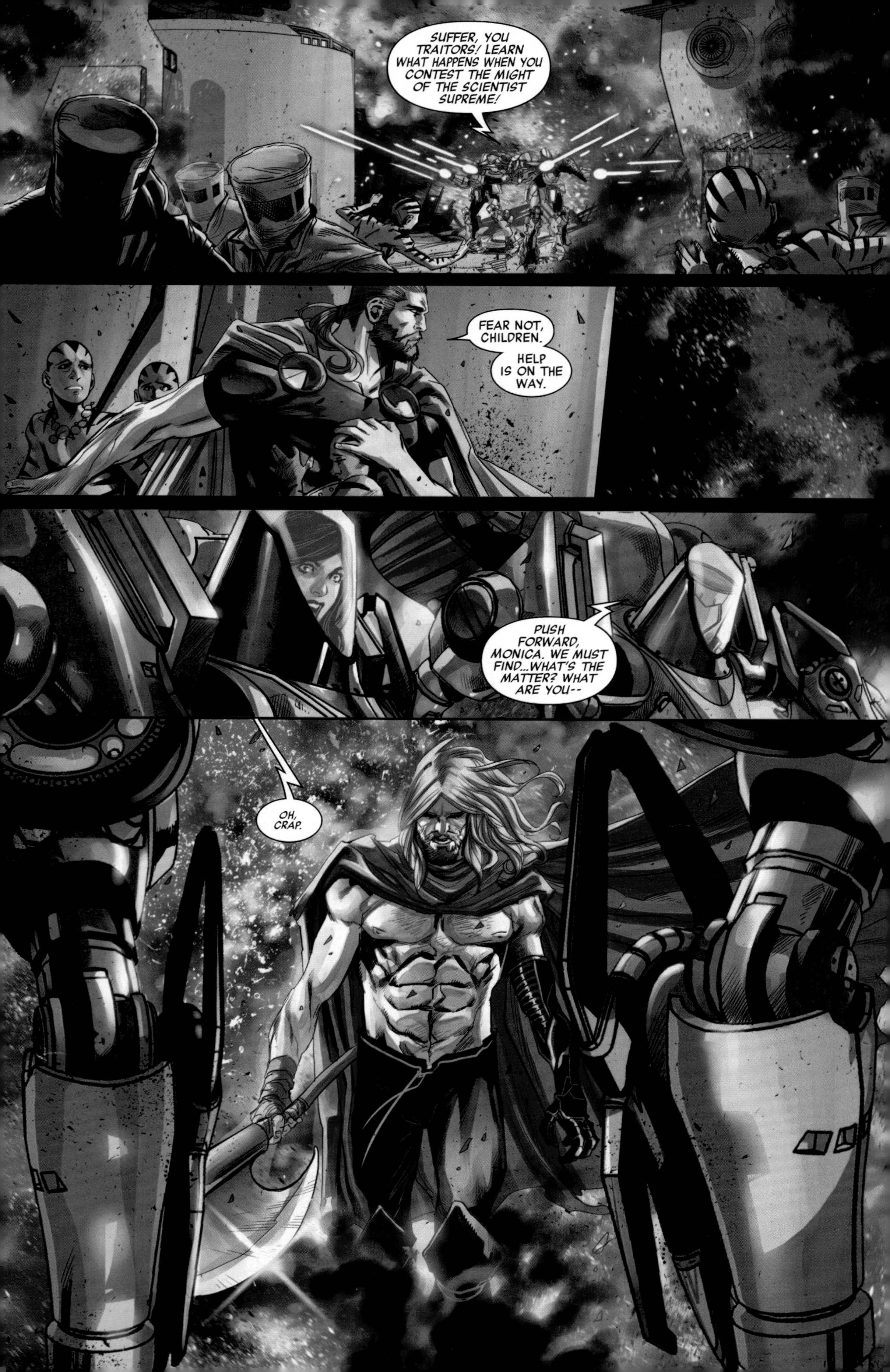
SUFFER, YOU TRAITORS! LEARN WHAT HAPPENS WHEN YOU CONTEST THE MIGHT OF THE SCIENTIST SUPREME!
FEAR NOT, CHILDREN.
HELP IS ON THE WAY.
PUSH FORWARD, MONICA. WE MUST FIND...WHAT'S THE MATTER? WHAT ARE YOU--
OH, CRAP.

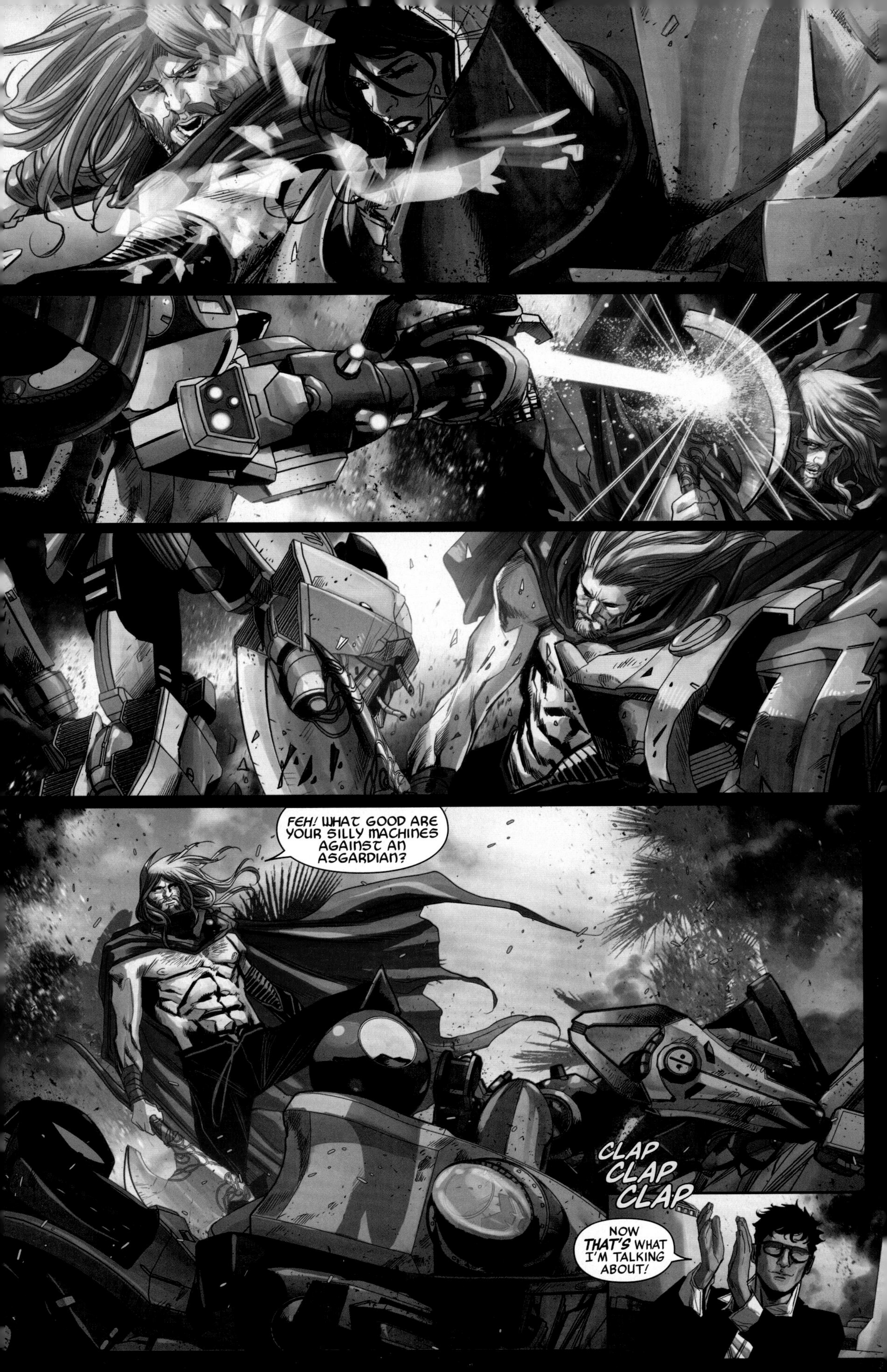
FEH! WHAT GOOD ARE YOUR SILLY MACHINES AGAINST AN ASGARDIAN?
CLAP CLAP CLAP
NOW THAT'S WHAT I'M TALKING ABOUT!

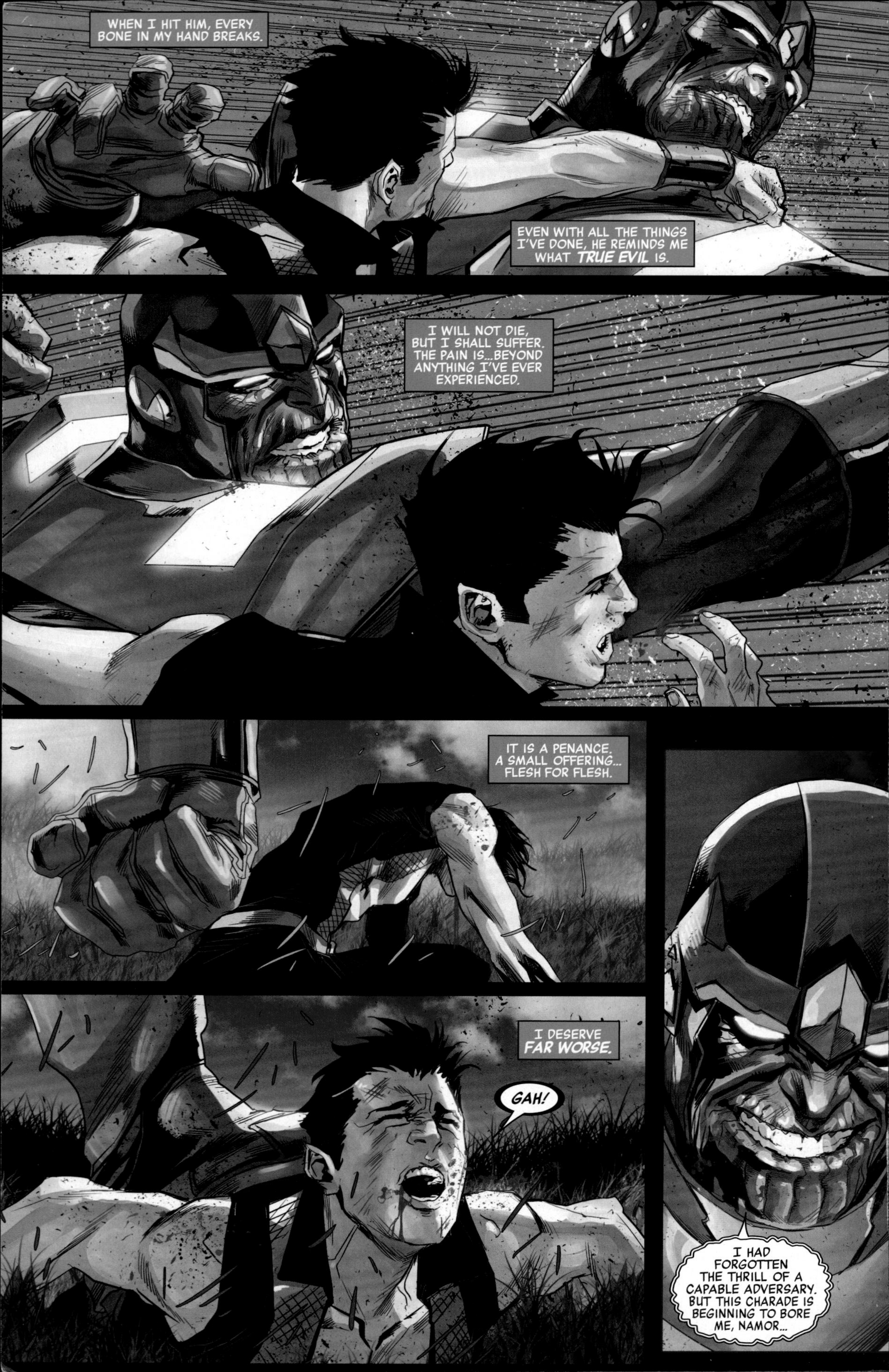
WHEN I HIT HIM, EVERY BONE IN MY HAND BREAKS.
EVEN WITH ALL THE THINGS I'VE DONE, HE REMINDS ME WHAT TRUE EVIL IS.
I WILL NOT DIE, BUT I SHALL SUFFER. THE PAIN IS...BEYOND ANYTHING I'VE EVER EXPERIENCED.
IT IS A PENANCE. A SMALL OFFERING... FLESH FOR FLESH.
I DESERVE FAR WORSE.
GAH!
I HAD FORGOTTEN THE THRILL OF A CAPABLE ADVERSARY. BUT THIS CHARADE IS BEGINNING TO BORE ME, NAMOR...

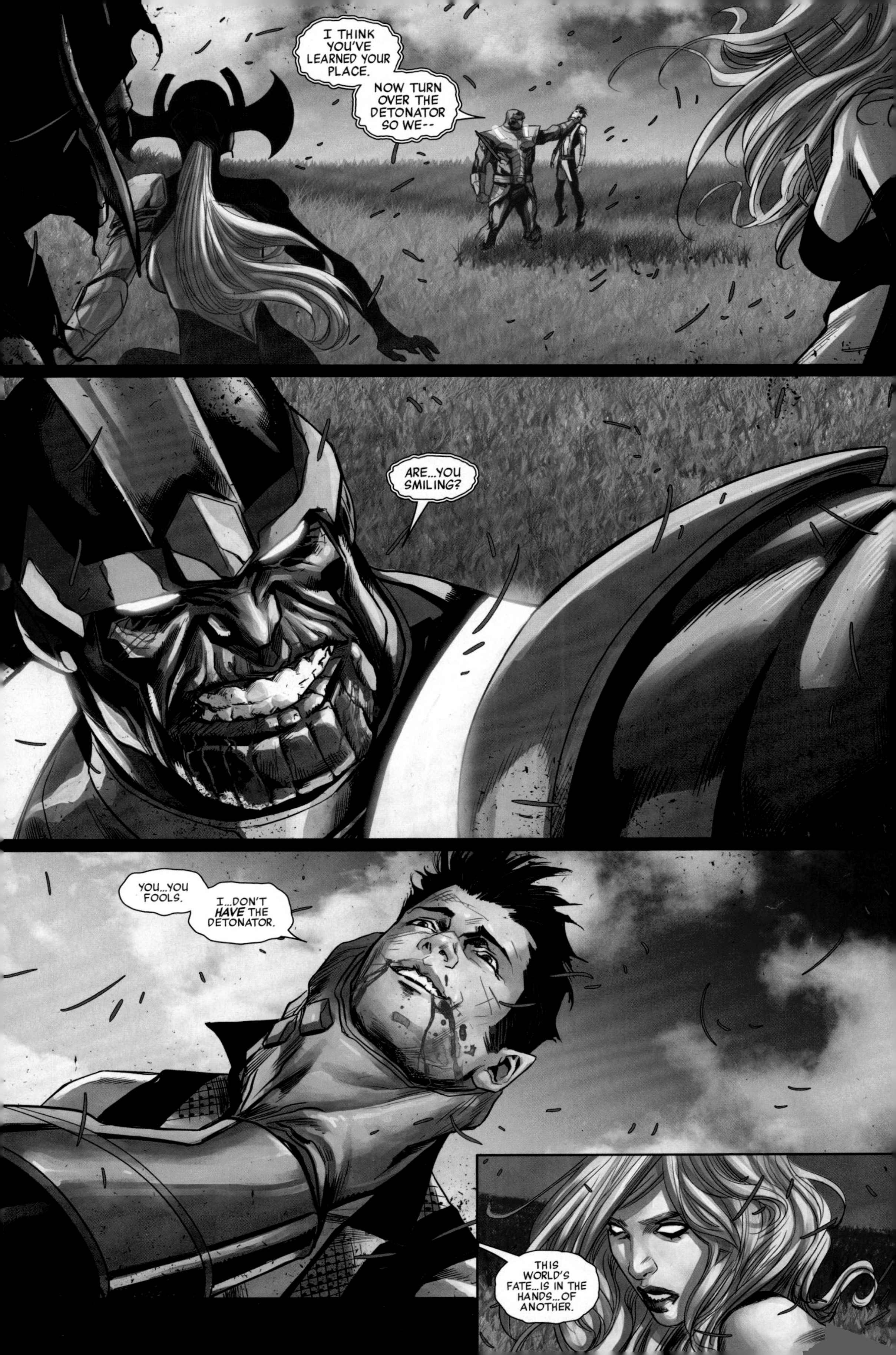
I THINK YOU'VE LEARNED YOUR PLACE.
NOW TURN OVER THE DETONATOR SO WE--
ARE...YOU SMILING?
YOU...YOU FOOLS.
I...DON'T *HAVE* THE DETONATOR.
THIS WORLD'S FATE...IS IN THE HANDS...OF ANOTHER.

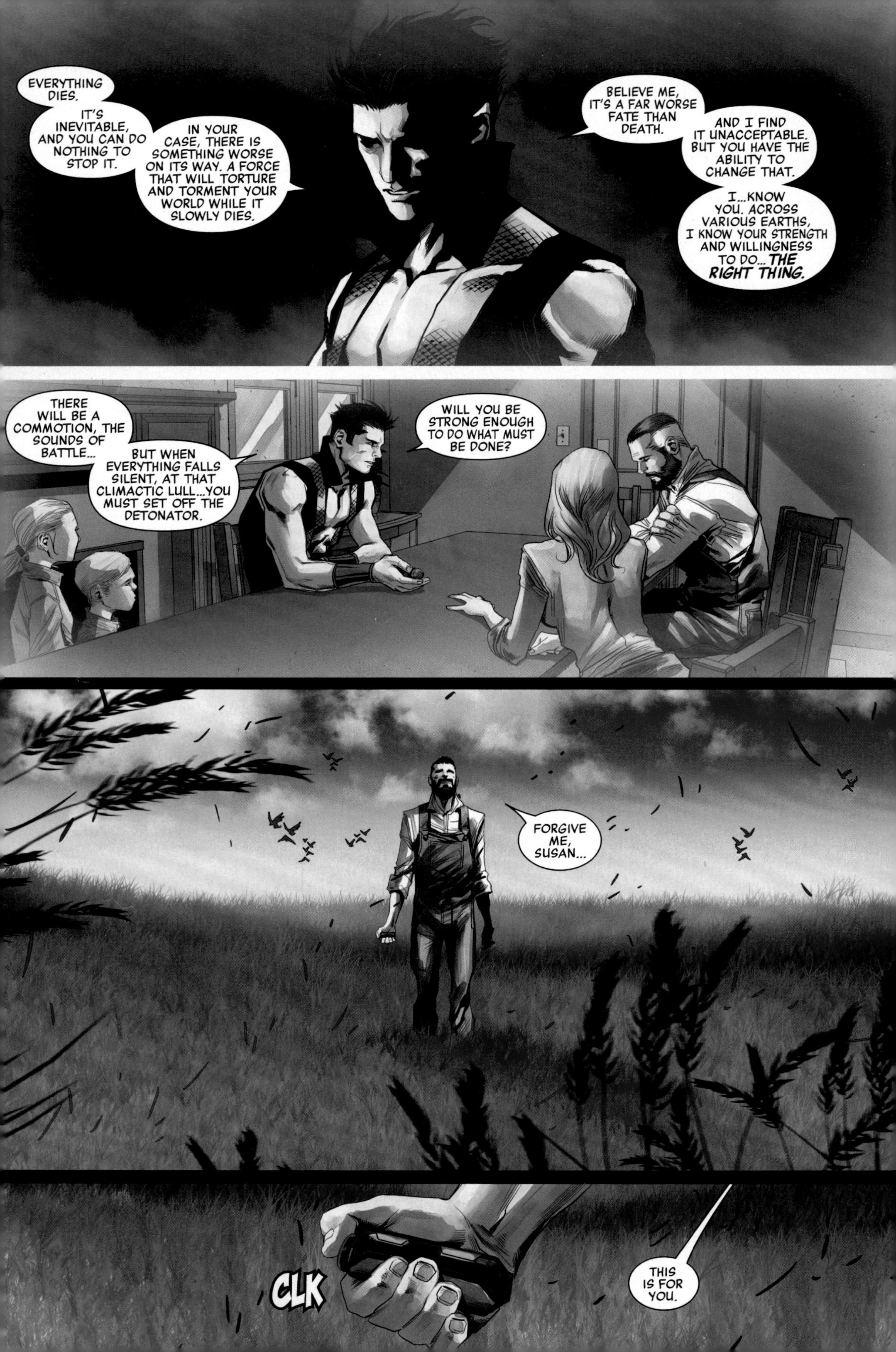

EVERYTHING DIES.
IT'S INEVITABLE, AND YOU CAN DO NOTHING TO STOP IT.
IN YOUR CASE, THERE IS SOMETHING WORSE ON ITS WAY. A FORCE THAT WILL TORTURE AND TORMENT YOUR WORLD WHILE IT SLOWLY DIES.
BELIEVE ME, IT'S A FAR WORSE FATE THAN DEATH.
AND I FIND IT UNACCEPTABLE. BUT YOU HAVE THE ABILITY TO CHANGE THAT.
I...KNOW YOU. ACROSS VARIOUS EARTHS, I KNOW YOUR STRENGTH AND WILLINGNESS TO DO...THE RIGHT THING.
THERE WILL BE A COMMOTION, THE SOUNDS OF BATTLE...
BUT WHEN EVERYTHING FALLS SILENT, AT THAT CLIMACTIC LULL...YOU MUST SET OFF THE DETONATOR.
WILL YOU BE STRONG ENOUGH TO DO WHAT MUST BE DONE?
FORGIVE ME, SUSAN...
CLK
THIS IS FOR YOU.

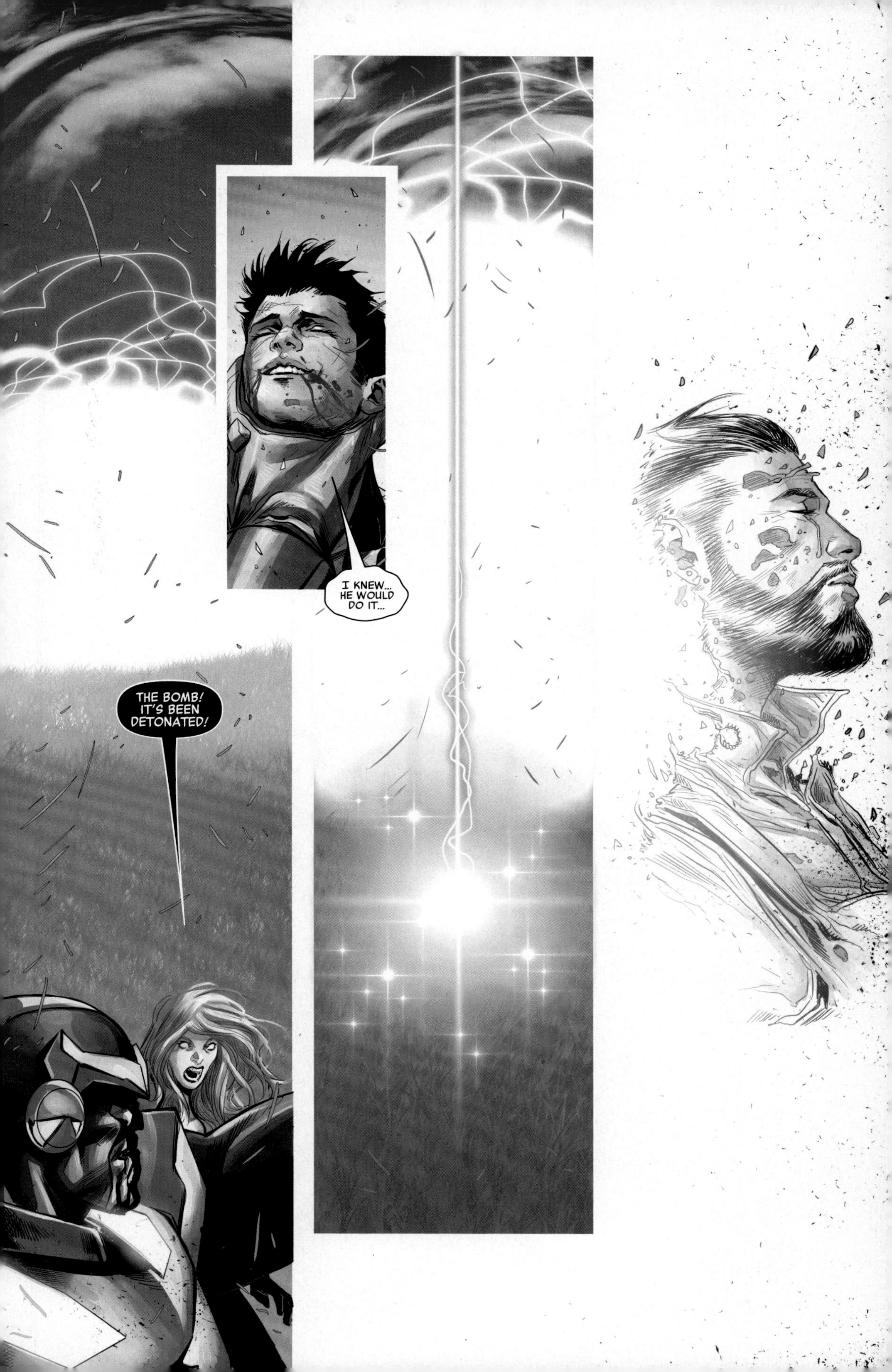
I KNEW... HE WOULD DO IT...
THE BOMB! IT'S BEEN DETONATED!

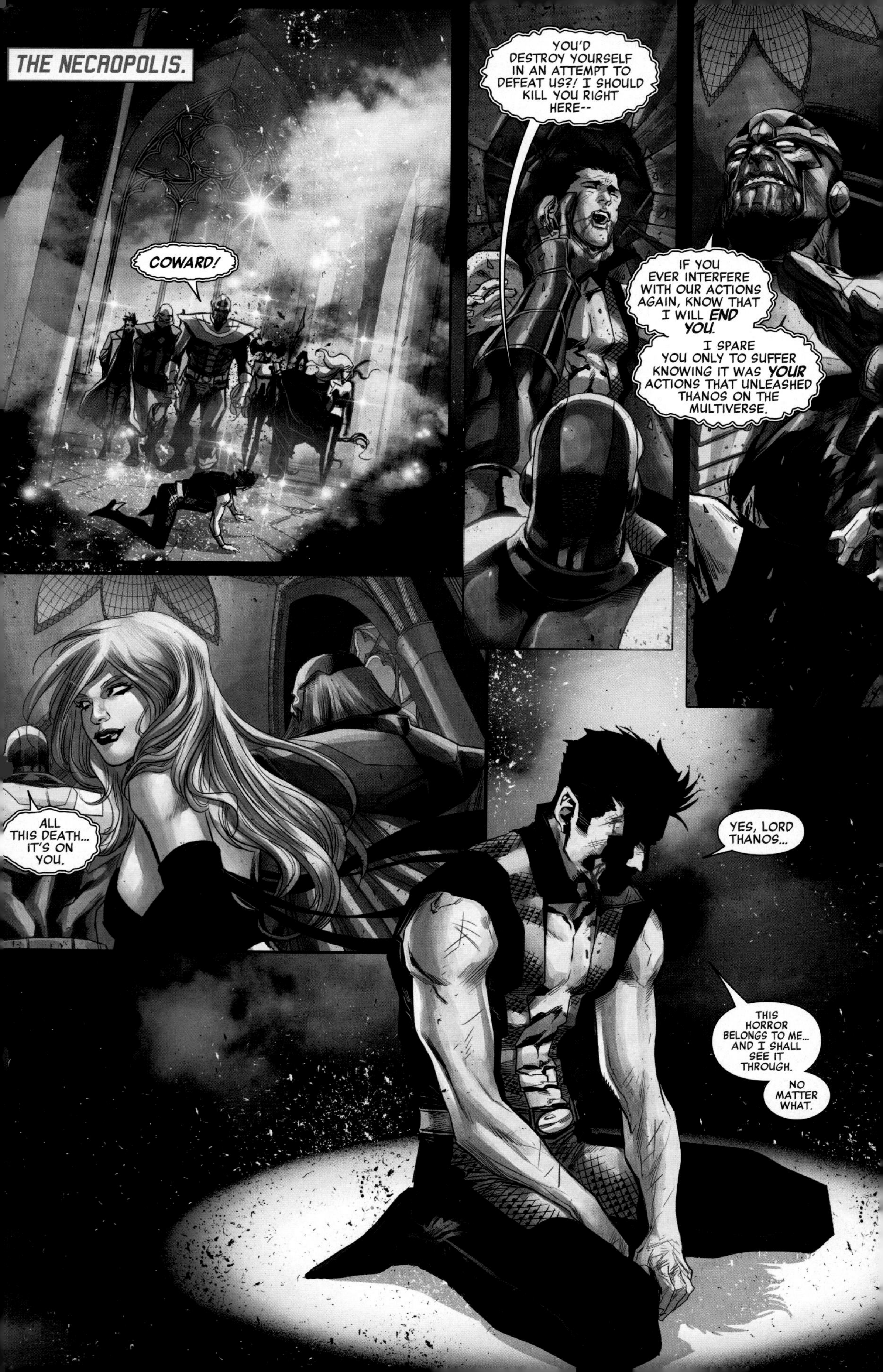
THE NECROPOLIS.
COWARD!
YOU'D DESTROY YOURSELF IN AN ATTEMPT TO DEFEAT US?! I SHOULD KILL YOU RIGHT HERE--
IF YOU EVER INTERFERE WITH OUR ACTIONS AGAIN, KNOW THAT I WILL END YOU.
I SPARE YOU ONLY TO SUFFER KNOWING IT WAS YOUR ACTIONS THAT UNLEASHED THANOS ON THE MULTIVERSE.
ALL THIS DEATH... IT'S ON YOU.
YES, LORD THANOS...
THIS HORROR BELONGS TO ME... AND I SHALL SEE IT THROUGH.
NO MATTER WHAT.

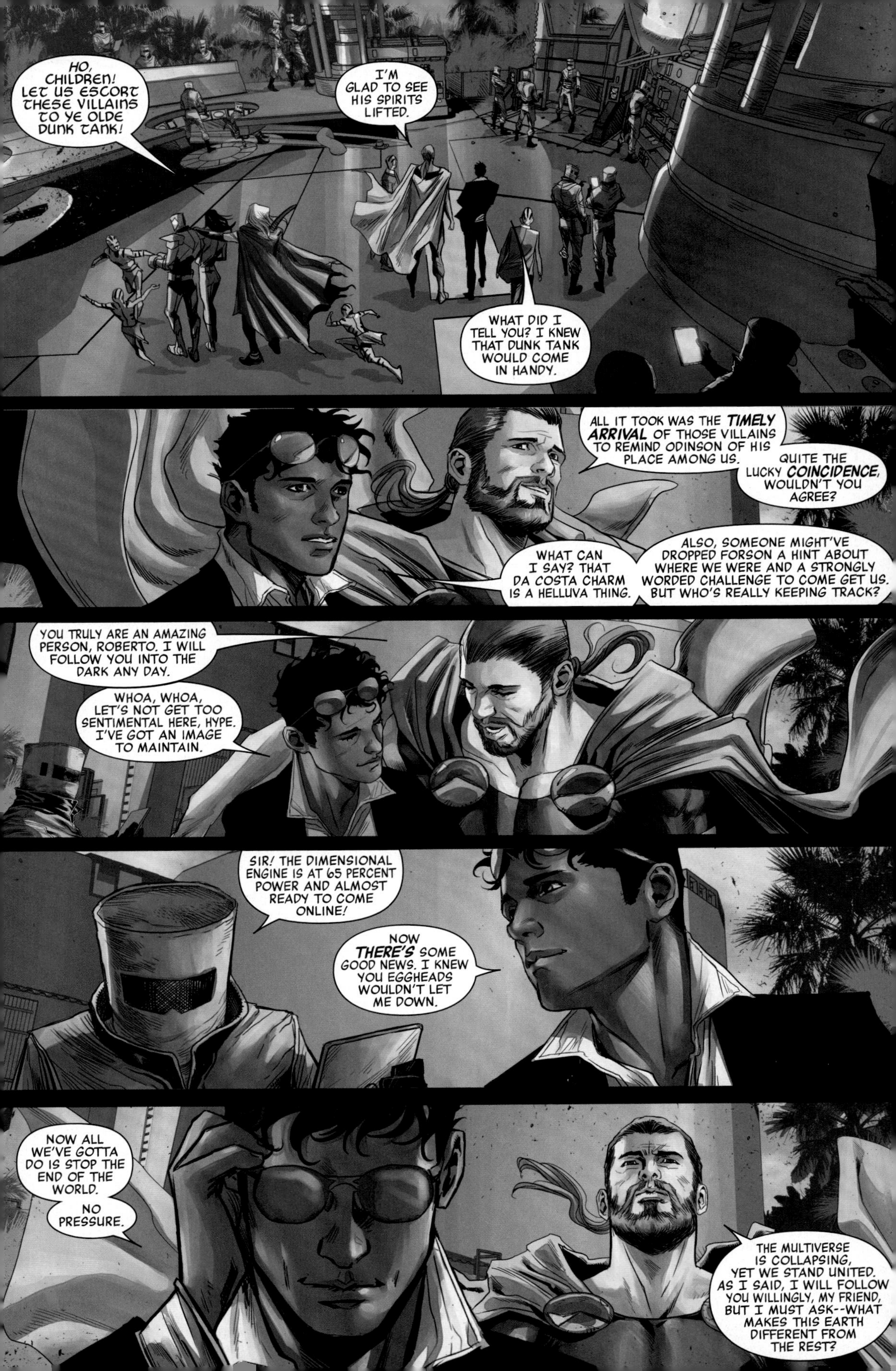
HO, CHILDREN! LET US ESCORT THESE VILLAINS TO YE OLDE DUNK TANK!
I'M GLAD TO SEE HIS SPIRITS LIFTED.
WHAT DID I TELL YOU? I KNEW THAT DUNK TANK WOULD COME IN HANDY.
ALL IT TOOK WAS THE TIMELY ARRIVAL OF THOSE VILLAINS TO REMIND ODINSON OF HIS PLACE AMONG US.
QUITE THE LUCKY COINCIDENCE, WOULDN'T YOU AGREE?
WHAT CAN I SAY? THAT DA COSTA CHARM IS A HELLUVA THING.
ALSO, SOMEONE MIGHT'VE DROPPED FORSON A HINT ABOUT WHERE WE WERE AND A STRONGLY WORDED CHALLENGE TO COME GET US. BUT WHO'S REALLY KEEPING TRACK?
YOU TRULY ARE AN AMAZING PERSON, ROBERTO. I WILL FOLLOW YOU INTO THE DARK ANY DAY.
WHOA, WHOA, LET'S NOT GET TOO SENTIMENTAL HERE, HYPE. I'VE GOT AN IMAGE TO MAINTAIN.
SIR! THE DIMENSIONAL ENGINE IS AT 65 PERCENT POWER AND ALMOST READY TO COME ONLINE!
NOW THERE'S SOME GOOD NEWS. I KNEW YOU EGGHEADS WOULDN'T LET ME DOWN.
NOW ALL WE'VE GOTTA DO IS STOP THE END OF THE WORLD.
NO PRESSURE.
THE MULTIVERSE IS COLLAPSING, YET WE STAND UNITED. AS I SAID, I WILL FOLLOW YOU WILLINGLY, MY FRIEND, BUT I MUST ASK--WHAT MAKES THIS EARTH DIFFERENT FROM THE REST?

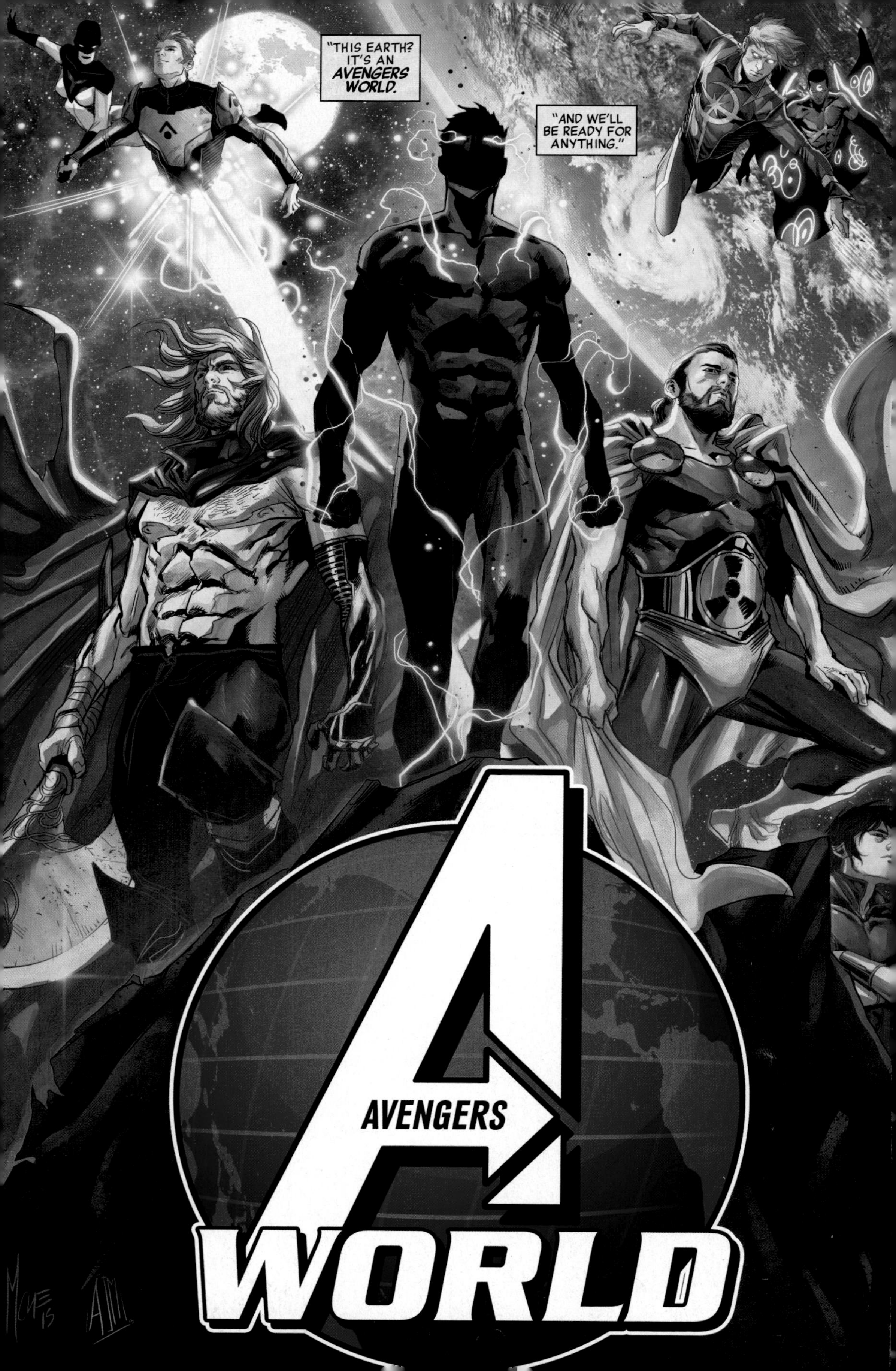
"THIS EARTH? IT'S AN AVENGERS WORLD.
"AND WE'LL BE READY FOR ANYTHING."
AVENGERS
WORLD

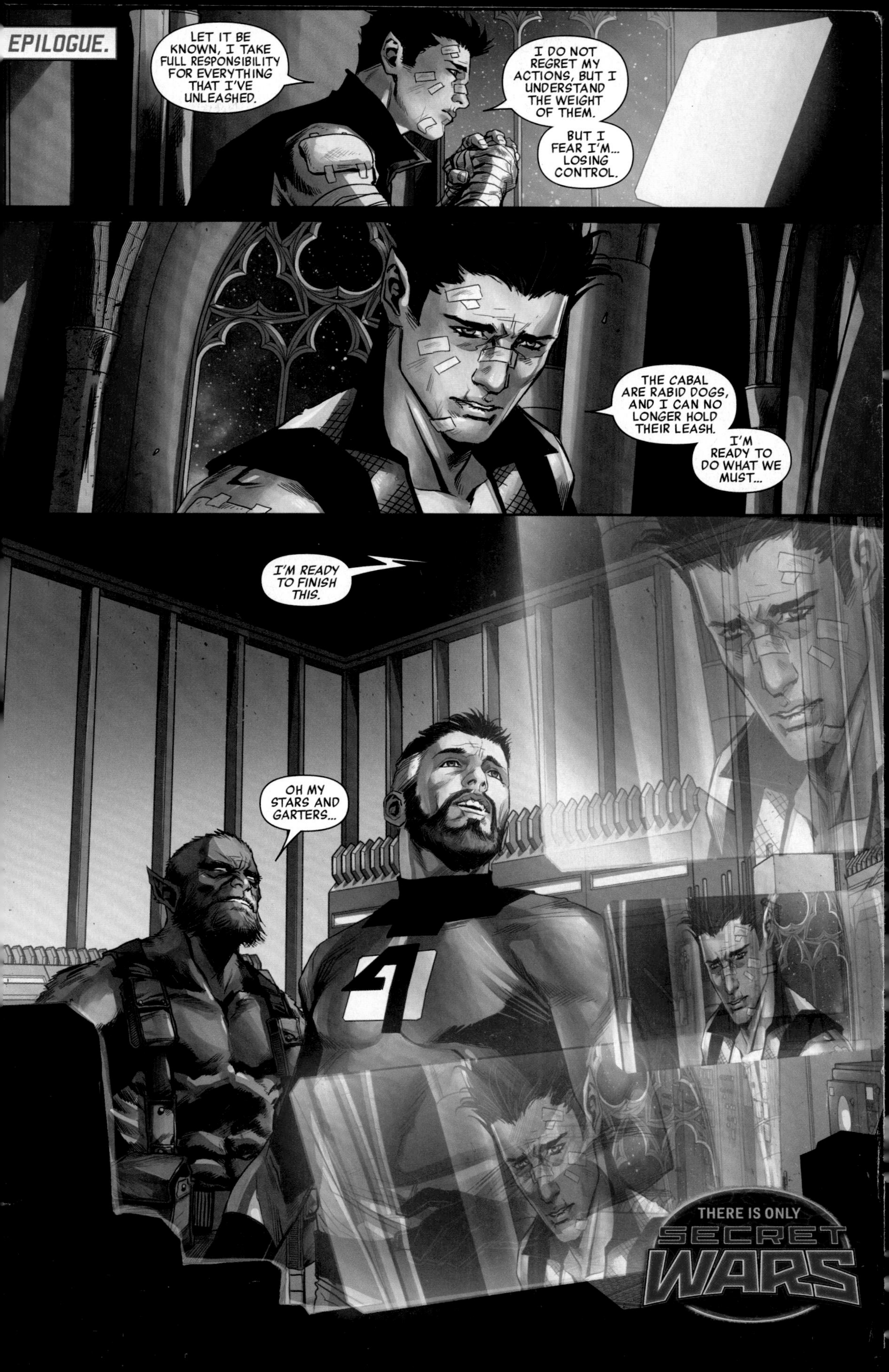
EPILOGUE.
LET IT BE KNOWN, I TAKE FULL RESPONSIBILITY FOR EVERYTHING THAT I'VE UNLEASHED.
I DO NOT REGRET MY ACTIONS, BUT I UNDERSTAND THE WEIGHT OF THEM.
BUT I FEAR I'M... LOSING CONTROL.
THE CABAL ARE RABID DOGS, AND I CAN NO LONGER HOLD THEIR LEASH.
I'M READY TO DO WHAT WE MUST...
I'M READY TO FINISH THIS.
OH MY STARS AND GARTERS...
THERE IS ONLY
SECRET
WARS

***Avengers World #18,* page 1 Art**
by Marco Checchetto

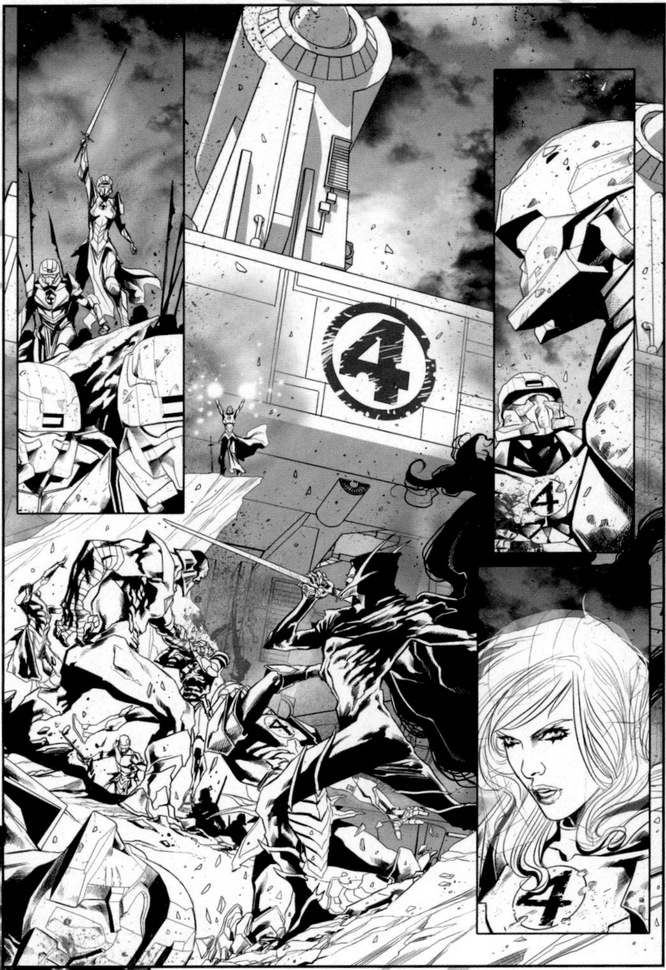

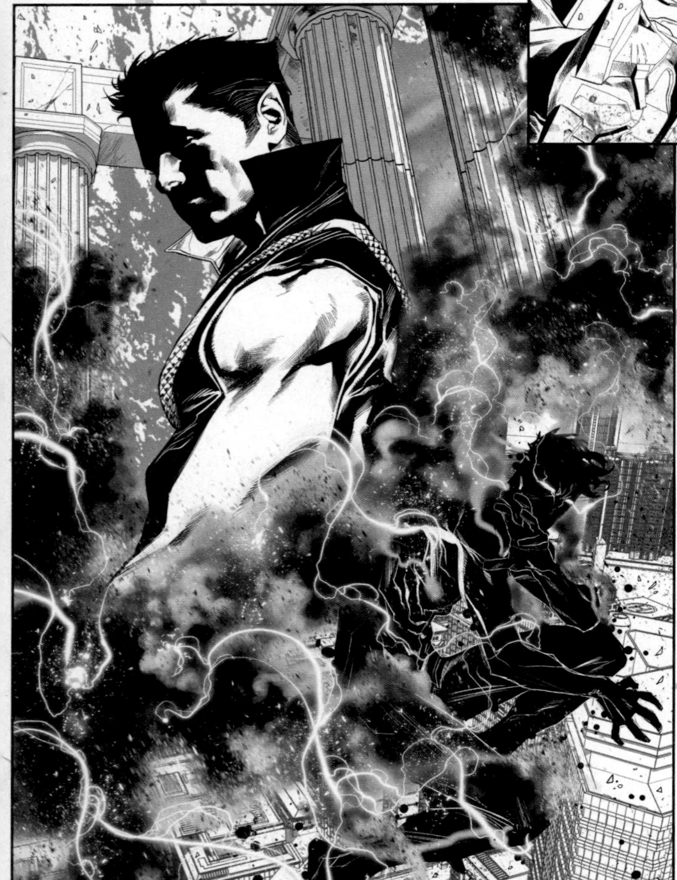

***Avengers World #18,* page 20 Art**
by Marco Checchetto